THE SOURCES OF HISTORY
STUDIES IN THE USES
OF HISTORICAL EVIDENCE

GENERAL EDITOR: G. R. ELTON

SOURCES FOR ANCIENT HISTORY

THE SOURCES OF HISTORY

STUDIES IN THE USES OF HISTORICAL EVIDENCE
GENERAL EDITOR: G. R. ELTON

The purpose of this series of books is, broadly, to present to students and readers of history some understanding of the materials from which history must be written and of the problems which these raise. The books will endeavour to bring out the inescapable links between historical sources and historical reconstruction, will help to define promising lines of fruitful research, and will illumine the realities of historical knowledge. Each volume will be concerned with a logical span in the history of a given nation, civilization or area, or with a meaningful historical theme, and it will confine itself to all the primary material extant for that sector. These materials it will consider from the point of view of two crucial questions: what can we know, and what have we no right to expect to learn, from what the past has left behind?

Sources for Ancient History

Edited by

MICHAEL CRAWFORD

Professor of Ancient History,
University College London

with contributions from

EMILIO GABBA

FERGUS MILLAR

ANTHONY SNODGRASS

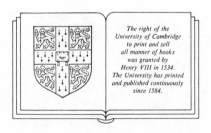

The right of the
University of Cambridge
to print and sell
all manner of books
was granted by
Henry VIII in 1534.
The University has printed
and published continuously
since 1584.

CAMBRIDGE UNIVERSITY PRESS

CAMBRIDGE

LONDON   NEW YORK   NEW ROCHELLE

MELBOURNE   SYDNEY

Published by the Press Syndicate of the University of Cambridge
The Pitt Building, Trumpington Street, Cambridge CB2 1RP
32 East 57th Street, New York, NY 10022, USA
10 Stamford Road, Oakleigh, Melbourne 3166, Australia

First published 1983
Reprinted 1985

Printed in Great Britain at
the University Press, Cambridge

Library of Congress catalogue card number: 82-23656

British Library Cataloguing in Publication Data

Ancient Greece and Rome – (The sources of history)
1. Greece – History – To 146 BC
2. Rome – History – To 476
I. Crawford, Michael   II. Gabba, Emilio
III. Millar, Fergus   IV. Snodgrass, Anthony   V. Series
938   DF12

ISBN 0 521 24782 9 hard covers
ISBN 0 521 28958 0 paperback

Contents

Illustrations

Abbreviations

ABSA	Annual of the British School at Athens
AE	L'Année Epigraphique
AIIN	Annali dell'Istituto Italiano di Numismatica
AJA	American Journal of Archaeology
ANRW	Aufstieg und Niedergang der römischen Welt
BCH	Bulletin de Correspondance Hellénique
BICS	Bulletin of the Institute of Classical Studies
BSFN	Bulletin de la Société Française de Numismatique
CIL	Corpus Inscriptionum Latinarum
CIS	Corpus Inscriptionum Semiticarum
CRAI	Comptes Rendus de d'Académie des Inscriptions et Belles Lettres
FGrHst	Die Fragmente der griechischen Historiker
FIRA	Fontes Iuris Romani Antejustiniani
HSCPh	Harvard Studies in Classical Philology
IG	Inscriptiones Graecae
IGCH	Inventory of Greek Coin Hoards
ILS	Inscriptiones Latinae Selectae
JdI	Jahrbuch des deutschen archäologischen Instituts
JHS	Journal of Hellenic Studies
JRS	Journal of Roman Studies
MEFRA	Mélanges de l'Ecole Française de Rome (Antiquité)
NC.	Numismatic Chronicle
NNÅ	Nordisk Numismatisk Årsskrift
Num.Medd.	Numismatiska Meddelanden
P. Bremen	Die Bremer Papyri
PBSR	Papers of the British School at Rome
PIR	Prosopographia Imperii Romani (second edition)
P. Oxy.	The Oxyrhynchus Papyri

QT	Quaderni Ticinesi di Numismatica e Antichità Classiche
RN	Revue Numismatique
RRC	(M.H. Crawford,) Roman Republican Coinage
RRCH	(M.H. Crawford,) Roman Republican Coin Hoards
SEG	Supplementum Epigraphicum Graecum
SM	Schweizer Münzblätter
SNR	Schweizerische Numismatische Rundschau
Syll.	Sylloge Inscriptionum Graecarum
TAPhA	Transactions of the American Philological Society
YCS	Yale Classical Studies
ZfN	Zeitschrift für Numismatik
ZPE	Zeitschrift für Papyrologie und Epigrafik

Introduction

If a scholar wishes to create a picture of a modern society in all its aspects, there is little of what he needs to know that he cannot find out, although there may still be much that he cannot understand. For the history of Greece and Rome, there is a great deal which is simply unknowable.

Towards the end of the Archaic age of Greece, there developed the writing of works of history which are recognisably the ancestors of those written today; from this point on there is an unbroken sequence of works by Greek and, later, Roman historians down to the end of antiquity. The investigation and characterisation of this historiographical tradition is among the first tasks which face a modern historian of the ancient world. But only a tiny part of what once existed survived the wreck of that world; in addition, the range of interest of historians in antiquity was rather narrow and it was limited, with a few exceptions, to political history; even where their interest was wider, they took for granted much that we wish to know, on economic conditions and even on political institutions. Moreover, there was a general tendency to explain all human actions largely in moral terms.

Much may, of course, also be learned from literary works besides the historical – epic poetry, tragic or comic plays, speeches, philosophical treatises, personal poetry; but many of these works are, like histories, the product of a restricted social class and share its limited vision, although they may also be unconsciously revealing of its assumptions and preconceptions.

Furthermore, the literary products of the Graeco-Roman world are in varying degrees alien to us and pose considerable problems of interpretation, quite apart from the difficulties caused by overt or covert bias; the inferences which a historian may make on the basis of these texts must be controlled by knowledge of the intellectual traditions from which they spring.

But even if this and other difficulties (notably linguistic) in handling ancient sources are surmounted, the problem remains of how to mitigate the effect of the limited range of interest of ancient authors and of the loss of much of what they did produce. Some help may be derived from the documentary material produced in antiquity, ranging from long texts to tiny seal impressions, material which was the product of officials organising public activities, or heads of families organising their affairs, or individuals leaving their mark on the world. Such material was often inscribed on stone or bronze or other durable substance; much of it has avoided destruction and is indeed being discovered in increasing quantities. In Egypt, because of the dry climate, many documents written on papyrus have survived. These texts, often fragmentary and hard to understand, may nonetheless enormously deepen our knowledge of the ancient world.

Beyond this, the evidence of archaeology and numismatics may also be very relevant; the sites of ancient settlements and the objects excavated there provide a great deal of information on the material culture of Greek and Roman society; coins survive in enormous numbers from about 600 BC onwards and, because they were produced by ancient states and functioned in an economic context, they provide evidence of particular significance for an important aspect of the ancient world which is also ill understood.

But even with all the available explicit evidence put to use, there is a long way to go; and in discussing the sources for ancient history it must be remembered that often the most important evidence is that drawn from the well-documented practice of another age or society. The Mediterranean world of the Greek and Roman periods can be seen to resemble Mediterranean societies of a later age, in some areas even of our own, for the lands and their climates have changed little.

In all this, it is important to approach the ancient world with questions and directions of research in mind, since mere accumulation of material or parallels is rarely rewarding. In this context, one can go far beyond the largely moral categories of explanation common in antiquity, though one must always be careful not to impose modern categories or preconceptions on a very alien world. This caution is particularly important where our suggested explanation involves the attribution of motives; the thought structure of the ancients was very different from our own.

Above all, one must remember that the ancient world in its various phases was a complex society; it is necessary to learn to think in correlates; an explanation of one event, be it never so ingenious, is of no use if it involves impossible consequences elsewhere in the structure.

The editor would like to thank Peter Brunt and Paul Cartledge for helpful comments.

CHAPTER 1

Literature

All written texts provide evidence of the ideas, opinions, interests and levels of education of their authors, of the extent of their freedom and of the nature of their conditioning. Furthermore, insofar as a text is a work of literature, it bears the mark of a particular personality and of his unique interpretative vision; it reflects also the culture, the taste and the ideological, political and literary currents of the time; it *may* be representative of the historical context in which it is created and of political, social and economic factors. In approaching literary (and other) texts it is, of course, crucial to attempt to understand the intentions behind their creation and the means used to achieve these intentions; but the later history and transmission of a work are also anchored in the most diverse geographical and cultural contexts, which may enrich or alter its significance. A further problem arises from the likelihood of mistakes in the course of the copying of literary texts in antiquity and the Middle Ages. The preservation of a text which is at all close to its original is very rare; the recently discovered papyrus from Qasr Ibrim, which contains two virtually complete elegies of Gallus, is a case in point (*JRS* 69 (1979), 125–5). In fact, the very survival of ancient literature is often the result of mere chance or of interests quite unrelated to the intentions of the authors concerned.

The historian approaches ancient literary texts with historiographical interests, using methodological approaches of great diversity; these interests and approaches derive basically from problems and pressures belonging to the society of the historian, to his political leanings, to his moral sense. If one remains attached to traditional models, which derive in the

I

final analysis from the concerns of ancient historiography itself, the central aim in dealing with ancient texts will be the reconstruction of historical events, in the widest sense of the words; the actual subject-matter may be historiography, political history or the history of ideas, economic or social history, legal or institutional history, military history, cultural history. Alternatively, a historian may attempt a more global approach, with a view to reconstructing every changing aspect of human life, individual and collective, spiritual and material, of behaviour and mentality, the life style of every level in its social and environmental context. Finally, a historian may base a synchronic analysis of an anthropological or sociological kind on the ancient sources. No doubt these three approaches do not in fact exhaust the possibilities which face a historian of antiquity; but it is clear that even these imply that one may wish to use the whole of the ancient literary material for historical purposes. The use made of it will obviously differ according to the aims of the historian; the legitimacy of this use does not depend on the nature and validity of his approach, but on his respect for certain rules of critical method which are generally recognised as irreplaceable and indispensable. The following discussion does not set out to explain these rules of critical method, which are taken for granted, or to expound the ways in which the texts may be used, since these obviously depend on the interests of individual historians. I propose here, with the use of examples which inevitably reflect my own interests, to indicate something of the content of the ancient sources, their public, their intention, their approach and their rationale, dealing both with internal problems and with historical contexts; I propose also to deal with what the texts, without explicit statement, presuppose or reveal incidentally.

An ancient text, particularly a historical text, can then be read in at least two ways.[1] Insofar as a historical text deliberately provides information on matters more or less

---

[1] M.Liverani, 'Memorandum on the approach to historiographic texts', *Orientalia* 42 (1973 = Gelb Volume), 178–94.

accessible to its author, a modern scholar may use this information, provided he is satisfied as to its adequacy and authenticity or is aware of the extent of any distortion; the use he makes of this information for his own historical reconstruction may, of course, not present the facts as narrated by the ancient text. On the other hand, the same ancient text, quite apart from the validity and significance of the information which it sets out to provide, is in itself a historical document, since the narrative approach and the impact of the personality of the author may permit us to learn something of his historical and cultural context. This does not mean that one has to reduce history to the history of historiography (although this may often happen for historical periods which are widely separated from the dates when their vicissitudes were recorded) or that one has to give precedence to the study and reconstruction of the cultural and literary parameters of a historical work; what is necessary is an overall view of a historical text, since the two ways in which it may be read are not mutually exclusive, but mutually reinforcing.

HISTORIOGRAPHY

Historiography in antiquity dealt with important and noteworthy events, or at any rate those regarded as such, according to principles, interests, aims and tastes of great diversity; these events vary according to the social ambience in which a work is composed, according to its intended public, according to the historiographical tradition to which it belongs. It is not the case that what the ancients regarded as a historical subject is so for us or *vice versa*; and there is also always the risk of reading an ancient work and attributing to it an intention which was completely lacking. Most important of all, historiography in antiquity is not in any obvious sense a single subject and does not develop in a linear and homogeneous way, although its different strands obviously have affinities with one another. The most important point to consider is the category of readers regarded as his public by the author; the content and form of historical narrative

Emilio Gabba

depend on the types of readers envisaged and on their interests.[2] Thus, for instance, the style of Thucydides, compact and allusive, even obscure, contrasts with the expansive approach of Theopompus, Timaeus or Roman annalistic history. Polybius IX, 1–7 explains with absolute clarity that the pragmatic character of his work is intended to make it useful to readers who are men of affairs; precisely because he regards this as the most valuable aspect of history, he does not appreciate other types, which he knows and lists, but which are intended for a different public, of no interest to him (see p. 12).

The aim of Herodotus – the 'father of history', writing in the third quarter of the fifth century BC – was to record the great and remarkable deeds and varied achievements of mankind, and the diverse fates of different communities, to preserve their memory; he also provides important and interesting information on many peoples and countries, on religious practice and social behaviour. The world of Herodotus is derived from and linked with that of the epic poems of Homer and of Hesiod; *their* world had seen the development of the notion of truth and falsehood, and of the personality of an author with a capacity for judgement and criticism.[3] But Herodotus must also be seen in the context of practical concerns, geographical and ethnographical, themselves linked to the phenomenon of Greek colonisation; these concerns had largely dominated the earliest scientific enquiry of the Greeks. Although the evidence is not as secure as is often believed, it seems likely that the work of Herodotus was designed to be read in public; in any case, it presupposed an enquiring and interested public, though not necessarily one which possessed specialised knowledge or which was politically involved. It is important to realise that it is we who read

[2] A.Momigliano, 'The historians of the Classical world and their audiences: some suggestions', *Annali Scuola Normale Pisa* 8 (1978), 59–75.
[3] H.Strassburger, 'Die Wesensbestimmung der Geschichte durch die antike Geschichtsschreibung', *Sb. wiss.Gesellschaft an der J.W.Goethe-Universität Frankfurt-am-Main* 5.3 (1966), 47–97; 'Homer und die Geschichtsschreibung', *Sb. Heidelb.Akad.,Phil.–hist.Kl.* (1972), 1.

4

Herodotus as a cultural historian, projecting backwards the kind of conscious historiographical reflection which developed under the influence of Herodotus in the fourth century BC with Ephorus and Theopompus (see p. 10).

The centrality of the Persian Wars, which gives the *Histories* of Herodotus the appearance of a nationalist work, must not, in any case, be allowed to diminish the importance (even the chronological priority, according to Dionysius, *de Thuc.* 5) of another strand, that of local history; based on religious and secular records, this strand is full of political overtones, albeit restricted to that of individual *poleis*.[4] This approach to history was to acquire an apparatus of learning and to undergo important changes in the Hellenistic period; it sometimes became official in character, in particular with its concern for traditions of liberty and independence in the face of the levelling effect of the Hellenistic monarchies. Eventually, one reaction to Roman power was the writing of ever more learned local history. It remains a complex problem to determine the extent to which local history was used by general history.

The history of Thucydides has a quite different aim from that of Herodotus: it consists in the analysis on a political level of events of outstanding importance, an analysis which may be compared with that of the author of the tract 'On the *politeia* of the Athenians'; but Thucydides is a statesman, and the events analysed are regarded as far more important than any earlier occurrences. The analysis is developed in a narrative in which the historical material is selected and organised according to an interpretation which contributes to the basic aim; the reader will be a man of affairs who can benefit from the combined narrative and analysis of the historian, himself rich in experience, because of similarities or analogies between future and past events, because of the unchangeability of human nature (Thuc. I 22,4).

---

[4] S. Gozzoli, 'Una teoria antica sull'origine della storiografia greca', *Studi Classici e Orientali* 19–20 (1970–1), 158–211; H. Verdin, 'Notes sur l'attitude des historiens grecs à l'égard de la tradition locale', *Ancient Society* I (1970), 183–200.

Emilio Gabba

Thucydides' unavoidable reference to epic poetry (I 21) and even the link with Herodotus (whose narrative is picked up in the chapters of the 'Pentekontaeteia' (I, 89–118, covering 480 to 435 BC)) do not, however, indicate a conscious desire to follow a model or continue the work of a predecessor. Emphasis on the 'unity' of subject-matter between Herodotus and Thucydides and their study in sequence represent a later approach and misrepresent the originally different ways of understanding and narrating history which the two men offered. It is clear that Herodotus and Thucydides stand at the beginnings of two different historiographical traditions, even if borrowing and assimilation occurred.

Both in the case of Thucydides and in that of his successors, political history naturally focuses on contemporary events, with various consequences for their subject matter and for their principles of method and interpretation. Thus, the presence together in historical narrative, with equal status, of events and speeches is not only to be regarded as reflecting the practice of epic poetry; the practice in history derives its legitimacy and plausibility from the actual forms of Greek democratic political behaviour, where open debate played the largest part in the formation of public opinion and in decision making. (It is worth noting that the classicising return of Dionysius of Halicarnassus in the age of Augustus to traditional forms of speech marked a noble attempt to restore the values of the age of freedom before Alexander.) In this context, the closeness of the speeches to what was actually said (Thuc. I 22, I) is perhaps less important than the historiographical significance of the speeches themselves (see Polybius XII 25a,3–5 for polemic against Timaeus over invented speeches).[5] An analogous consideration is also valid for the political life of the Roman Republic and justifies the presence of speeches in early Roman historiography (naturally, following Greek models); Dionysius took them over thence, but he also knew well the political role of speeches and their analytical role in history (*Roman Antiquities* VII

---

[5] F.W.Walbank, *Speeches in Greek Historians* (Oxford, 1965).

66,3). The most accurate reports of speeches are to be found in Cato, who inserted his own speeches in his historical writing, guaranteeing thereby the diffusion of his political views as well. Cato's intended public will have been among other Romans and Italians of the middling sort, at whom also his 'On agriculture' was aimed; his pronouncements hostile to the nobility are to be understood against this background. In this general context the explanation of the decline of eloquence in terms of the loss of political freedom, developed under the Empire, is perfectly comprehensible.

The central position accorded to contemporary events, regarded as more important than any earlier occurrence, had some effect on the failure of the Greek world to elaborate an idea of moral and material progress, continuous and infinite, involving whole communities. Awareness of technical and scientific progress accompanying the different phases of human civilisation is something quite different. Notions of technical or scientific development, and of development in political and military institutions, are used to interpret the *past*, to describe the different phases of human civilisation, coinciding as they did with the gradual acquisition of stability, security, wealth and power – to explain, that is, arrival in the *present*, which is regarded as the highest point of development; no attempt is made to look beyond this point and there is no prospect of a further growth in power or of a higher cultural level. In fact, we are always faced with a conception of history where historical investigation invariably ends by concentrating on a contemporary historical or political problem. In other words, a biological view of history leads the historian to regard himself as being at the highest point of development, never on the way up, though occasionally in a period of decline. This type of analysis of the past appears in the 'Archaiologia' of Thucydides (1 2–19) and again in general terms in the account of the rise and development of the Athenian Empire in the fifth century BC. By its very nature, it cannot be applied to the *future*, which is rather conceived either as a period of decadence (so Polybius, who knew perfectly well the nature and extent of the cultural and political development of his own age) or as in some way a repetition of earlier human experience of history; it is precisely for this reason that history could be useful. (Some historians held that history went in cycles, a theory which obviously accommodated the idea of periods of decadence in the future.)

History as a source of instruction will only be possible if it is written by a man of affairs, expounding his own view of history to other men of affairs. The result, as emerges clearly in the cases of Thucydides and Polybius, was a limitation of the subject-matter of history to political and military matters and to the internal political history of one *polis* or state. Thucydides limited Greek history to the conflict between Athens and Sparta; Polybius eliminated almost completely the cultural aspects of history. This type of history presupposes that the historian belongs to the political ruling class, because only so can he be competent in political and military matters. The fact that some historians – Thucydides, Timaeus, Polybius, Josephus – were men of affairs who were exiled is relevant insofar as exile may have sharpened their historical sensibility and enlarged their horizon of experience.

The competence of the historian and man of affairs is the result of direct knowledge and experience of military, political and geographical matters; as a result, this type of history is predominantly the history of the present and displays only a limited interest in the origins of a people or a *polis*. The necessary competence cannot be based only on theory or on earlier historical works, as is the case with armchair historians. Since historical narrative has the precise function of allowing political forecasting, the demand for truth, the search for causes, the concern with documentation – all are vital for a proper analysis of events (Polybius XII 25b; 25d–26d). Other types of history obviously lay less stress on these requirements. The writing of history, then, is for Thucydides and Polybius an activity, to be undertaken by men of affairs, not by way of recreation, but as a fundamental duty; for political experience is indispensable for the writing of a history which can, in turn, form part of an education for politics (Polybius XII 28, 1–5). For Sallust, writing the preface to the *De coniuratione Catilinae*, reflection on history is itself a political act and a continuation of political activity.

Lying behind this correspondence between historian and man of affairs are both the theory and the practice of Greek and Roman political life; one is both an actor in and a spectator of political life and thus knows it from the inside. Thucydides, Polybius, Cato, and the Roman senators who wrote history in the second and first centuries BC all fit this mould. The accessibility of the history of the Greek *poleis* and of the Roman Republic is tied to the openness of decision making, which took place in popular assemblies or at least in councils of state; the resulting history is a history of political activity, at home and abroad, military action, rebellion – cause, intention and aim can always be known. Insurmountable difficulties arise with this type of history when governing classes, such as Roman senators, lose the power of decision making and hence also the possibility of knowing about it. Decline in political eloquence, no longer necessary when open debate has disappeared, corresponds to a reduction in the importance of history; this has now to limit itself to simple narration of facts, with little chance of establishing their causes, since decision making now rests in the hands of others. This state of affairs lies behind the political and historical drama of the contrast between senatorial freedom and despotic power which forms the theme of the history of Tacitus. The same state of affairs is also discussed, though now from a detached point of view, by Cassius Dio in the Severan age (LIII 19); for him the difference between history of the Empire and history of the Republic resides finally in the fact that it was impossible for a senatorial historian under the Empire to penetrate the secret decisions of the emperor, to check and compare different versions of events, to master the vast problems of Empire (history, like politics, was now three-dimensional). It only remained to be disbelievingly content with the official version of events and to attach importance to banal episodes involving the emperor and the Senate (LXXII 18,3–4 = III, p. 300 Boissevain).[6] It was

---

[6] E.Gabba, 'Sulla Storia Romana di Cassio Dione', *Rivista Storica Italiana* 67 (1955), 325–30.

no longer possible to expect of the governing class of a world-wide empire the moral awareness which the senatorial nobility retained during the first century AD. Imperial history became the history of the emperors, and has remained so to this day.

It is worth remarking that early in the eighteenth century the Count of Boulainvilliers, the defender of the historical and political function of the French nobility against the encroachments of monarchical power, took up the theme of Cassius Dio in similar terms and considered, among the difficulties faced by free historical enquiry under absolute monarchies, that of penetrating the secrecy of royal decisions; although the difficulty was not insurmountable in France, it was necessary largely to limit oneself to the narration of events without discovering their causes.[7]

The class of men of affairs, to which Thucydides and Polybius belonged, was of course limited in size; but even this group was not as a whole capable of complex and profound historical and political analysis. Nor was it easy to maintain the high level achieved by Thucydides. Xenophon, who continued his work, is much his inferior and his own interpretative approach is reductive and indeed banal.

On the other hand, the example of Herodotus was already available to indicate the possibility and the validity of a historical approach less politically involved, not limited to wars between and internal conflicts within *poleis*, and above all more varied and more open to a larger circle of readers interested in cultural history, in the history of institutions and of customs, in a wider geographical and human horizon, readers who sought in history also moral edification. Institutional history, based on rich antiquarian documentation often of local origin, also made possible the systematic studies and sociological generalisations of Aristotle and the anthropological constructions of Dicaearchus. The history of Ephorus and, in particular, of Theopompus, while retaining

---

[7] M.de Boulainvilliers, *Lettres sur les Anciens Parlemens de France que l'on nomme Etats-Généraux* I (London, 1753), 1–7.

a critical methodology, was aimed at an audience of educated general readers and consciously offered a history of civilisation or a world history, with an approach which went beyond the narrow limits of Greece itself. The model of Theopompus was taken up by Dionysius of Halicarnassus in the age of Augustus, openly critical of the 'factual' history of Polybius (*epist. ad Pomp.* 6,1–8) and, in particular, polemicising against a conception of history as a history of military action (*Roman Antiquities* I 8,1–3; V 48,1).[8]

The ancient discussion on the superiority of history over epideictic oratory, already to be found in Ephorus and taken up by Timaeus (note the sarcastic comments of Polybius XII 28,7–9), is probably evidence for an awareness of the fact that the two literary genres had a single aim, the formation and instruction of a serious public opinion – in other words, a large-scale pedagogical function.

It was clearly also the intention of someone like Dionysius to fulfil this function, as it had been earlier of Theopompus and Timaeus; for they aimed not simply at describing the outcome of an event or outlining the political analysis which it might suggest, but also at characterising the event itself as it evolved (Dionysius, *Roman Antiquities* V 56,1; VII 66,2–3). The paradigmatic importance of an event, and hence its educational value and the lesson to be drawn, does not depend solely on its outcome, but precisely on following the entire process: causation, behaviour of those involved, changing vicissitudes. Hence the necessity of filling in any gaps in the process, for instance by the introduction of speeches; these are of course invented but rest on a necessary hypothesis, given the author's general intuition about the event and about its probable evolution in a particular social context. A similar procedure in general terms was followed by the Roman historians who in the course of writing their annals attempted in all seriousness to reconstruct the unknown archaic phase of Roman history; they did so by

---

[8] S.Gozzoli, 'Polibio e Dionigi d'Alicarnasso', *Studie Classici e Orientali* 25 (1976), 149–76; E.Noè, in *Ricerche di storiografia greca di età romana* (Pisa, 1979), 21–116.

using the political and ideological models of contemporary public life, convinced that institutions and problems were substantially unchanged. (In a sense, they were simply standing on its head the notion that future history was to be a repetition of the past.) The close link between annalistic history and the law and legal history (the same person was often a historian and a jurist) gave this assumption plausibility.

Deliberately writing in opposition to Polybius and attempting to provide as complete a picture as possible, Dionysius also made much of the mythical and legendary part of the story of Rome; he went so far as to posit an early Hellenisation of the city and at the same time, in Book I of his *Roman Antiquities*, provided a synthesis between antiquarian research into institutions and historical investigation of origins.[9]

Ephorus and Theopompus used a broader canvas, not so much for the sake of following the example of Herodotus as because the declining power of the Greek *poleis* reduced the importance of the history of their wars. Greek history in Ephorus, a history of the succession of different hegemonies, envisages and foresees the end of the period of the *poleis* and the appearance of universal history, inevitably dominated by cultural history.

To a certain extent the Macedonian monarchy had already been a unifying element in Greek history, even before the conquests of Alexander; these had then opened up new historical prospects and suggested both a content for history in which the exotic and the abnormal predominated, and a new means of attracting readers. The genre of dramatic history (whatever its origin) attempted to achieve the emotional participation of the reader in the situations and events of the story; this was possible, among other reasons, because the social and cultural horizons of this reader were much wider

[9] E.Gabba, 'Dionigi e la "Storia di Roma arcaica"', in *Actes IX Congrès Budé* I (Paris, 1975), 218–29.

and more diverse than those of earlier readers of history.[10] A clash with the renascent pragmatic history championed by Polybius was inevitable. But it is also necessary to remember that Polybius regarded himself as belonging to a line of historians who were experts and specialists, diplomats and generals; the line goes from Nearchus and Ptolemy, generals of Alexander, to Caesar. (It remains true that the methodological argument between Polybius and the dramatic historian Phylarchus involved also a political split between the Achaean politican who admired Aratus and a historian who admired the reforming kings of third-century Sparta.)

The Hellenistic monarchies were in the end unable to inspire a universal vision of Greek history, which tended increasingly to concentrate on the politics of equilibrium between the great powers. Polybius turned to Rome as the centre of Mediterranean history, following the precocious intuition of Timaeus that what mattered in history was now occurring in the West; this intuition had also been adopted and used by the earliest Roman historians at the end of the third century BC, presenting Rome to the Greek world on the occasion of the clash between Rome and Carthage. It is also worth noting that Polybius added a third element to the polarity between Rome and the Hellenistic monarchies – a third force composed of the Greek federal states; they were based on a political formula which went beyond the narrow limits of the *polis* and which might have shown the way to organise large territorial states on the basis of free institutions.

Meanwhile, the writing of history under the Hellenistic monarchies followed two paths, both charged with political and ideological significance.[11] There were on the one hand monographs on political history, with the personalities of the individual kings at their centre, redolent of the Alexander

---

[10] B.L.Ullman, 'History and tragedy', *TAPhA* 83 (1942), 25–53; F.W.Walbank, 'Tragic history : a reconsideration', *BICS* 2 (1955), 4–14; *idem*, 'History and tragedy', *Historia* 9(1960), 216–34.

[11] K.Rosen, 'Politische Ziele in der frühen hellenistischen Geschichtsschreibung', *Hermes* 107 (1979), 460–77.

tradition; there were also biographies, providing for the new taste for individual histories, in contrast to the collective stories of the *poleis*. On the other hand, the Hellenistic states, to assert their own continuity with the past, made much of the traditions and local history of the regions now under their control. Manetho in Egypt and Berossus in Babylonia are the best examples of this tendency, supported as they were by the power of the state; and it was in Egypt that the state organized the translation into Greek of the sacred books of its Jewish subjects.[12] Hecataeus of Abdera, Megasthenes and Agatharcides imported into historical research the scientific approach of philosophical and anthropological analysis, naturally with an interest in the East.[13] At the same time, the texts of the earliest Greek historians of all, the so-called *logographoi*, were republished with additions, while remaining under their original names; the intention was to satisfy the public demand for the exotic, but the effect was to mystify later scholars.[14]

New tastes and new cultural interests correspond, as we have seen, to a wider, though not a deeper, public interest in history. Extracts from histories and anthologies of historical writing had already been published in the fourth century, following a procedure widely used in other fields; they covered specific themes of an extraordinary or miraculous nature, geographical, scientific or social. Such works were usually published under the name of the author from whom the excerpts were made, despite the fact that supplementary material was often added, with the result that they now raise insoluble problems of paternity. The existence of the anthologies indicates a shift of interest away from the history of which the extracts had originally been a part towards paradoxography; this change of taste certainly corresponds to the cultural demands of social strata which had not earlier

[12] E.J.Bickerman, 'Origines gentium', *Class.Philol.* 47 (1952), 65–81.
[13] S.Gozzoli, 'Etnografia e politica in Agatarchide', *Athenaeum* 56 (1978), 54–79.
[14] B.Virgilio, 'Logografia greca e storiografia locale pseudepigraphos in età ellenistica', *Studi Classici e Orientali* 29 (1979), 1–37.

read history. We are faced with a strand of literary activity of the greatest importance, popular pseudo-history; side by side with more refined literature, it persisted through the whole of the Hellenistic and Roman periods. In a certain sense its ultimate product was the fanciful biographies of the *Historia Augusta* (see p. 50), written for the ignorant new ruling classes of the fourth century AD; it was for them also that résumés of Roman history were composed.

It is significant that in the same climate of paradoxographical literature the 'novel' is born and develops; the novel in antiquity is in fact a form of history. Before it took up the vicissitudes in love and the adventures of unknown persons (in the second century AD), it was a tale of invented and miraculous events in the lives of great men: Alexander, Ninus and Semiramis, Hannibal. The ancient historical novel was the result of a process of free invention which certainly did not expect to take anyone in; paradoxography likewise was a literary genre which chose odd stories to narrate and in some cases actually invented them together with the names of alleged authorities; in these stories it is often easy to see political overtones, linked with crude, but efficient, attempts to mould public opinion by playing on credulity and superstition.

In other words, beside 'elevated' history there was always 'historical' writing of a more popular kind; the former was aimed at an upper class which was limited in size, but held political power; the latter, however, was no less interested in influencing public opinion.[15] It is, for instance, well known that in all ancient wars polemical versions and political slogans were circulated among the people; it is also well known that in order to make them more authoritative such stories and slogans were often circulated by centres of prophecy or were linked with famous cult centres, and that they exploited ancient myths and hallowed traditions. One thinks of the role

---

[15] M.Sordi (ed.), *Propaganda e persuasione occulta nell'antichità; Storiografia e propaganda; I canali della propaganda nel mondo antico* (Univ. Cattolica del S.Cuore, Milan, Contributi Istituto Storia Antica, vols. II, III, IV; Milan, 1974, 1975, 1976).

of the so-called Sibylline oracles – part erudite, part popular –at least from the end of the third century BC onwards in the Greek East; they were usually, though not always, anti-Roman. Elements of this material of course sometimes penetrated into history proper. (By contrast, the rumours which figure so prominently in the work of Tacitus are never of popular origin, but are suggestions and opinions originating and developing among the upper class, usually in opposition to the official line; sometimes the rumours are even of official origin.)

The main effect of the existence of the material I have been describing was to make possible popular 'history', with a cruder and (at any rate to us) more evident propaganda content. One thinks of the elaboration in a Seleucid context of anti-Jewish slanders, which created an entire literature, and of the anti-Roman nonsense accepted even by a historian like Antisthenes of Rhodes, cited by Polybius (XVI 14) and actually preserved by a paradoxographer of the Hadrianic age.

It is not always easy to make the conceptual distinction between this kind of fantasy history and a piece of deliberate (but plausible) falsification introduced into a serious historical narrative. It is for this reason that a historian of the calibre of Eduard Schwartz made the mistake of abandoning as 'romance' much Greek historical writing of the Imperial age.[16] This difficulty of ours explains why the pragmatic history of Polybius, reacting against the alternative approach to history, is closer to the ideal of the modern historian, despite its limitation to political and military affairs. One must, however, never lose sight of the remarkable and revealing fact that the tendency to fantasy and escapism existed beside the demand for scientific rigour, manifest not only in history of the Polybian kind, but also in the erudite and technical literature of the Hellenistic age.

---

[16] E.Gabba, 'Ed.Schwartz e la storiografia greca dell'età imperiale', *Annali Scuola Normale Pisa* 9 (1979), 1033–49.

The history of Livy, a man of learning and not a politician, is in a certain sense a retreat from the ideal which saw the man of affairs and the historian as one and the same, *res gestae* and *historia rerum gestarum* as two sides of the same coin. The work belongs rather to the strand of history aiming at moral education, though it follows an independent line. As emerges clearly from the preface, Livy shared the pessimistic vision of Sallust and viewed the present with anxiety and disenchantment: in this sense he was out of tune with the Augustan age. The difference is that Sallust had set out to examine as a politician those moments of recent Roman history in which the corruption of the ruling oligarchy was most apparent; that corruption was the source of a graver disease which had affected the whole body politic. Sallust attempted to analyse the social, economic and moral causes of the decline, placing them in a broader anthropological context; he saw no way out in the future, writing as he did in the midst of the civil wars of the triumviral period. Livy also had no concrete suggestions for resolving the crisis, although its gravity and scale were clear to him behind the façade of the Augustan restoration. His pessimism was in a sense deeper than that of Sallust, since Rome had now emerged from the civil wars; but their end, apparently auguring well, made no difference to the decadence which Livy observed, not from the point of view of a politician, but with hopeless nostalgia for a lost past. An account of the whole history of Rome is thus for Livy the best way to show how the spectacular rise of the city was always aided (and can now be historically explained) by the presence of precisely those values whose disappearance brought on the crisis. A fact of history, the rise of Rome and her decline, was thus seen by Livy as a moral problem. It is, of course, obvious that the idealisation of Rome before the onset of moral and political decline could only be seen in the context of a conservative ethic; this involved the extolling of the great civic virtues, individual and collective, which were in the first instance the heritage of the governing oligarchy and were then imitated by the entire citizen body. Hence Livy's instinctive acceptance of the senatorial ideology; but at the same time he was far from sharing the approach and the political involvement of annalistic history written by senatorial historians (p. 20). At the same time, locked in his moral dilemma, he was only very slightly troubled by the problem of the relationship between the new regime and the traditional governing class (to which he did not belong); he also largely lacked the broad imperial interest which one glimpses in the ideological presuppositions of his contemporary Dionysius of Halicarnassus.

Dionysius' return to classicism, whose theoretical basis is laid in the initial chapters of the first book of his *De antiquis oratoribus*, is exemplified in his historical writing; it had various aims. First and foremost, it took up the classical literary tradition at the point where it was fragmented at the beginning of the Hellenistic period; it was a unifying point of reference for the Greek upper classes favoured by Rome; it saw in Roman rule a cultural and political system which permitted the renaissance of true Greek traditions. Dionysius' aim was clear, though his belief that it could be achieved may have seemed illusory to some; nonetheless, his careful approach in a certain sense made historical reflection possible for the Greek upper classes of the Empire, both for senators and for members of the imperial bureauracy; they went on to write Roman and other history from a firmly imperial viewpoint: Arrian, Appian, Cassius Dio and Herodian all went far beyond the approach of Tacitus, confined to the clash between senatorial liberty and imperial despotism. Dionysius also provided the formal historical scheme adopted by the *Jewish Antiquities* of Flavius Josephus.

The position of Josephus is peculiar for a number of reasons.[17] He was a figure of the greatest importance in the Jewish revolt of AD 66 and then in the 60s wrote a history of the war in Aramaic, now lost, for his fellow Jews living in Parthia, followed by a version in Greek for the Jewish upper classes of the Diaspora. Josephus' intention was to present

---

[17] P. Vidal-Naquet, *Il buon uso del tradimento. Flavio Giuseppe e la Guerra Giudaica* (trad. ital.) (Rome, 1980).

them with his own interpretation of the tragedy, combining characteristically Jewish motifs such as prophecy with strands from Greek history writing, especially that of Polybius: political and social concerns prevail over religious. The other writings of Josephus belonged rather to the last decade of the century, and there was a good reason for his renewed activity. The *Antiquities* are, in intention, for a wider public; they are an attempt to make the Jewish world and its history known and above all to explain the logic and the circumstances of coexistence between Jews and pagans. It was a political problem; both for Palestine and for the Diaspora it was necessary to characterise the links between the world and culture of the Jews and the various political powers with whom the Jewish people had to live or to whom it was subjected: Persians, Macedonians, Ptolemies, Seleucids and finally Romans. Rome is the central reality: respect for and recognition of its power and of the monarchy were already present in the earlier Jewish writer Philo (as also in the author of the *Letter to Aristeas*); but why did the need to *explain* suddenly become urgent in the Domitianic age? Is it symptomatic of the doubts and uncertainties, discontents and anxieties, which form the prelude to the revolt of the Diaspora under Trajan? It is interesting that Josephus should also have felt the need to continue the polemic against the Egyptian Apion begun by Philo, with a defence valid for ever of Jewish culture and religion. The polemic was conducted largely with arguments Greek in character: textual sources which prove, among other things, the greater antiquity of Jewish civilisation in relation to Greek (a few years later Philo of Byblus boasted of the chronological priority of Semitic and Phoenician civilisations, p. 35). A motive can also be found in the fact that two decades after the events Justus of Tiberias felt the need to attack Josephus for his activities in Galilee in AD 66–7, impelling him to attempt a reply, often unconvincing. Both Justus and Josephus, in his *Autobiography*, appeal to the Jewish audience of the Diaspora, for whom this ancient quarrel still had or was recovering meaning.

Any piece of historical writing, which has a minimum of political commitment and aims at least at some ideal, naturally attempts to establish its own interpretative approach in the reconstruction of the past, in the choice and elaboration of themes and facts, and in the organisation and disposition of the narrative. Some distortion of the past thus always takes place; its extent often cannot be assessed in the absence of comparative material, but it may be attributed to the influence of the political and social ambience of the historian, especially if the historian is also a man of affairs. Nonetheless, except for a few cases of excessive subservience to particular interests, the distortion cannot really be classified as propaganda. Insofar as propaganda existed in antiquity it was not channelled through history writing; instead, coins, inscriptions, statues (as of emperors in public places) served its ends, or used literary productions more widely diffused than works of history, such as oracles and (during the civil wars at Rome) open letters, magisterial edicts, pamphlets, documents of varying authenticity, or the circulation of suspicions and rumours. Roman annalistic history, before and after Sulla, evidently reflects the political beliefs and the ideology of the senatorial nobility and sometimes betrays traces of conflicts within that oligarchy. The occurrence of political, juridical and religious problems simply provides evidence of the cultural homogeneity of history writing under the Republic. It is even doubtful if the history of Velleius, openly admiring the regime of Tiberius and of Sejanus, can really be called propaganda, as has sometimes been done.

There is a tendency to regard as a propagandist an author who has deliberately made himself the spokesman of a public figure, disseminating and justifying his activities and his aims. Claudian could thus be regarded as the propagandist of Stilicho.[18] The argument is an important one, because if Claudian were the official propagandist of Stilicho, it would

---

[18] A.Cameron, *Claudian. Poetry and Propaganda at the Court of Honorius* (Oxford, 1970).

be possible to engage in a process of historical reconstruction and move from Claudian to the aims of Stilicho. It has also been suggested, in a more sweeping but perhaps less rigorous argument, that one should take into account in this context the attempts, assisted by the natural human disposition to conform, to influence or direct public opinion, with the help of intellectuals and by means 'of the organisation of cultural activity; such attempts of course relate largely to the educated. In this way, ideas, arguments, historical and other interpretations, all reflecting the point of view of the powers-that-be, were put into circulation, a fact of which historians writing under the Roman Empire were already aware. The approach was occasionally adopted by politicians towards the end of the Republic, systematically under the Empire: chapter 21 of *The Roman Revolution* of Sir Ronald Syme is called 'The organisation of opinion'. The extent to which Horace reflects the ideology of the principate is well known:[19] after all, the *Carmen Saeculare* was commissioned by the *princeps*. Later, Quintilian discussed the theoretical problems of the relationship between political power, intellectual activity and education.[20] The public functions of a *rhetor*, from Dio Chrysostom to the representatives of the Second Sophistic movement (see p. 41 n.39) and on to Libanius and Themistius in the fourth century, are clear enough; they finally received the stamp of official recognition with the authors of the Latin panegyrics of the fourth century. (By way of contrast, in the published form of the *Panegyric* of Pliny there are clear traces of deliberate detachment from the conventional approach demanded by the theme.)

Despite all this, the direct influence of the powers-that-be on the writing of history and on literature in general should not be exaggerated, following the analogies of the modern world; similarly, of course, one may be sceptical about the effectiveness of intellectual opposition to the principate.[21]

---

[19] A.La Penna, *Orazio e l'ideologia del Principato* (Turin, 1963).
[20] I.Lana, *Studi sul pensiero politico antico* (Naples, 1973), 427ff.
[21] M.I.Finley, 'Censura nell'antichità classica', *Belfagor* 32 (1977), 605–22.

Emilio Gabba

If we consider as a whole what one might call professional Greek and Roman histories, we observe that the problems discussed are to a large extent those of modern historians of antiquity also; nor is the observation as banal as one might at first sight suppose. The relationship between the Greek world and the East in the Archaic and Classical periods; the emergence and development of the Athenian Empire; the decline of the *poleis* and the emergence of the monarchies; Greek expansion in the East; the Hellenisation of the East; the rise of Rome and the reasons for her expansion; the causes of the civil wars in Italy; the crisis of the Republic and the establishment of the principate; the dramatic collapse of Palestinian Judaism; the transition from principate to dominate; the decline of the Empire in the fourth century; from Herodotus to Ammianus Marcellinus, the problems developed by historians in antiquity are largely our problems also, despite differences in perspective and approach and different solutions. The interpretation of history in Eusebius, already to be found in Melito of Sardis in the second century, regards the whole of pagan history down to Augustus as the indispensable process whereby the world was united in preparation for the coming of Christ; this interpretation dominated historical and political analysis in the medieval West. Similarly, a universalist vision of ancient history, which underlies the work of Orosius, appealed to a wider audience than that of the early fifth century and in due course, along with *The City of God* of Augustine, influenced the 'Discours sur l'histoire universelle' of Bossuet.

One may accept that the coincidence we have observed is to a large extent the result of the fact that the themes which interest us actually derive from those of history in antiquity; it remains true, however, that some problems which were central in antiquity have now no interest: the problem of the origins of Rome, in the form in which it was posed in antiquity, is to us simply a historiographical problem. For one now investigates the origins of Rome in the first instance with the help of archaeology and anthropology, even if some of the results actually confirm the literary tradition.

There is no doubt that history in antiquity, in the context of the problems which it analysed, favoured military, political and institutional affairs. It is open to question, however, whether economic affairs are really missing altogether. One may answer both yes and no. In our sense of the term, they are missing: one never finds economic factors at the centre of historical analysis or as the central element in historical interpretation, nor even an independent treatment of economic change. On the other hand, a writer like Polybius knew very well that a state needed the economic capacity to sustain its hegemonial aims and that economic factors played a part in political history. Josephus noted the social and economic causes of the Jewish revolt, though his perspective was not an economic one. In his account of human civilisation, Thucydides showed that economic factors (trade, the accumulation of wealth, the building of cities) were fundamental and governed the historical process. Leaving aside his moralising account of the corrosive effect of wealth, Sallust was yet well aware of the decisive effect of economic factors on the crisis of the Republic. If one looks carefully at the annalistic histories written after Sulla, one observes that in their reconstruction of early Roman society, naturally based on contemporary analogies, the problem of the land is at the forefront; one finds in particular an interest in the origin and development of great estates and in the changing use of *ager publicus*.

There is nothing of the kind in Greek history writing, despite the fact that problems of the land often stood at the centre of the stage in Greek history. The tradition preserved by Appian on the Gracchan crisis belongs in the Roman sphere; it assigns a great deal of importance to social and economic factors (decline of the peasantry, new forms of exploitation of the soil, rural impoverishment), albeit inserted into a political framework. Appian was equally aware that a knowledge of the economic potential of the Empire was essential to a historical account of it and devoted a special monograph to the subject (Praef. 61).

Moving outside the field of history writing, where we find scattered pieces of information on economic history, there occurred with Xenophon and Aristotle some specific analysis of problems of economics and economic history; this, however, did not go beyond general remarks on the one hand and practical suggestions on the other, without really achieving the status of a technical theory. Similarly, philosophical analyses of the value and use of wealth, sometimes in separate treatises, are informative about mental attitudes rather than about economic factors as such.

To sum up: the different types of history in antiquity aimed at different readers, had different aims, were composed according to different principles. It is in the first instance this fact which determines the varying value and meaning of Greek and Roman works of history. Even the information preserved in a single historical genre is often of quite variable value; the criteria of each historian's choice must be individually established. Things which seem of the greatest importance to us may be left out by a historian of the highest quality as irrelevant to his interpretative approach, an approach which *we* must understand and evaluate. Information was also sometimes omitted because it did not fit the patriotic vision of the author or because the political consequences were simply unimaginable. Thus, we know of the Gallic capture of the Capitol from some lines of Silius Italicus (*Punica* I 525ff., IV 150ff., VI 655ff.), though it perhaps occurred in Ennius (*Annales* 164–5 v); there is no trace in the standard annalistic accounts which offer a quite different version.[22] Similarly, the tradition that Rome actually surrendered to Porsenna does not turn up before Pliny and Tacitus (*NH* XXXIV 139; *Hist.* III 72). An example of the second possibility may be found in the tradition of an equal distribution of two *jugera* of land to every citizen by Romulus when the city was founded;[23] this tradition is known to us from antiquarian sources and from the technical literature on land-

---

[22] O. Skutsch, 'The Fall of the Capitol', *JRS* 43 (1953), 77–9.
[23] E. Gabba, 'Per la tradizione dell'*heredium* romuleo', *Rend. Ist. Lombardo* 112 (1978), 250–8.

surveying, but does not occur in the annalistic versions, which could not have explained how this original equality related to the equally original division of the citizen body into patricians and plebeians, of vastly differing wealth. Many things are ignored by historians of contemporary events as obviously known to their readers. Thus one ancient writer on military technique lamented the fact that historians of earlier ages, interested only in wars themselves, had left out many details potentially interesting to posterity. This failing was accentuated precisely by the overwhelming interest of historians in contemporary affairs. Again, an exalted vision of history excluded some matters as being apparently unfitting to the dignity of the subject.

One ancient writer on the theory of history writing, who held that the sole duty of the historian was 'to say exactly how things happened' (Lucian, *De conscribenda historia* 39; Ranke almost certainly derived his dictum from him), was right to insist above all on the need for impartiality and independence in a historian; but one must not miss the irony and the oddity of Lucian's comparison between the sudden flowering of 'popular' and romantic history, even with its literary pretensions, and the magnificent Thucydidean model, aimed at citizens involved in political activity. It would be equally odd to compare the content and historical method of the *Bellum Hispaniense* and Caesar's *De bello civili*: the former is a vigorous and ingenuous product of a Caesarian official, remarkable evidence of his ideology and moral code; the latter is a work of art, designed for high political ends.

Furthermore, objectivity, even if achieved, was always confined within the narration of a chosen sequence of facts; this choice corresponded to an established perspective and was itself an act of interpretation. In any case, we know how difficult it is to distinguish between facts and their interpretations, which are for us further facts. It is, of course, reasonable for a modern scholar to examine, as and when necessary, the sources of a historian in antiquity; the research involved is legitimate insofar as it brings us closer to a source contemporary with the events described or at least recreates an earlier source. But it is more to the point that source criticism enables us to establish the ways in which thought and interpretation are influenced and develop. The changes made to an earlier source reveal the emergence of new values; the very choice of sources by an author may be of the highest significance. Why did Fabius Pictor, when dealing with the tradition concerning the founder of his own city, follow or at least cite an obscure local historian of the Hellenistic age, Diocles of Peparethus, when it is likely that he knew an indigenous tradition? The answer is to be sought in the intentions of the first Roman historian, writing in Greek, for Greeks, the story of his city.

HOMER

The peculiar educational and cultural value of the Homeric poems for the Greek world at all periods was the result of the fact that they enshrined the whole collective wisdom of a culture; naturally, attitudes to the poems varied from one period to another. Furthermore, not everyone in antiquity accepted the conventional evaluation of the poems: Xenophanes criticised Homer and Hesiod for presenting the gods with all the vices of human beings (Fr. 11 Diels-Kranz), and Plato wished to exclude all poetry, including Homer, from his ideal state, despite his recognition of the extent to which Homer had been 'the educator of Greece and someone who deserved to be taken up and studied in order to administer and educate the world' (*Respublica* 606e–607a). From the historiographical point of view, of even greater importance is the debate which arose in the learned world of the Hellenistic age on the value of the information in Homer on the geography and (implicitly) early history of the Greek world and the Mediterranean. This debate is known to us essentially from the first book of Strabo's *Geography*, written under Augustus and Tiberius; the book is devoted to extended polemic against Eratosthenes who claimed that the poet had no educational intention and in consequence no concern for scientific and technical accuracy: his only intention was to entertain, and it was impossible to find any certain information in Homer's fantasy narrative, even if *some* precise geographical knowledge lay behind it. The existence of nuggets of historical and geographical truth in Homer, even if surrounded by passages of free invention, had already been recognised by Polybius (III 2, 1–4, 8; see F. W. Walbank, *Commentary* III, pp. 577–87). This view was then given extensive theoretical treatment by Strabo, with a defence to the last detail of Homer's veracity; this approach carried with it not only belief in the historicity of the two events which form the themes of the poems, the Trojan War and the voyages of Odysseus, but also in the geographical, topographical and historical reality of events, places and areas. Strabo attributes to Homer deep knowledge and scientific experience, while allowing him a certain liberty in adjusting the position of peoples and places and a certain margin for poetical embellishment (Strabo I 1, 1–10; 2, 1ff.). Strabo is well aware of the fact that different theories had been propounded on the wanderings of Odysseus and on their localisation, even by those convinced of the substantial historicity of the story; but more important, because it reveals the ideological importance of the defence of Homer's veracity, is the remark at I 2, 8 on the political and educational value of an invented narrative, provided it had a social or political purpose and tended towards history. Such a narrative belonged to a cultural stage before the development of history and philosophy, both of limited appeal, while poetry was an affair of the people, as emerged from the existence of verse plays and from the even more extensive knowledge of Homer among ordinary people. Despite his date Strabo's reasoning reveals an attitude which was decisive for the way in which the Greeks reconstructed their past and for the way in which their approach to historical analysis followed the Homeric model for understanding history and representing its unfolding.

Strabo's argument draws attention to the political value placed in Greece on geography, or at the very least to the close connection between geographical exploration and the exercise of political power, as evident to Strabo (I 2, I) as it had been to Polybius (XXXIV 5,7 for his critique of Pytheas), Agatharcides, Posidonius[24] and Alexander Polyhistor. The fact that the greatest geographer of the Augustan age could reaffirm the prior claims of Homer as a geographer obviously implies the reassertion of the values of the Classical tradition, in the same way and at the same time as Dionysius of Halicarnassus was expounding his views on oratory (p. 18).

Acceptance of Homer as a historical source and the direct or indirect association of the whole of Greek myth and legend with the Homeric world meant that myths and legends were generally accepted as part and parcel of early Greek history and furnished a detailed framework for it. Not even Thucydides was able to dissociate himself from this point of view, both accepting the historical reality of the Trojan War and using the data of epic poetry as evidence for his reconstruction of the development of civilisation in Greece. In the realm of ideas, the Homeric poems, especially the *Iliad*, and the historical vision enshrined in them were of the greatest importance in promoting the growth of Greek national sentiment (later exploited by Isocrates), although it is not possible to hold that such a sense lay behind their composition.

As far as the *Odyssey* is concerned, the problem of the localisation and identification of the places mentioned has been the subject of a long debate in modern times (with some scholars even imagining the existence of an earlier Phoenician *periplous*), a debate which still goes on, even if its terms are now more concrete and involve the process of Greek colonisation in the eastern and central Mediterranean and especially in Sicily and Magna Graecia (not to mention attempts to localise places and events connected with the myth of the Argonauts).

In fact, as far as we are concerned, the chief significance of the Homeric epic for the study of history lies in the problematic nature of its composition. This is not the place even for a brief account of the complexities of the origin of epic: the long

---

[24] A.Momigliano, *Alien Wisdom. The limits of Hellenization* (Cambridge, 1975), 22ff.

process of composition, initially oral, but eventually influenced by the adoption of writing in Greece and the developing literacy of poets and audience; the process of transmission, also oral, and successive modifications of the poems as a
result; the formulaic technique; problems of language; problems of publication. These and other such questions naturally
raise problems of chronology which are not easy to resolve
and which involve problems of method. The way in which
the poems were composed over a long period of time involves for a start the presumption, which is easy to verify, of a
number of precise moments of major creative activity. The
problem then arises – and it is this which concerns historians
– of the unity and historicity of the society described in the
Homeric poems; that is, do the poems refer to a single
historical period and, if so, to which? In fact, the analysis of
the material culture and of the social and economic institutions of the poems permits at once the rejection of the unitary
hypothesis and the separation of the aristocratic, warrior
world of the *Iliad* from the world of Odysseus, more developed, open to the sea and to the West, marked by mercantile
and individualistic elements; two different social systems
have been juxtaposed. This juxtaposition is certainly artificial
and the origins of the two systems are to be sought in
different historical situations. Comparison with external evidence, specially archaeological, seems at first sight to place
the two systems in the late Mycenaean period on the one
hand and in the age of the 'poet' shortly before 700 BC,
apparently with the deliberate exclusion of material from the
intervening period.

This interpretative approach allows one to reject as
methodologically false any theory involving a global analysis
of the 'Homeric' world. But the decipherment of the Linear
B script of the Mycenaean tablets poses the problem of the
relationship between Mycenaean and 'Homeric' worlds.
Here also one must begin by observing that the linking of
individual passages, phrases or words of the poems with data
from the tablets can never lead to general conclusions valid
for the poems as a whole; the process is in any case dubious,

since the tablets are the product of a bureaucratic administration, wholly different from the social class which forms the subject-matter of epic. This does not mean, of course, that there are not in epic fragmentary Mycenaean survivals which can be securely identified, or that one cannot *compare* the picture presented by the poems with the picture emerging from the tablets. At this point one must observe that the formation of epic in the so-called Dark Ages produced a picture of a long-past heroic age whose events and personalities were nostalgically evoked as superhuman. This poetic evocation of the past finally supplanted the actual memory of events, less remarkable on every count. The process of evocation also invested the past with a primitive aspect, quite uncharacteristic of the highly organised Mycenaean world which is emerging from the tablets. In other words, an interpretation such as that of M.I.Finley may largely be accepted, despite criticism levelled against it: a comparison between the Mycenaean and the 'Homeric' worlds shows that there was a complete break between the Mycenaean world and later ages and that Homer is no guide to the former.

Asking in different terms the question of Eratosthenes, whether Homer could be used as a historical source, and developing what we know from comparative evidence of oral composition, we may legitimately ask to what extent the centre piece of epic, the Trojan War, was an historical event; that is, can such an event be *remembered* for generations in its essentials, without the changes, exaggerations, distortions, falsifications readily documented in other spheres? It is impossible for archaeology to confirm a historical event such as the war fought by the Greeks against Troy; the same is true, *a fortiori*, of the Mycenaean tablets; the fact that the historicity of the war was accepted in antiquity does not help, since the ancients were confronted with an unshakable tradition. In any case, not all accepted the whole of the tradition on the war, such as its causes and outcome; beside Eratosthenes stands Dio of Prusa. He held the paradoxical view that the responsibility for the war lay with the Greeks (see *Oratio*

Troiana (XI), I, pp. 115–54 von Arnim); that the Trojans really won; and that they then sent out the men who settled the West (including Aeneas). Dio insisted on the function fulfilled by the Trojan story in rousing panhellenic sentiment at the time of the Persian Wars. This function no longer existed under the Roman Empire, and as a result Dio felt able at last to establish the truth. Dio's disenchantment with the Homeric tradition is accompanied by seriousness of approach and by a pro-Roman aim.[25]

Some support for the notion of Greek involvement in Asiatic affairs towards the end of the second millennium has been sought in a connection between the 'Achaioi' of epic and the land called 'Ahhijawa' in Hittite documents; but, once again, no confirmation can be found for the specific incident of the Trojan War, even if some general participation of Greek elements in warlike episodes in Asia (perhaps in connection with an invasion from the North?) produced the notion of a grand expedition, as presented in the *Iliad* and *Odyssey*.

The search for Mycenaean elements in the Homeric poems has produced interesting results in a number of fields – language, social usage, concepts, material culture – but no general conclusions may be drawn. It even seems that in some cases memories of *early* Mycenaean periods have been preserved, before the twelfth century: thus the famous helmet ornamented with boars' tusks of *Iliad* x 261ff. and the tower-like shield of Ajax, covering his entire body and quite different from a normal shield. Ajax himself seems to stem from a very early context and does not appear in the Catalogue of Ships. Thus the notion of early elements being preserved embedded in later strata is confirmed, and so is at the same time a Mycenaean core to the poems. A widely held view goes on to consider the Catalogue of Ships and the Catalogue of Trojans as Mycenaean survivals. If this were true of the former, it would be a remarkable document of united action

---

[25] P. Desideri, *Dione di Prusa. Un intellettuale greco nell'Impero Romano* (Florence, 1979), 431–4, 465–8.

against Troy by the Greek world and provide important evidence of the extent of geographical knowledge, since the epithets attached to different places seem not to be formulaic, but rather to be precise. There is no doubt that the Catalogue of Ships does not fit its setting in the *Iliad*: it does not make sense to provide a general description of the Greeks at Troy at an advanced stage of the war; there are numerous discrepancies with the rest of the poem; and there are omissions. The Catalogue appears, therefore, to have been composed and transmitted separately and inserted into the *Iliad* at a late stage. Attempts at dating it have been based on attempts to identify places and peoples mentioned in it, with little prospect of success, since many were already unknown to the scholars of the Hellenistic age. The Mycenaean character of the list is hypothesised on the basis of the fact that all identifiable places were inhabited in the Mycenaean period; some were destroyed at the end of the Mycenaean period and not reoccupied; some lost their autonomy after the beginning of the seventh century BC (the latest likely moment for the insertion of the Catalogue into the *Iliad*). But it must be said that, impressive as they are, the archaeological arguments are not decisive and can indeed be stood on their head; fragmentary recollections of an earlier age may have been deliberately inserted in the poems. Furthermore, there is no way of deciding whether the intention of the Catalogue was to describe a real present or past situation or to create a more or less archaising reconstruction.

Even greater difficulties arise with political details, such as the kingdoms of Agamemnon, Achilles and Odysseus, described in quite different terms in the Catalogue and in the rest of the *Iliad*; with Pylos there is the problem of the conflict between the Catalogue and the tablets. Opposed to the view which sees the Catalogue as describing a situation which vanished with the end of Mycenaean civilisation is another view which seeks to show that the Catalogue fits the divisions of Archaic Greece (though not for Thessaly or Ithaca). On the one hand, we should have a Catalogue based on a Mycenaean document (an army list, a geographical list or a list based on Achaean memories of the expedition), orally transmitted and somewhat modified over centuries; on the other, we should have a Catalogue based on an early guide-book, datable to the seventh century, perhaps put out by Delphi for sacred envoys announcing the festivals, listing their hosts. An argument for a Delphic origin is the alleged similarity between epithets attached to different places in the Catalogue and the style of the oracle. This last theory, propounded by A.Giovannini, at least succeeds in providing a partial explanation for the order in which places occur, beginning oddly with Boeotia.

The problem is far from resolution and exemplifies to perfection the difficulties involved in using what for the ancients was historically the most important part of the *Iliad*. The position is similar with the Catalogue of Trojans, complicated by hypotheses involving comparisons with Hittite texts. We cannot be sure whether the lack of knowledge of anything beyond the coast of Asia Minor is the result of ignorance in the Mycenaean world or of the still limited knowledge possessed by the Greek colonial age.

If, however, we separate research on the Homeric poems from research on the historical reality of the events described, the historical use of the poems is both safest and most profitable when it is concerned with the analysis of aspects of family, social and political life, institutions and norms, ethical principles, religious behaviour, material culture, economic factors; the similes in the poems are particularly revealing.[26]

[26] *Archaeologia Homerica*, eds. F.Matz and H.-G.Buchholtz (Göttingen, 1967 onwards;) C.M.Bowra, *Heroic Poetry*, (London, 1952); O.Carruba, 'Ahhijawa e altri nomi di popoli e di paesi dell' Anatolia Occidentale', *Athenaeum* 42 (1964), 269–98; *A Companion to Homer*, edd. A.J.B.Wace and F.H.Stubbings (London, 1962); P.de Fidio, 'Le categorie sociali e professionali del mondo omerico', *Annali Istituto Ital. Studi Storici* 2 (1970), 1–71; M. I .Finley, *The World of Odysseus* (London, 1978); *idem*, 'Homer and Mycenae', *Historia* 6 (1957), 133–59; *idem*, 'The Trojan War', *JHS* 84 (1964), 1–9; A.Giovannini, *Etude historique sur les origines du Catalogue des vaisseaux* (Bern, 1969); E.A.Havelock, *Preface to Plato* (Cambridge, Mass., 1963); G.Jachmann, *Der Homerische Schiffskatalog und die Ilias* (Cologne, 1958); G.S.Kirk, *The Songs of Homer* (Cam-

Emilio Gabba

EARLY GREEK POETRY

The world that emerges from the works of Hesiod, which belong to the early seventh century BC, is already very different from the world of Odysseus, even if some elements of continuity show how things have developed. In contrast to epic, largely impersonal, Hesiod presents his own personality – with autobiographical elements which have a clear spatial, temporal and social reference – his own ideas and his own feelings: we are clearly on the way towards lyric poetry (p. 36) and its marked individualism. Hesiodic society can be characterised in economic and cultural terms which are clear and quite different from those which relate to the Homeric poems. Beside large-scale aristocratic land-holding there exist small-scale peasant properties; and, even if institutional and juridical norms have not yet developed, the problem of the alienation of land is there and we can glimpse the existence of complex social problems, no doubt linked to the beginning of the colonising movement and foreshadowing the tensions of the age of Solon. Beside the self-sufficiency of agriculture in Hesiod there exists also commercial activity, complementary to agriculture and integrated with it, engaged in the disposal of agricultural surpluses. Commerce in Hesiod is a phase of aristocratic commerce, similar to the commerce which appears in the Homeric poems; this is indeed one of the factors which detach the worlds of the poems from the heroic age proper. (In a later period commerce in the Greek world will become largely autonomous.) It is important to note that if one reads the Hesiodic *Works and Days* in their social and economic context they are relevant to a much wider world than that of Boeotia – closer to that of Cyme in Asia, whence Hesiod's family derived.[27]

bridge, 1962); H. L. Lorimer, *Homer and the Monuments* (Oxford, 1950); A. Mele, *Società e lavoro nei poemi omerici*, (Naples, 1968); D. L. Page, *The Homeric Odyssey*, (Oxford, 1955); idem, *History and Homeric Iliad* (Berkeley and Los Angeles, 1959); R.H.Simpson and J.F.Lazenby, *The Catalogue of the Ships in Homer's Iliad* (Oxford, 1970); A.M.Snodgrass, *The Dark Age of Greece* (Edinburgh, 1971); idem, 'An historical Homeric society?' *JHS* 94 (1974), 114–25.

[27] Ed. Will, 'Aux origines du régime foncier grec. Homère, Hésiode et

The same breadth of cultural horizons appears also in the *Theogony*. Hesiod's cosmology, especially in the light of the discovery of the Hittite epic of Kumarbi (of Hurrian origin, from the middle of the second millennium), is clearly influenced by oriental borrowings. This fact means that scholars have had to reconsider the problem of oriental influence on and oriental borrowings in early Greek philosophy and history and related literary activity.[28] It is worth remembering that precisely this problem was raised at the beginning of the second century AD in the 'Phoenician History' of Philo of Byblos (p. 19), who argued that the *Theogony* was a Greek translation from Sanchuniathon who lived before the Trojan War. Further, Dionysius of Halicarnassus regarded the adoption in history of forms characteristic of temple records, themselves to be regarded as of Phoenician origin, as lying at the origin of Greek local history.

On a different tack, the emergence, with Hesiod, of the personality of the poet and of his own mental processes, along with the centrality of his own social experience, is clearly reflected in the new demand for 'truth', going beyond reliance on the inspiration of the Muses, who were, of course, present everywhere and so could provide truthful information. Hesiod, however, knew that the Muses could also provide false, even though plausible, information (*Theogony* 27–8). This newly developing critical sensibility involves a distinction between true and false as a principle of knowledge and is the necessary premise of critical, historical analysis.[29]

l'arrière-plan Mycénien', *Revue des Etudes Grecques* 59 (1957), 5–50; M. Detienne, *Crise agraire et attitude religieuse chez Hesiode* (Brussels, 1963); A.Mele, *Il commercio greco arcaico. Prexis ed emporie* (Naples, 1979).

[28] P.Walcot, 'Hesiod and the didactic literature of the Near East', *Revue des Etudes Grecques* 75 (1962), 13–36; G.Arrighetti, 'Cosmologia mitica di Omero e Esiodo', *Studi Classici e Orientali* 15 (1966), 1–60; M.L.West, *Early Greek Philosophy and the Orient* (Oxford, 1971).

[29] S.Accamé, 'L'invocazione alla Musa e la "verità" in Omero e in Esiodo', *Rivista Filol.Istr.Class.* 91 (1963), 257–81, 385–415; *idem*, 'L'ispirazione della Musa e gli albori della critica storica nell'età arcaica', *Rivista Filol. Istr.Class.* 92 (1964), 129–56, 257–87.

The case of Hesiod is in a certain sense paradigmatic of the possibilities offered by the reading of a literary work with historical questions in mind – his poems are not historical and are not even interested in problems of a political character. The exercise is all the more important in this case, since there are no detailed historical narratives for this period, while the text of Hesiod allows us to grasp complex political and social problems. Other literary texts may also casually preserve information or data otherwise unknown. Thus, an attempt by the Romans to colonise Corsica is noticed in the *Historia Plantarum* of Theophrastus (v 8,1); the information is now generally regarded as reliable and the fact related to what is known of the Roman and Etruscan worlds of the fifth and fourth centuries BC. In a Greek love-story, probably of the third century AD, the *Ethiopica* of Heliodorus, there occurs one of the most realistic descriptions of heavily armed cavalry (IX 15,6). One could easily multiply examples. In addition, a text may allude to something with which it has no concern; an ancient reader would at once have recognised the allusion, an attentive modern reader may recover not necessarily the precise allusion but at least its context. Thus two frivolous poems of Catullus (114 and 115), relating to a notorious officer of Caesar's, Mamurra, allow one to recon-struct a page of late Republican agrarian history.[30]

On a more general level, the world of lyric poetry, whether Greek or Roman, precisely because it is character-ised by self-assertion and full of references to individuals and particular situations, gives the modern scholar a good chance of glimpsing the outlines of historical situations, local and general: the fragments of Alcaeus are the most important source for the internal history of Lesbos in the sixth century BC. One passage from him is the only contemporary Greek evidence for the campaign of Nebuchadnezzar in Syria Palaestina at the beginning of the sixth century: the brother of Alcaeus, Antimenidas, must have taken part in it as a

---

[30] P.Harvey, 'Catullus 114–115; Mentula, *bonus agricola*', *Historia* 28 (1979), 329–45.

mercenary (there is actually a mention of the city of Ascalon).[31]

It is worth noting in passing that the historical exploitation of poetic texts in addition (naturally) to Homer, was known in antiquity also. Thus Callinus was used by Strabo for the Cimmerian invasion of Asia Minor in the seventh century and more generally for the geography of the region (Fr. 2,3,5,7 West). Tyrtaeus was used for Spartan history first by Aristotle and then by Strabo, Plutarch and Pausanias;[32] modern scholars, of course, may not agree with the interpretations of the ancients. In any case, the value of the texts of Tyrtaeus and Alcman for the internal history of Sparta in the archaic period, as well as for its political and military history, before the community turned in on itself in the sixth century, is outstanding.

The problems become complex in the case of a poet who had a specific political line to follow and therefore aimed at a public greater than that of a normal lyric poet: Solon is a case in point, which is relevant also to ancient techniques of history writing. The poems of Solon, both the purely ethical ones and the more overtly political ones, were certainly always known in antiquity, but no doubt were seen in the context of a vague tradition of Solon as a wise man, within an aristocratic and religious ambience. The poems were thus not initially used as historical sources. Only in the fourth century BC, as a result of research on Attic history and in particular because of the efforts of Aristotle, did the poems become the subject of philological study and historical investigation; the aim of this investigation was, with clear ideological and political goals, to reconstruct and interpret the little known earliest phase of Athenian history. The poems of Solon, as a result, were studied because of the documentary evidence they provided for constitutional, social and economic history

---

[31] D.Page, *Sappho and Alcaeus. An introduction to the study of ancient Lesbian poetry* (Oxford, 1955), 149–243; for Ascalon: B 16 (Lobel and Page, *Poetarum Lesbiorum Fragmenta*, 1955).

[32] U.Cozzoli, *Proprietà fondiaria ed esercito nello stato spartano dell'età classica* (Rome, 1979), 34–5.

and attracted interpretations which diverged even on specific facts: the disagreement between Aristotle and Androtion on the nature of the *seisachtheia* is a case in point, a disagreement which finds echoes in modern controversies. The same poems were then the foundation of the biography by Plutarch and lie behind all modern work. The result has been unfortunate. Because of the existence of his political and ethical poems – which must be taken together in order fully to understand the man and his time – Solon not only symbolises the problems and ideals and indeed history of Athens in the early sixth century BC, but also actually impresses his own individual mould on that history.[33]

It is clear that in the world of learning of the second half of the fourth century the poems of Solon were valued as documentary sources for historical enquiry because they allowed ideologically oriented reconstructions of a little known phase of early Athenian history. The ideological and political purposes served by the verses of Tyrtaeus cited by Lycurgus in the speech against Leocrates (107 = Fr. 10 West) are much the same; Homer, Euripides and Simonides were also cited by Lycurgus, and other Attic orators had similar ends in view in their frequent citations of documents, often false, of the great period of the Persian Wars.[34]

VERNACULAR LITERATURE

In a sense, we may find the case simpler when a literary text, whether circulated officially or not, is occasioned by a particular event known to us and illustrates that event or at least indicates the way in which it was seen at the time. One thinks of the *Eclogues* of Vergil, many of the *Odes* of Horace, of the traces of contemporary history (including the history of social customs, moral ideas and local pride) in the poems of Ovid.[35]

If one wants an analogous example in a quite different

---

[33] G.Ferrara, *La politica di Solone* (Naples, 1964), esp. 33 and n.26.

[34] Chr. Habicht, 'Falsche Urkunden zur Geschichte Athens im Zeitalter der Perserkriege', *Hermes* 89 (1961), 1–35.

[35] R.Syme, *History in Ovid* (Oxford, 1978).

literary genre, the little piece by Lucian, 'Alexander or The False Prophet', may be compared with other literary texts and with inscriptions relating to the Roman protagonist in the story; the piece thus sheds light on obscure aspects of the relationship between a Roman governor and local groups, involving cult activity among other things. The mocking tone of the piece should also be seen in the light of Lucian's ambiguous attitude to Rome. It does not follow, however, that an author is necessarily politically involved even if he participates consciously in the system of his time, as Propertius did; and to attempt to read Lucretius in political terms, as has been done, is almost certainly a mistake. On the other hand, the epic poem of Lucan openly faces, at a particular historical moment, the problem of the civil wars and the origins of the principate; obviously the author did not intend at the same time to provide us with the means of reconstructing any of the lost Livian account.

In any case, it is often politically uninvolved authors who in the end enable us to understand particular social groups with their tastes and life styles and norms of behaviour, to identify and characterise the different social classes of antiquity and their particular mentalities. Thus, the *Silvae* of Statius reflect as a whole a homogeneous social milieu, of high status, apparently contented, portrayed with realism and yet with some idealisation, that is, with the negative side removed; the poems are thus a perfect mirror of the culture, moral code, life style and behaviour of the class concerned. One sees clearly in this mirror, in fact, the type of the freedman in the service of the court, along with his social and juridical position, his functions, his attitude to power. The resulting portrait must be viewed in the light of the entire problem of the position of freedmen in the apparatus of the Imperial state from Augustus to Trajan, the tensions with the traditional governing classes (one thinks of Tacitus and the Younger Pliny), the problems involved in the organisation of power, the difficulties in the way of efficient administration, the influence of Stoic ethics.[36]

[36] G.Lotito, 'Il tipo etico del liberto funzionario di corte (Stazio, *Silvae* III 3 e v 1)', *Dialoghi di Archeologia* 8 (1974–5), 275–383.

By way of contrast, in a literature of a completely different type, of a popular kind, it has been possible to treat 'the moral attitudes of the *Fables* of Aesop as those of the lower classes in antiquity.'[37]

It is in general important to remember that the nature of the ancient literary tradition makes it difficult to write 'l'histoire des mentalités' of antiquity, involving access to popular and collective patterns of thought; what the tradition does do is encourage a history of ideas revolving round individual thinkers. In other words, while it is impossible in this situation to construct an 'objective' history of the phenomena, one can grasp how they appeared, transformed according to the point of view of particular observers. Thus, we can only with enormous difficulty understand the mentality of a slave or a member of the lower classes, since we perceive it as represented by the literature of the upper classes, in other words of owners or patrons. For this reason, Christian literature, often written for a popular readership and at the same time less formal and less individualist, allows us to approach closer to the social and cultural aspects of collective patterns of thought in antiquity (see p. 72).

The autobiography of Trimalchion in the novel of Petronius, as analysed by P. Veyne,[38] shows what one can discover in terms of social and economic history, on behaviour and mentality, from an apparently frivolous and marginal text. The upward mobility of an Asiatic slave, first financial administrator for a senator, then his heir, takes the form of the sale of the inherited land, enrichment by running the risks of maritime commerce, finally the purchase of land once more and the attempt to appear with the characteristics and tastes of the aristocrat. The caricature of reality and in particular of the moral attitudes of the upper classes (one is reminded of the famous passage in Tacitus, *Annals* III 55) and of those of rich freedmen reveals much about Roman Imperial

[37] A. La Penna, *Società* 17 (1961), 459–537.
[38] 'Vie de Trimalcion', *Annales* 16 (1961), 213–47. A better interpretation in J.H. D'Arms, *Commerce and Social Standing in Ancient Rome* (Cambridge, Mass., 1982), 97–120.

society of the first century AD and about basic tendencies in the Roman economy. To a certain extent, the frank and ironical treatment of Petronius may be compared and contrasted ·with, but also complemented by, the picture in the *Silvae* of Statius.

Texts such as the *Metamorphoses* of Apuleius are susceptible to a similar analysis, as also the Greek novels of the Second Sophistic movement; the former is full of information on provincial life, and both are revealing of customs and life styles among different classes and areas, despite the conventional character of many of the novels.

A quite different approach to an understanding of Roman society, in particular urban society, may be made by way of the rhetorical exercises of the Elder Seneca, rooted in reality and full of material on legal affairs.[39]

PLUTARCH

The legitimacy of the use for historical purposes of texts which their authors envisaged as having quite different ends depends on a clear understanding of what these intended ends were, since they necessarily influenced the form of the texts and impressed their characteristics on them. The case of Plutarch is significant. At the beginning of his work he makes the peremptory assertion that he proposes to write biography and not history (1 1–3). The notion reappears in the biography of Nicias (1 5). A distinction between biography and history had already been discussed by Polybius (x 21), but not that of Plutarch; Polybius distinguished the eulogistic character of biography from pragmatic history. For Plutarch, the difference between the two genres lay in the

---

[39] For the Sophistic movement, see G.W.Bowersock, *Greek Sophists in the Roman Empire* (Oxford, 1969). E.L.Bowie, 'Greeks and their past in the Second Sophistic', *Past and Present* 46 (1970), 1–41 = M.I.Finley (ed.), *Studies in Ancient Society* (London, 1974), 166–209; G.W.Bowersock (ed.), *Approaches to the Second Sophistic* (University Park, 1974); *YCS* 27 (1982). For the practice of rhetoric see F.Lanfranchi, *Il diritto nei retori Romani* (Milan, 1938); S.F.Bonner, *Roman Declamation in the Late Republic and Early Empire* (Liverpool, 1949).

fact that in order to delineate the moral outlook of his subject, penetrate the innermost recesses of his mind, and portray the essential aspects of his life, it was legitimate to choose those historical events connected with the subject which served his purpose and omit the rest; in fact to leave aside events which might be of the greatest historical importance. On the contrary, the biographer preferred apparently minor details, which revealed the character and attitudes of his subject. The clear distinction, then, which the ancient world made between biography (whenever exactly this may have appeared) and history proper is a central problem in the study of history writing in antiquity;[40] the distinction presumably relates to the establishment of the different literary genres as a whole.[41]

It is important to remark at this point that, given Plutarch's declaration, one cannot and must not expect from him what he did not intend to produce, a work of history. The observation appears banal, but is not. It is clear enough that Plutarch not only used more or less fully the material he found useful, but also slanted and arranged it according to his general biographical interests, and those specific to individual biographies and the pairs of which they formed part. It is not surprising, then, if there are contradictions within individual biographies, depending on the traditions chosen at one moment or another to illustrate particular aspects of the character of the subject. Furthermore, the need to establish links between the two people covered in parallel will often have had a considerable effect on the treatment of one or the other, without our necessarily being able to identify the effect. The problem is worst of all in the unparalleled case of the linking of the two reforming Spartan kings of the third century BC, Agis and Cleomenes, with the two Gracchi. The effect of the comparison is already manifest in the association of the two people who make up each pair, the necessary preliminary to the comparison of the two pairs.

[40] A. Momigliano, *The Development of Greek Biography* (Cambridge, Mass., 1971).
[41] L. E. Rossi, 'I generi letterari e le loro leggi scritte e non scritte nelle letterature classiche', *BICS* 18 (1971), 69–94.

The difficulties in the way of a proper use of the 'historical' content of Plutarch's *Lives* are then clear enough, since this content was selected and arranged with quite different ends in view from those of the modern historian. Apart from anything else Plutarch will have had to take account of the traditional rules for the genre of biography, while our attempts to extract and use material usually ignores completely the general meaning of Plutarch's work, although this is actually what one needs to be clear about.

It is customary to deny that there was any political side to the comparison between Greeks and Romans and to hold that Plutarch had only a literary, moral and educational intention, leading him to describe character and psychology.[42] I do not find this interpretation convincing. It is understandable that the genre of biography should have required comparative material to highlight the subject; but the presentation of pairs of biographies of persons from the two different worlds and cultures which made up the Roman Empire, and which are treated on a basis of equality, seems to transform the literary and moral aspect and gives it a political direction; by not favouring one or other culture, Plutarch recognised Latin culture as being the equal of Greek. In any case, the act of comparison affects the content of the *Lives*, and it is not paradoxical to talk rather of Plutarch as using historical method in some of the essays in the *Moralia*; these are less literary in their intention and character and allow a better acquaintance with the scale and diversity of Plutarch's reading and of the materials which were used in a worked-up form in the *Lives*: a good example is the essay 'On the virtues of women.'[43]

Other essays in the *Moralia* are perhaps more directly relevant to an understanding of Plutarch's attitude to the Roman Empire. Thus 'Political advice' contains the reflections of an intellectual directed towards younger members of the Greek

---

[42] E.g. J.Palm, *Rom, Römertum und Imperium in der griechischen Literatur der Kaiserzeit* (Lund, 1959); C.P.Jones, *Plutarch and Rome* (Oxford, 1971).
[43] Ph.A.Stadter, *Plutarch's Historical Methods. An analysis of the Mulierum Virtutes* (Cambridge, Mass., 1965).

cities, once free and independent, now part of the Roman Empire; the work contains practical suggestions on how to behave in relation to the ruling power. These practical suggestions share with the differently intentioned speeches of Dio of Prusa the distinction of being the most precious evidence for Greek attitudes to Rome at the turn of the first and second centuries. As we have already seen (p. 18), politically involved history written by other members of the Greek upper classes shows a quite different level of acceptance of Roman rule and integration into it. Looking at Plutarch's essay from a different point of view, one can learn much from it on the conditions of the Greek cities under the Empire (to be compared particularly with the rich epigraphic harvest, pp. 113–21); on the administration of the Empire, as far as it concerned the cities; on the real or supposed attitudes of part of the Greek upper classes. It is in this way that the essay helps to clarify the meaning of the *Lives*.

Literary activity of the scale and diversity of Plutarch's was naturally based on a wide reading of Greek sources (on his own admission Plutarch knew little Latin); these sources were then exploited for his polished productions. Plutarch does refer to his sources and there is usually no reason to doubt direct acquaintance; but more often there is no open acknowledgement of his indebtedness. An ancient author, in fact, usually cited a source by name when he wished deliberately to distance himself from it or to engage in polemic with it. In general, the re-use in one's own text of material from earlier authors was not regarded as plagiarism; this is something which is true of prose as well as of poetry. On the contrary, the insertion of phrases or verses from someone else was regarded as an allusion, often complimentary, which the reader was expected to notice. Furthermore, citations were usually made from memory, on the basis of earlier extensive reading, and one cannot hold that they were made *verbatim*: mistakes and changes (many no doubt unrecognised by us) are not to be regarded as deliberate or intentional. Naturally also, citations may often be secondhand, taken from florilegia or commentaries which presented material already sorted into categories: historical material, and also mythological, was often exploited to provide *exempla* for orators and essayists. Nor must one forget the case of Seneca, documented by Quintilian (*Inst.Or.* X 1,128), where an error was committed, despite Seneca's erudition and learning, by someone to whom he had entrusted a particular piece of research. The Elder Pliny, on the other hand, used only his own researches.

The problem of the way in which the ancients cited other authors has many other sides. A work of literature, whether historical or not, had in the first instance artistic ends; one had therefore to adapt citations, whether of an earlier author, of a document or of an inscription. It is very rare for a citation, particularly a long one, to be *verbatim*. A well-known example is offered by the comparison between the text of Tacitus, *Annals* XI 24, with the speech of the Emperor Claudius in the Senate, on the admission of Gauls to office, as re-worked by the historian, and the authentic (if fragmentary) text preserved in an inscription from Lugdunum (*ILS* 212). Short inscriptions do occur in historical texts, for instance in Livy, as supporting evidence. Dionysius, for his own ends, repeats a long passage of Fabius Pictor, adding his own comments, but there is no way of knowing whether the citation is a literal one.[44] (The citation of documents and depositions in speeches in court belongs in a different sphere.)

In a historical work like Josephus' *Jewish Antiquities*, the extensive citation of documents conferring privileges on the Jews granted by various powers relates closely to the aims of the work and is an integral part of it. The example of Josephus was followed on an even grander scale by Eusebius in his *Ecclesiastical History*. One must thus not confuse the case of antiquarian compilations without literary pretensions, like the *De lingua Latina* of Varro or the *Deipnosophistae* of Athenaeus; both were largely composed by stringing

---

[44] *F.Gr.Hist.* 809 F 13b; note the typographical devices used by Jacoby to distinguish what he regards as authentic quotations.

together *verbatim* quotations. The same point applies to the learned 'guide-book' of Pausanias (and, no doubt, also to the earlier works of Polemo of Ilium).

While on the subject of citations, it is worth remarking on the case of Alexander Polyhistor, who, as far as one can tell from his 'On the Jews', compiled genuine historical anthologies; the narrative was composed of passages of earlier authors chronologically arranged and provided with linking passages. Some process like this lies behind the *Origo gentis Romanae*.

PRIVATE TEXTS

We have seen that an author or a single work may provide direct or indirect evidence for a whole age, or for a historical moment, with all its social, political and cultural overtones. The nature of the relationship between an author and the society in which he lives is itself a difficult historical problem; for too often we try to reconstruct the social context of a work from the work itself, which we can only really understand against a known background. In theory, the relationship between an author and his society ought to be closer the more public the character is of his work; that is to say, the nature of the relationship is affected by the intended audience of the work. This observation is not just theoretical, it can help us in our historical use of the work in question. The truth is that our use of a work for historical purposes ought to take account of an infinity of factors influencing it; endless differing analyses of ancient texts follow from that perception.

The classic example of the fragility of any assertion about the context of a work, however true in itself, is provided by the *Meditations* of Marcus Aurelius.[45] What we have is a written soliloquy. Author and audience are the same; the author is alone with his conscience. Let us leave aside for the moment the terrible problem of how the text was preserved

---

[45] P.A.Brunt, 'Marcus Aurelius in his Meditations', *JRS* 64 (1974), 1–20.

and transmitted. The reflections of the emperor are entirely
personal and not directed to anyone else; they concern fundamentally the divine order of the universe and man's position within it. It is against this background that the emperor
places his reference to his personal experiences and preoccu-
pations and his historical allusions (probably unconscious):[46]
that is, against a psychological background. For someone
interested in events, a knowledge of the psychology of the
emperor may be of no interest; in fact, however, the mentality of the emperor helps one to understand his behaviour
and his actions. The sincerity of the reflections involves
serious problems when one brings in different historical
interpretations of the same emperor; we have a classic case
of the difficulties of comparing disparate types of documentation.

Similar comments could be made in the case of private
letters, such as the letters of Cicero, usually and in theory
presupposing the recipient to be the only reader. Open letters, reports in the form of letters (such as those from one
Christian community to another) and official messages to
governments or their agents obviously fall into a different
category. However, even private letters, especially if their
subject-matter was political in nature, could be widely circulated; they could then be preserved in official records and so
find their way into works of history, like the letters cited by
Sallust in the *De coniuratione Catilinae*. In such cases, wide
circulation was sometimes intended by the writer, sometimes
criticised as an indiscretion. Cicero projected a publication of
a selection of his letters, perhaps for purely literary ends; he
kept, it seems, copies of his letters and carefully preserved
letters which he received – all this shows clearly that the texts
of letters were regarded as valuable documentary material. It
has indeed been suggested that the publication of Cicero's
extensive correspondence was the result of a secret political
manoeuvre, but the arguments, with all their subtlety, lack

---

[46] IX 2 contains the famous mention of the plague; the mention of the
Christians at XI 3 is regarded by Brunt as an interpolation: see *Studies in
Latin Literature and Roman History* I (Brussels, 1979), 483–98.

plausibility.[47] Certainly it was only much later that the letters of Cicero acquired literary value, serving as a model for a long series of collections of letters – Seneca, the Younger Pliny, Fronto, etc.

Whatever criterion was used in making the selection which *was* made, and despite the possibility of changes and improvements to the original texts, there is no doubt that the letters of Cicero allow us to see, sometimes to our embarrassment, much of his private life and to follow parts of his political life day by day, as if with a diary. The value of this absolutely unique material is such that it is difficult and perhaps even impossible to institute a meaningful comparison with historical narratives of the same events; these, naturally, are neither able nor bound to go into such minute detail and have quite different methods of approach and literary objectives. We are faced yet again with the problem of comparing classes of source material which are not homogeneous.

PSEUDEPIGRAPHA

The problem of the relationship of a work to its historical context, a problem concerning its meaning, can be complicated both by uncertainties over dating and by deliberate ascriptions of invented dates; the latter occurrence involves the necessity of establishing the reason for the deception *and* the correct date, as with the *Historia Augusta*. It is even more difficult to find a secure date for, and hence to understand, literature which by its very nature cannot have a single contingent validity and which is made to be added to and adapted: all apocalyptic writing falls into this category, also writings attributed to a Sibylline oracle,[48] and much Jewish writ-

---

[47] J.Carcopino, *Les secrets de la correspondance de Cicéron* I–II (Paris, 1947), argued for publication in the triumviral period, with Atticus partially responsible; the date of publication, but not the alleged purpose, is accepted by A.Piganiol, *Scripta Minora* II (Brussels, 1973), 348–50. For a dating in the Neronian period: D.R.Shackleton Bailey, *Cicero's Letters to Atticus* I (Cambridge, 1965), 59–76.

[48] A.Peretti, *La Sibilla Babilonese nella propaganda ellenistica* (Florence,

ing of the Hellenistic period (often only known to us through Christian intermediaries). Such writing is deliberately time-less, idealising the past and often claiming authorship which it does not possess in order to enhance its authority (compare p. 14); by the very nature of its function at one moment and its potential function in the future, it cannot fulfil our demand for accuracy or offer any coherence beyond that of the cultural and religious milieu which saw its birth and development.[49]

Properly speaking, one cannot say that pseudepigraphical material of a religious nature is a forgery, even if it is often categorised thus. Anonymity was common enough in the literature of the ancient orient; and the attribution of a text to a revered earlier figure, whether mythical or historical, had precisely the intention of guaranteeing the text's acceptance and of giving it everlasting value. The claim to divine inspir-ation, whether by a Sibyl or a Muse, is characteristic both of religious literature and of Archaic Greek poetry and guaran-tees the truthfulness of the author; as we have already seen (p. 35), in the Greek world the claim was superseded by an author's growing awareness of his own individuality and personality.

It is a serious mistake of method to associate under the general name of forgery a vast and heterogeneous range of literary production. Nor is it easy or indeed possible to find a single explanation for all literary forgeries outside a simplistic psychological one. In general, people famous for whatever reason (sages, politicians, saints) are often named as the authors of collections of letters, sometimes put together from respectable material, or form the subjects of biographies full of invented details, which met the demands of an inquisitive public or one which wanted to know ever more of someone it admired or venerated. If it was legitimate for a historian to reconstruct in *his* work a speech probably delivered by a politician, with some approximation to reality, what was

1942); V. Nikiprowetzky, *La troisième Sibylle* (Paris and The Hague, 1970).
[49] P. Vidal-Naquet (n.17), 109–23.

wrong with circulating speeches which famous people, even contemporaries, must have delivered on important occasions? Cicero was free to prefer a version on the death of Coriolanus which disagreed with that handed down in Roman annals, but which allowed him to draw a neat parallel with the death of Themistocles; Atticus replied with a certain indifference that 'orators were allowed to lie in their accounts of events in order to produce a good effect' (*Brutus* 43). Not only orators, as we have seen.

Political polemic, claims to priority, local pride often stand behind forgeries of one kind or another, historical, literary, philosophical, religious. Anaximenes even went so far as to issue a bitter political pamphlet which he attributed to his enemy Theopompus, in order to discredit him.[50] But the parade of learning in the *Historia Augusta*, as in many paradoxographical works, was intended to give an air of respectability to exotic and often deliberately incoherent narratives.[51]

THE ATHENIAN DEMOCRACY

The considerations advanced in the preceding paragraphs are valid for literature, whether popular or sophisticated, without any official aspect, that is, not written to fulfil a commission or for a particular occasion. Let us now consider commissioned pieces, in the first instance those forming part of Greek lyric or choral poetry. The poet is no longer free, as Hesiod, for instance, had been but is governed by the demands of the patron who at the same time is a representative of the intended audience. The society and milieus concerned are aristocratic. The occasion determines the celebratory and encomiastic character which the poetry inevitably

---

[50] *F. Gr.Hist.* 72 T 6 (= Paus.VI 19, 5); F 20–1.

[51] E.J.Bickerman, 'Faux littéraires dans l'Antiquité classique. En marge d'un livre récent', *Rivista Filol.Istr.Class.* 101 (1973), 22–41; idem, *Pseudepigrapha* I (Entretiens sur l'Antiquité Classique 18, Fondation Hardt, Geneva, 1972); W.H.Speyer, *Bücherfunde in der Glaubenswerbung der Antike* (Göttingen, 1970); idem, *Die literarische Fälschung im heidnischen und christlichen Altertum* (Munich, 1971).

takes on. The important place given to myths, the presentation of aristocratic ideals, the portrayal of aristocratic society, even political allusions, all belong in a framework of tradition and convention which is the same for Pindar, Simonides and Bacchylides, despite some differences in their conceptions of the world, man and moral values.

The official position of the literary genre of tragedy in the cultural and social life of the Athenian *polis* makes it *a priori* likely that it was related to a particular political situation and had a substantially 'political' character. Choice of theme, fantasising elaborations and adaptations of myth, precise attitudes of the poets towards major religious, moral or human problems of society – all probably or certainly reflect cultural and even political choices, though ones which we cannot always detect with certainty, in part because we do not know the precise chronology of the plays. In other words, it is usually hard to identify certain references or allusions to known historical events or to detect attitudes otherwise known as those of particular politicians – hence the diverse theories of modern scholars. Equally, it is dangerous to identify *tout court* mythical figures with contemporary politicians; and naturally it is not always possible to say if allusions or references were intended by the author, seen by the audience or imagined by ancient or modern commentators. Naturally it is always uncertain whether an attitude of the poet is to be related to the attitudes of his fellow citizens and, if so, how – in agreement or in opposition. One must even be cautious in attempting to characterise the developing political attitudes of the three great tragedians of the fifth century BC.

However, one must not be too sceptical or negative. The choice of contemporary themes by Phrynichus and, even more, Aeschylus shows clearly the wish of the authors to express views of contemporary relevance. It is possible that both tragedians held a political position close to that of Themistocles – that is democratic, in relation both to external and to internal affairs. Certainly the *Persae* of Aeschylus, beside the major theme of divine justice, offers a highly sympathetic interpretation of Persia and the Persian state, though not of the policy of Xerxes; the interpretation is of the highest interest, because it is linked to a vision of Athens which places the *polis* at the centre of Greek affairs. It is reasonable to argue that Aeschylus here provides evidence of an important contemporary mode of thought and value system, even if it is not reasonable to hold that Aeschylus wished to serve particular political ends. Nor should one forget, either here or with the other tragedians, the more or less open or concealed polemic, in an artistic context, over the treatment of similar subjects.

In general, it is easier to discover links with external affairs: the praise of Argos in the *Supplices* and the *Eumenides* (458 BC) must relate to the alliance of that city with Athens of 461: Agamemnon is made king of Argos instead of Mycenae. It is more difficult to identify allusions to internal affairs. The obviously negative view of a 'tyrant' (in the other tragedians, as well as in Aeschylus) may not always be evidence of democratic sympathies and of fear of elements within oligarchic circles aiming at tyranny. Are there references, as is often said, to social conflicts and political differences within the *polis*? There is no way of deciding; praise of democracy is obvious and understandable enough; but it is not easy to say what the political significance is of the clearly positive evaluation of the Areopagus by Aeschylus, precisely at the moment when the powers of that body were being dramatically limited by the reforms of Ephialtes; least of all must one try and fit Aeschylus into a neat and unequivocal position. At the very least, however, the play reveals the existence of impassioned discussions, to which the poet was no stranger.

On the other hand, it seems most unlikely that the famous passage in the *Prometheus Vinctus*, praising human progress and technical skill, seen as part of the vision of a 'democratic' Aeschylus, is evidence of an appreciation of the rising working classes. Aeschylus perhaps reflects the proud awareness, to be found also in Thucydides, of the cultural progress of his own time; the beginnings, however, are in Aeschylus the result of divine intervention.

The fact that Sophocles took an active part in the political life of Athens, even holding office, does not make the historical interpretation of his tragedies any easier, not least because we are not in a position to establish with any certainty the political group to which he belonged. The solutions offered or considered by Sophocles in the *Antigone* for the great human and social problems, such as the clash between the city and the family and their respective demands, or the defence in the *Oedipus Rex* of traditional religion, are precious evidence of a particular spiritual and cultural atmosphere, of discussions of supreme values, of the involvement, achieved or intended, in these discussions of the people as a whole, certainly of the attitudes and ideals of the poet. But it is quite impossible to say what if any his political aims were, beyond a passionate reaffirmation of basic principles. Uncertainties over dating complicate the task of establishing links. The second *stasimon* of the *Oedipus Rex* (lines 872–910), with its powerful defence of the political and religious traditions of Athens, has been related to the harrowing position of Athens before the oligarchical coup of 411 BC; allusions have been discussed to the profanation of the Mysteries and to Alcibiades, and have been used as an argument for dating the tragedy to between 415 and 411; but an alternative date around 430 demonstrates the ambivalent nature of the interpretations offered and the uncertainty of identifications of mythical personages with contemporary personalities (usually quite unnecessary except in terms of the modern obsession with complete exposition).

The historical use of tragedy is on safer ground when it pursues an understanding of an astonishingly lively milieu, in social, political and cultural terms, and of an age passionately involved in dramatic choices. These points are even more valid for the tragedies of Euripides, which closely reflect human reality and seem also to follow more closely than other plays the social changes and the shifts in public opinion which accompanied the political situation as it unfolded during the Peloponnesian War. Hence a number of hostile evaluations of the poet.

Euripides' sensitivity to change (the person of Menelaus, for instance, appears as a different character in different dramas) seems to indicate a deliberate wish for tragedy to reflect the attitude of mind of the people as a whole, whose spokesman the poet thus becomes; his attitude is now warlike, now opposed to war; naturally certain themes remain constant, such as Euripides' patriotism, his praise for Athens as the cradle of liberty, his political moderation, his sincere belief in democracy. It may well be true that the chorus of the *Andromache* (lines 465–85), in lamenting the loss of the enlightened guidance of one man, refers to Pericles; and there is no conflict with the praise in the *Supplices* for Theseus as the far-off mythical founder of the Athenian democracy, a democracy clearly 'moderate' in character. In this sense, the individual character of Euripidean tragedy provides confirmation perhaps of the loyalty of (and of the need for) the middle classes of Athenian society.

But it is dangerous to go further and seek to interpret as a critique of the social structure of the *polis* what are simply the normal motifs of an attack in moralising terms on wealth and corruption. On a more general level, one must say that it is very hard to identify in the fantasising or rationalising transformation of myth reflections of contemporary social and economic conditions – which are, on the other hand, the necessary and determining background of Attic comedy. In tragedy, we are much more closely bound to the political and moral aims and objectives of the author, whether these are implicit or explicit; we are at the same time much more limited in our ability really to understand these aims and objectives.[52]

[52] E. Delebecque, *Euripide et la guerre du Péloponnèse* (Paris, 1951); V. Di Benedetto, *Euripide. Teatro e società* (Turin, 1971); W. Eberhardt, 'Die griechische Tragödie und der Staat', *Die Antike* 20 (1944), 87–114; V. Ehrenberg, *Sophocles and Pericles*, (Oxford, 1954); J. H. Finley, 'Politics and early Greek tragedy', *HSCPh* 71 (1966), 1–13; R. Goossens, *Euripide et Athènes* (Brussels, 1962); R. Guerrini, 'La morte di Euristeo e le implicazioni etico-politiche negli Eraclidi di Euripide', *Athenaeum* 50 (1972), 45–67; D. Lanza, *Il tiranno e il suc pubblico*, (Turin, 1977); A. Pickard-Cambridge, *The Dramatic Festivals of Athens*[2] (Oxford, 1968); A. J. Podlecki, *The Political Background of Aeschylean Tragedy*, (Ann Arbor,

The use for historical purposes of so-called Old Comedy may be of various kinds. In the first place, there is the general political significance of comedy itself in the Athenian social and cultural context. Meanings are much more wide-ranging and explicit than is the case with tragedy; for the people as a whole played its part by sharing the views of the author, in the sense that the author, by free and open discussion of political themes, sought deliberately to be an exponent and interpreter of widely-held opinions. The freedom of speech, even licence, of Old Comedy was a concrete realisation of what has been rightly called a way of removing all barriers between audience and author.

In this sense Old Comedy is the correlate of the developed democratic regime of the age of Pericles and of the Peloponnesian War, marked by popular participation on a large scale; comedy is indissolubly linked to this atmosphere and to this way of engaging in politics. It is not for nothing that comedy belongs precisely in this period; indeed political criticism is still alien to one of the earliest comedians, Crates; and the genre of comedy declined as the particular political system which had given it birth declined. The last comedies of Aristophanes himself (the *Ecclesiazusae*, with its limited references to the contemporary political situation, and the *Plutus*, important for its reflection of new aspects of Athenian religious feeling) are evidence of the clear abandonment of earlier political themes.

Comedy, then, is a necessary aspect of the democratic regime, precisely because of its critical and polemical function, often taking the form of violent personal attacks (beginning with the titles, as with some of the plays of Plato the Comedian). The famous passage of the 'Old Oligarch' (Pseudo-Xenophon II 18), where the author remarks that the

1966); F.Sartori, 'Echi politici ne "I Persiani" di Eschilo', *Atti Istituto Veneto* 128 (1969–70), 771–97; G.Thomson, *Aeschylus and Athens. A study in the social origins of drama* (London, 1941); P.Walcot, *Greek Drama in its Theatrical and Social Context* (Cardiff, 1976); T.B.L.Webster, *Political Interpretations in Greek Literature* (Manchester, 1948).

'people' encouraged political attacks on the rich, the noble and the powerful, and indeed against the popular politician making his way up, is very revealing of the nature and origin of the personal attacks of the comedians. What is involved is the expression of murmurs, resentments, dissatisfaction directed against the powers-that-be, an expression which naturally often reappears in comedy under a moralising guise, with attacks on corruption, profiteering and so on, and with laments for an idealised past. Authors could also sometimes direct their shafts against their audience, that is, against the people; but their targets are normally the powerful, who tolerated the authors' freedom of speech, at any rate within very wide limits, though action was occasionally taken; they did so because it was better for manifestations of popular public opinion, of whatever kind, to find a fundamentally harmless outlet in comedy. One is moved to compare the relationship which developed in Rome between *princeps* and *plebs*, in amphitheatre and circus. Furthermore, the powerful will not have underestimated the publicity which was certainly given to their persons and actions.

It follows from all this that it is pointless to regard the comedians as being reactionary or anti-democratic or even in opposition. Being 'against' was part of the game. This does not mean that criticism in comedy of Pericles and his political and military leadership of Athens did not have its counterpart in real life; but what one cannot do is make the comedians members of a particular political party or even followers of a particular line, such as that of Kimon, as has been suggested for Cratinus. Furthermore, no contradiction is involved when Aristophanes, usually regarded as an opponent of the democratic system, appears in the *Clouds* as opposed to oligarchy; Aristophanes was neither anti-democratic nor anti-oligarchic, nor did he wish to represent the country against the town – he simply registered momentary swings of public opinion, for that was the function of comedy.

What is important for us who wish to use comedy for historical purposes is that because comedy lived with the continual unfolding of Athenian history in the second half of the fifth century it allows us (both with the fragments of lost comedies and with the complete comedies of Aristophanes) to see the diversity of popular reaction to pleasant or unpleasant happenings, at home and abroad, and to weigh the extent of popular involvement in every aspect of the life of the *polis* and of the discussions arising out of it.

The comedian, then, may be from time to time a spokesman for pacifist or warlike sentiments; he will be against the exploitation of war, precisely because he will pick up any grumbles that there are. This is one aspect, perhaps the most important, of the professionalism of the comedian; there was also literary, rather than ideological, polemic between different comedians; parody of other literary genres, such as tragedy; literary and dramatic caricatures. Acting as spokesman for general attitudes does not however involve the *elimination* of personal commitment and awareness: the *Demes* of Eupolis (412 BC), with its sad longing for the energetic political leaders of the past in a moment of defeat and dislocation after the Sicilian disaster, seems to reveal deep commitment on the part of the author.

Our relatively good knowledge of the chronology of the comedies, and hence of their historical context and their relationship with the contemporary events which are mentioned or discussed, gives us a full and lively acquaintance with changes in public opinion; above all, we can see what forms were taken by spontaneous popular reaction at Athens.

Up to this point, a historical analysis of Attic comedy finds itself exploring the aims of the author himself and making use of the expressions of public opinion which he had deliberately taken over. But we have open to us another and equally important way of using Attic comedy as a historical source. It has been observed that in order to be understood by the audience the wild, even absurd, unreality of much of comedy would need to be fitted into a framework of some kind. The realistic aspect of comedy derived from its presentation of a social milieu which related to the social and economic behaviour as well as to the political perceptions of the audience; a contributory factor was the presentation of popular feelings, collective and individual, in the face of concrete political, social and economic factors. If a modern historian can grasp the reflection of reality in Attic comedy he will be able to reconstruct the actuality of Athenian society and economy. It was this that V.Ehrenberg attempted to do in a justly famous book, *The People of Aristophanes*, which attempts a sociological analysis of the Athens of the comedies of Aristophanes. The methodological introduction by Ehrenberg is very important. An attempt to reconstruct from Old Comedy and in particular from Aristophanes the attitudes and mentalities of the different social classes of Athens in the context of their society and economy means an approach to the complex stratification of Athenian society and its pattern of behaviour; but it does not follow that one will understand the social and economic context itself, still less the rationale of that context. Aristophanes is not a theoretician, but an acute and realistic observer. The greatest difficulty is to distinguish what elements in Attic comedy are distorted or exaggerated (the problem also exists, of course, for New Comedy and for Plautus), to what extent a character is invented, how typical an attitude is. But in any case, the basic problems of the plays, which form the basis of the plots, reflect real problems; the same problems are presupposed by other literary genres and are as a result only partially comprehensible – Attic comedy alone reveals them to us.[53]

[53] A.Bellesort, *Athènes et son théâtre* (Paris, 1954); R.Cantarella, 'Atene. La polis e il teatro', *Dioniso* 39 (1965), 39–55; M.Croiset, *Aristophane et les parties de Athènes* (Paris, 1906); K.J.Dover, *Aristophanic Comedy* (London, 1972); V.Ehrenberg, *The People of Aristophanes. A sociology of Old Attic Comedy* (Oxford, 1951); G. Nicosia, *Economia e politica di Atene attraverso Aristofane*² (Rome, 1935); G. Norwood, *Greek Comedy* (London, 1931); L.E.Rossi, 'Il dramma satirico attico. Forma, fortuna e funzione di un genere letterario antico', *Dialoghi di Archeologia* 6 (1972), 248–302; J.Schwarze, *Die Beurteilung des Perikles durch die Attische Komödie und ihre historische und historiographische Bedeutung* (Munich, 1971); V.A.Sirago, 'Campagna e contadini attici durante la Guerra Archidamica', *Orpheus* 8 (1961), 9–52; F.Turato, *Il problema storico delle "Nuvole" di Aristofane* (Padua, 1972).

ORATORY

The fact that oratory flourished in the Greek *poleis* and at Rome was closely dependent, as the ancients well knew, on the open forms of government which existed, on the ways in which political matters were handled, on the organisation of the judicial system. The person and the personality of the orator and the politician merged in the ancient democracies, and the art of persuasion was no more than the principal aspect of the process of informing the people of what they needed to know in order to come to a political or judicial decision – of moulding public opinion in general. The literary genre of oratory is predominantly public and political in character and this is equally true of so-called epideictic oratory, with its various educational and cultural aims. The nature of oratory as outlined above is confirmed by the inclusion of speeches in works of history (see p. 6). Furthermore, the majority of surviving forensic orations at Athens and at Rome relate to political cases or at least cases with political overtones.

As a result, the history of oratory at Rome in the *Brutus* of Cicero turns out to be in large measure political history. The rhetorical works of Cicero do not only discuss theory and method, but outline the general and technical education of a politician and reveal the ideals of the governing classes. An ostensibly theoretical work, like the *Rhetorica ad Herennium*, quite apart from the use of historical *exempla*, clearly belongs in a particular historical and cultural situation, that of the early first century BC; at that moment, the problems facing the schools of rhetoric were problems of political liberty.[54] The centrality in forensic oratory of legal problems, and of actual cases and the need for an orator to present them in detail to hearers with varying knowledge of the subject, means that forensic oratory is a major source of our knowledge of Attic law over much of its range and of social and

---

[54] J.-M.David, 'Promotion civique et droit à la parole: L.Licinius Crassus, les accusateurs et les rhéteurs latins', *MEFRA* 91 (1979), 135–81.

economic factors.[55] The speeches of Cicero allow us not only to see what his practice as a lawyer involved, but also what his legal thought was, in relation to the theories of his time, as E. Costa showed.[56]

It should be clear that a forensic or political speech presupposes adaptability to the minds of the audience, whether it be the people, a deliberative gathering of restricted membership, or a court. It is easy to spot major differences of tone and type of argument in the fragments of the speeches of Tiberius Gracchus on his agrarian bill or in the *Catilinarians* of Cicero, depending on whether the people or the Senate was being addressed. We almost never possess both sides of a case, although opposing arguments are often incorporated in the published version of a speech in the form of replies to foreseeable objections; the result is that it is often hard to identify the distortions made necessary by the demands of the case, even in forensic speeches. In political speeches, deliberate concealment of the central point at issue, silence on fundamental aspects of the case, distortion of the opposing view are all normal and make it hard to be sure of what is reliable. Furthermore, the Athenian custom of accepting commissions to write speeches for the defence of someone else makes it unlikely that one will acquire a certain knowledge of the political views of an orator; the custom also raises interesting questions of the relationship between advising orator and customer. In the most typical representative of the genre of epideictic oratory, Isocrates, the need or at least the wish to pronounce on a variety of political problems over a long period of time makes it difficult to trace a coherent development of his political ideas, apart from basic points such as patriotism, panhellenism, opposition to Persia, political moderation.

But the most complicated problem in the use of ancient speeches for historical purposes is that posed by the relationship between the published text and the speech actually

[55] E.g. E.Paoli, *Studi di diritto attico* (Florence, 1930); M.I.Finley, *Land and Credit in Ancient Athens 500–200 B.C* (New Brunswick, 1951).
[56] *Cicerone giureconsulto*[2] I–II (Bologna, 1927–8).

made. The problem obviously involves the question what exactly 'publication' of an ancient speech was. As far as Attic forensic oratory is concerned, the position is complicated by the nature of the relationship between the customer who has gone to law and the speech writer, since the former is the actual speaker. The various possibilities have been clarified in exemplary fashion by K.J. Dover.[57] One must note above all in the case of Attic oratory that the handling of a case by an acknowledged expert was treated as a precedent and that this encouraged the circulation of copies. It is readily understandable that it was on the texts of the Attic orators that Dionysius of Halicarnassus deployed his talents as an investigator of forgery. The problem is even more complex in the case of political speeches. At Athens, it was a long time before they were 'published', because they belonged to a particular moment in time and to a particular occasion, because the historical context was unique and preservation of the speech in consequence pointless. Such a speech was a fact of political history, and this is why historians felt it necessary at an early stage to introduce speeches into their works, deliberately anchored to the events which had occasioned them. We have already seen how the practice became in due course an element of the technique of history (p. 6).

It has been rightly observed that at Athens, as far as we can tell, the first published political speeches owed their publication to foreigners, probably because this was the only way in which they could influence the policy of the *polis*. The same motive will lie behind the pamphleteering of Ion of Chios and Stesimbrotus of Thasos and also the historical activity of Hellanicus of Mytilene. The publication of political speeches then became generalised when the themes appeared of wide interest and no longer relevant simply to an Athenian audience. Speeches and 'open letters' were directly addressed to political figures of the moment. What we cannot say is what political effect, if any, the publication of works by an Isocrates or a Demosthenes had, but no doubt the speeches

[57] *Lysias and the Corpus Lysiacum* (Berkeley and Los Angeles, 1968), 151ff.

helped to form Greek public opinion. Given this background, it is easy to understand how apocryphal letters attributed to famous persons came into existence. In general, publication of a speech prolonged its effective life as a political force. It was even possible for genuine speeches to be inserted into works of history in order to increase their circulation, as with Cato (p. 7).

What is not easy is to determine what changes the author or an editor may have made to a text at the moment of publication, and it is dangerously easy to see interpolations at every turn. Nonetheless, it has been plausibly argued that some speeches of Demosthenes as preserved summarise more than one speech actually delivered. And the *Fourth Catilinarian* of Cicero probably consists of remarks made at intervals during the famous sitting of the Senate on 5 December 63 BC. An analysis of a speech of Cicero's sometimes reveals substantial modifications;[58] apart from the famous case of the *pro Milone* (where there is independent testimony) a good example is provided by the *pro Roscio Amerino*. Remarks on and judgements of the conduct of Sulla fall clearly into two groups, those pronounced when Sulla was still alive and powerful, and the negative and ironical additions made after his death.

The publication of speeches was in the ancient world one of the outstanding means of spreading ideas and political opinions; it also makes the speeches effective in milieus different from those in which they were delivered. In a sense, a published speech belongs because of its aims to the genre of political literature, since it has the formation or influencing of an educated public opinion in mind. Cicero's treatise *De officiis* is perhaps the most important example of political literature: it retained a major position in the history of western thought and raises very interesting questions of method. The form taken by the *Nachleben* of the *De officiis*, already in antiquity, has had a major effect on the interpretation, under-

---

[58] J.Humbert, *Les plaidoyers écrits et les plaidoiries réelles de Cicéron* (Paris, n.d.).

standing and evaluation of the work; it has been taken as the highest exemplification of the ideal of *humanitas*, the legacy of antiquity and in particular of Cicero, as such even affecting educational practice. The *De officiis* has been seen as providing a model for ideal human behaviour in civilised society. On the other hand, the treatise is unashamedly a reworking of a similar treatise by the Stoic philosopher Panaetius, as far as the first two books are concerned. Modern research, understandably, has studied the *De officiis* in order to recover the thought of Panaetius and other Greek sources, to place them in the development of Stoicism, to identify the intended audience of the Stoic philosopher, to evaluate the scale and significance of Cicero's additions (in particular the use of *exempla* from Roman history, significantly selective).

The procedure is no doubt fundamentally legitimate, but the result in the end is a series of subjective and circular assertions, and the political and historical value of Cicero's work is lost sight of, a value which is quite independent of his debt to his sources. The *De officiis* was written at the end of 44 BC; it is a piece of anti-Caesarian polemic, from which it draws its most central themes: for example, the substantial continuity in the behaviour of Caesar between 63 and 44 BC, from the programme of Catiline to the measures on debt. The work is intended as a reaffirmation of loyalty towards a state governed by a regime controlled by a senatorial oligarchy; Cicero defends and propagates its traditional ideals and the proper behaviour which goes with them for a politically involved citizen; at the same time, Cicero reasserts the correctness of traditional forms of political life, beyond the degeneration and the corruption of the moment. Cicero offers the new classes of Roman Italy, emerging after the Social War, the political ideals of the golden age of Scipio Aemilianus, with some necessary changes; he is consequently engaged in a labour of general and political education. We do not need here to discuss whether the new classes concerned were in a position to accept political ideals and norms, which had been developed for an elite much smaller in size. Sallust, in the two monographs which he wrote soon afterwards, probably reacted deliberately against any attempt to offer as ethical and political ideals anything belonging to a past state which had dissolved in corruption and impotence: he offered in fact an evaluation and interpretation of the present situation without any solution for the future (p. 17). I do not wish to suggest that Sallust actually intended to reply to the view propounded by Cicero, my purpose is only to place the two different pieces of historical reflection in the same political and cultural climate. On the other hand, there are clear echoes of the *De officiis* in Horace, and in any case the treatise must be read in the first instance as a piece of political philosophy. It is true that the *De legibus* and the *De republica* are texts which display more evident involvement in a political goal, but the *De officiis* betrays much greater depth of feeling. The approach outlined is also that which must be applied to the bulk of the philosophical works of Seneca.[59]

COMEDY AND SOCIETY

What happens when a literary genre loses its political content and its official function may be well illustrated from New Comedy. The characters become stock types and the political overtones characteristic of Old Comedy disappear. New Comedy has no link with an involved political life in a democratic *polis*; but it does reflect the existence of new tastes and attitudes on the part of its audience, politically uninvolved and indifferent. Perhaps, however, there is a realistic element in the comedies of Menander, despite the prevalence of stock characters and psychological types and the use of fairly standard plots; this realistic element is precisely the investigation of individual psychology and individual behaviour in actual situations.

Among the typical figures of New Comedy is for example that of the mercenary soldier, drawn from contemporary reality, boastful and extravagant in the aftermath of victory.

---

[59] M.T.Griffin, *Seneca. A philosopher in politics* (Oxford, 1976); P.Grimal, *Sénèque ou la conscience de l'Empire* (Paris, 1978).

War was common at the end of the fourth century, and the professional soldier who was poor in times of peace and happy-go-lucky after the distribution of booty was easily ridiculed and caricatured – his psychology was distinctive and recognisable. The presence of the mercenary in the *polis* as portrayed by New Comedy may be compared with the abundant evidence of Hellenistic inscriptions.[60]

The question is often asked whether elements of change or of continuity are dominant in Greek and Athenian society as portrayed by Menander; the answer is ambiguous. There are elements of structural continuity, insofar as the *polis* and the family, religious practices and economic conditions still provide a basic framework which governs the lives of the characters. But within this apparently stable set-up there exist life styles (in which the countryside is central) and ways of thinking about life which are different; the change can be seen at both the individual and the collective level and is often reflected in changed legal rules. The comedies of Menander, together with the surviving Attic speeches on private law matters (p. 59), are a mine of information on contemporary society and often reveal the characteristic changes of the age of Alexander. Given the nature of the plots, family institutions are central, in particular marriage, adoption and inheritance; the position of women and slaves also figures prominently.[61] What is less clear is the extent to which the plays reflect contemporary values, given the fact that dramatic requirements will have impinged on their presentation; one can here, however, institute useful comparisons with contemporary philosophical analysis.

It is also worth considering along with the comedies of Menander the *Characters* of Theophrastus as products of Athenian society in the Hellenistic period. They also reveal a

---

[60] H.W.Parke, *Greek Mercenary Soldiers* (Oxford, 1933), 234–5; M.Launey, *Recherches sur les armées hellénistiques* II (Paris, 1950), 790ff.

[61] A.Martina, 'Aspetti sociali e giuridici della Samia di Menandro', *Atti Acc.Scienze Torino, Classe Sc.Morali* 107 (1973), 853–940; E.J.Bickerman, 'La conception du mariage à Athènes, *Bull.Instituto Dirritto Romano* 88 (1975), 1–28.

citizen more concerned with his private affairs, with new patterns of behaviour, new attitudes, new ideas. The description of different human types reflects a new interest in the individual as opposed to the *polis*, which also appears in the contemporary study of physiognomy and in the flourishing of biography. The human types are primarily those of a 'middle' class, fairly well-off, rarely those of the lower classes; indirect light is shed on the ideas and political inclinations of Theophrastus.[62]

The poems of the slightly later Theocritus are also revealing; they depend on the antithesis between city and country, and reflect a perceived contrast between the reality of daily life and its various experiences (as portrayed also, rather crudely, by Herodas) and a longing for escape into an Arcadian world, an imaginary poetical construction from elements of reality. Theocritus reveals the turmoil in the souls of men of the Hellenistic period, with their urge to escape and to fantasise, which explains also the new taste for certain types of historical narrative, full of romance and fantasy (p. 13).

The problem of how accurately Athenian society is portrayed in New Comedy and of how the portrayal is to be understood is even more acute if we turn to the Roman adaptations of New Comedy from Plautus onwards. It seems clear that we are faced with adaptations which are in a sense caricatures and which, if only because of the implicit comparison with the Roman world, have a political aspect completely missing from the originals. Nonetheless, it is not easy to see how the staging of Attic comedy was received, even given the changes necessitated by the different audience, or what cultural response it evoked in the Roman context, where anti-Greek sentiments were common. In this perspective, it is vital to know how far Plautus adhered to his Greek models and what changes he made, and to establish criteria based on style as well as subject-matter.[63] The question is also

---

[62] G.Bodei Giglioni, 'Immagini di una società. Analisi storica dei caratteri di Teofrasto', Athenaeum 58 (1980) 73–102.

[63] Ed. Fraenkel, *Elementi plautini in Plauto* (Florence, 1960); U.E.Paoli,

a vital one if one is to make serious use of the evidence of Plautus for the study of Roman society at the turn of the third and second centuries BC (the precise chronology of the plays also poses problems).

The complexity of the problems emerges from one example. The polemic against feminine luxury in the monologue of Megadorus in the *Aulularia* could permit a dating to about 195 BC and could suggest a historical context in the polemic surrounding the abolition of the Lex Oppia, which had limited the luxury spending of women. The monologue could reveal much of interest on the society and economy of Rome in this period; it contains a long list of trades and professions, which despite the element of caricature could show diversification of service trades and hence the existence of a wealthy clientele. But at the end of the monologue (lines 525ff.) there occurs the bizarre episode of a hungry soldier getting his pay from a rich citizen. Despite many ingenious attempts, the episode cannot be fitted into a Roman context; but it *can* be explained by comparing it with a passage in Aeneas Tacticus XIII concerned with the payment of mercenary soldiers precisely by rich citizens of Greek *poleis*. The episode is thus part of the military history of the fourth century and one must doubt whether any of the monologue of Megadorus, with all its social and economic overtones, relates to the Roman world of the early second century BC, rather than to the Greek world;[64] it will perhaps have provoked amazement and mirth in its Roman audience, precisely because of its strangeness.

The fact is that clear and certain criteria for the determination of changes made by Plautus do not exist, and it is perhaps better to consider each case individually rather than risk general solutions based on stylistic or literary considerations or on terms used in jest for public institutions. Here

---

Comici latini e diritto attico (Milan, 1962); G.Rotelli, 'Ricerca di un criterio metodologico per l'utilizzazione di Plauto', *Bull. Istituto Diritto Romano* 65 (1972), 97–132.

[64] E.Gabba, 'Sul *miles inpransus* dell' *Aulularia* di Plauto', *Rend. Ist. Lombardo* 113 (1979), 408–14.

again an example is helpful: lines 575–600 provide the best available evidence for the history of clientship at Rome and for the understanding of its role in Roman society at the beginning of the second century BC.[65]

TECHNICAL LITERATURE

Technical and scientific literature has its own distinctive characteristics, since it is for the most part not bound by the literary considerations which determine the nature of any work not aimed at a specialist audience. Works on medicine, natural science, geography, military science (in particular, techniques of siege and assault), land surveying – all are addressed to readers able to understand and use them; they are closely dependent on the results of new scientific and technical enquiry and, as a result, adapt easily to the actual requirements of the society or the milieu at which they are aimed – hence the fact that they can give us precious information on economic or political affairs. The other side of the coin is that for the most part new and improved methods and their benefits only achieved a limited penetration of those works in the same field which had literary pretensions, works which remained bound by traditional concepts and continued to purvey out-of-date material. One result of this fact is that scientific and technical innovations were little known outside the milieu in which they were achieved and that little use was made of them; it is also easy to see why geographical treatises of a literary kind continued to repeat for centuries without change the views of authors regarded as of fundamental importance: we have already observed the nature of the relationship between Strabo and his sources (p. 27).

The general points just made must be nuanced in terms of the importance and role of each discipline and its methodology in its social and cultural context. It is clear that some

---

[65] N.Rouland, *Pouvoir politique et dépendance personnelle dans l'Antiquité romaine* (Brussels, 1979), 261ff.

medical texts of the Hippocratic corpus provide the best evidence of the advances made by Greek science in the second half of the fifth century BC. The works provide evidence on problems of the history of science – medical methods, medical instruments, medical attitudes – and on problems of social history (the clinical histories of Books I and III of *Epidemics* are particularly revealing) as also on the role and social position of the doctor.

The influence of medical study of symptoms and their use for prognosis on the methods of history is clear in the case of Thucydides, particularly with reference to his insistence on the investigation of causation.[66] Furthermore, climatological theories as to the influence of geography on the physical and spiritual characteristics of peoples were easily transferred to ethnography and history; in these contexts the theories had a long history, involving attempts to evaluate the institutional bases and diverse political systems of different peoples. They also furnished the basis for comparative analysis of Greek and barbarian customs, laws and institutions (see, for instance, *Airs, waters, places* 11–24).

By way of contrast, in the second century AD, the doctor Galen and his prestigious position must be seen in the context of the Greek renaissance of the Second Sophistic (p. 41) and in that of high imperial society, with its intellectual tastes and cultural interests, in which philosophy, rhetoric and medicine were closely linked.[67]

The works on siege technique by Aeneas Tacticus (mid fourth century BC) and Philo of Byzantium (late third century BC) reveal both changed military practices deriving from quite new ways of planning and conducting military operations and a very high level of technical expertise. They also tell us much more than historical works proper of the social

---

[66] K. Weidauer, *Thukydides und die hippokratischen Schriften* (Heidelberg, 1954); D. L. Page, 'Thucydides' description of the Great Plague at Athens', *Classical Quarterly*, n.s. 3 (1953), 97–118; A. M. Parry, 'The language of Thucydides' description of the Plague', *BICS* 16 (1969), 106–18.

[67] G. W. Bowersock, *Greek Sophists in the Roman Empire* (Oxford, 1969), 59–75; M. Vegetti, 'Introduzione', in *Galeno. Opere scelte* (Turin, 1978).

Emilio Gabba

and political problems within Greek *poleis* of the period.[68] For
a variety of reasons, there was a decline in the Roman period
from the high technical level achieved in the Hellenistic
period in the conduct of military operations, despite the fact
that technical literature in Greek continued to appear in quantity down to the Byzantine period; Vitruvius depends on this
literature for his chapters on siege technique in Book x of his
De architectura. On the other hand, the *Epitoma rei militaris* of
Vegetius, written under Theodosius the Great, despite its use
of specialist Greek and Latin sources and its concern with the
problems of the time, is basically a literary work addressed to
the emperor. The curious piece by the so-called Anonymus
de rebus bellicis is also a work of political and institutional
analysis; it is concerned with fiscal and economic reform and
bizarre technical innovations in the military sphere.

(It must be said in passing, on the *De architectura* of Vitruvius, that it belongs in a particular historical context, that of
the age of Augustus, and has not only a technical purpose but
also an ideological one; one has only to look at the preface to
Book I. We are at the high point, the end of a long process of
development and urbanisation which had characterised the
whole of the first century BC in Italy. The internal organisation of the work makes it clear that political and social
considerations are uppermost and that Vitruvius has in mind
the programme of urban renewal of Caesar and Augustus.)

There is no doubt that technical military literature had
some direct effect on pragmatic history. The most obvious
example is that of Polybius (p. 8) who also wrote on tactics;
but one can also cite the case of Arrian: in both cases we are
dealing with historians who had considerable experience in
the command of armies. Elements drawn from technical
treatises are also to be found in the *Geography* of Strabo and in
the geographical books of the Elder Pliny; but, as we have
seen (p. 27), Strabo is predominantly a literary figure, and
one cannot claim that his treatment is always precise and

[68] H.Bengtson, 'Die griechische Polis bei Aeneas Tacticus', *Historia* 11
(1962), 458–68; Y.Garlan, 'Cités, armées et stratégie à l'époque hellénistique d'après l'oeuvre de Philon de Bysance', *Historia* 22 (1973), 16–33.

70

reliable; contemporaries will have looked elsewhere for such information, in guides to roads, descriptions of sea routes, administrative documents, maps, etc.

The best example of the complete isolation of technical treatises from literary activity is that of the Latin Gromatici; these were in all likelihood school texts on surveying, full of information on geometry and also on law, perhaps different from one area to another precisely because of the nature of educational requirements.[69] There is no modern critical edition, an indispensable preliminary to the use of these texts for historical purposes; yet they are our principal source for the processes of Romanisation in Italy and elsewhere, and for the reorganisation of agrarian and urban structures.

A category apart is that of official legal sources. The historical use of a text like the Codex Theodosianus must be preceded by a series of observations which are vital precisely because of the importance of the information in the Codex on the administrative apparatus of the Imperial state and on the political, social, economic, military and, of course, legal history of the Empire. It is necessary, therefore, in the first place, to understand the aims and intentions of the compilers, related as they were to contingent political needs, and the ways in which the texts were chosen by the commission established by Theodosius II and the material chosen then organised and reworked:[70] in other words, the way in which the material has been handed down to us (in itself a major historical problem) affects the way in which we can use it. Perhaps even more insidious is the sheer difficulty of using a text which expounds the decisions and norms adopted by the Imperial power; decisions and norms may state the absolute

---

[69] G.Tibiletti, *Storie locali dell'Italia romana* (Pavia, 1978), 317–19, 325–7; O.A.W.Dilke, *The Roman Land Surveyors* (Newton Abbot, 1971).

[70] Fundamental are J.Gaudemet, 'Aspects politiques de la Codification Theodosienne', in *Istituzioni giuridiche e realtà politiche nel Tardo Impero (III–IV sec.d.C.)* (Milano, 1976), 261–9; G.G.Archi, 'Nuove prospettive nello studio del Codice Teodosiano', *ibid.* 281–313. Cf. also V.Giuffrè, *'Iura ' e 'Arma'. Intorno al VII libro del Codice Teodosiano* (Naples, 1979).

converse of what was really the case. In other words, we must ask what the relationship was between the intentions of the Imperial power reflected in the Codex and in the changes made to earlier texts on the one hand, and the actual reality of Roman society in the fourth century AD on the other. There is a dangerous temptation to portray that society and its problems in terms of the aims of Imperial authority. We cannot be certain of knowing even approximately the outcome of the frequent repetition of imperial enactments – the mere fact of repetition reveals their ineffectiveness. Even Diocletian's edict on maximum prices lasted no more than a decade or so. The danger is that we may find ourselves portraying not Roman society but the solutions canvassed for its many problems without ever being implemented. It is of course true that it is important to understand the mentality of the emperor and his proposed solutions to problems and the means with which it seemed possible to implement them; but it is all one-sided. To take one fundamental problem, we have been rightly warned[71] against seeing fourth-century society as characterised by the static nature which imperial legislation was attempting to impose. This legislation itself shows precisely the opposite (and other sources confirm the picture) – namely that there was considerable social mobility, perhaps more than in the first two centuries of the Empire. Similar analyses could be applied to material preserved in the Codex on other problems and perhaps could make possible a more subtle picture of the whole of fourth-century society.

CHRISTIAN LITERATURE

The democratisation of culture in the late Empire must be seen as the result of the working of Christianity on local cultures which had been at the fringes of classical Graeco-Roman culture; the process involved the active and direct

---

[71] A.H.M.Jones, in *The Conflict between Paganism and Christianity in the Fourth Century*, ed. A.Momigliano (Oxford, 1963), 34–5; R.MacMullen, 'Social mobility and the Theodosian Code', *JRS* 54 (1964), 49–53.

participation in religious activity of all social strata, including the lowest, and hence also their participation, at least indirectly, in the political life of the Imperial state; the basic truth of this proposition is only modified by the existence of centrifugal tendencies.[72] The nature of the achievement of Christianity is clear in the bulk of ancient Christian literature, which is characterised by the existence of a much stronger popular element than is pagan literature; its impact was as a result much wider. The best example is provided by hagiography, where a literary aspect is combined with lively popular elements; the roots of hagiography lie in biography and paradoxography (p. 15), yet it is a substantially new literary genre, its wide diffusion evidence of the level of popular intelligence, of popular fantasies, of popular taste.[73] Within hagiography, acts of the martyrs are of particular interest; their origin is problematic and is related to the complicated question of the extent to which judicial proceedings in the Imperial period were recorded and handed down; but in any case, their popular nature is clear from the vast circulation they enjoyed for purposes of instruction and education (Eusebius, *Ecclesiastical History* v, praef. 2); the acts then served as material for polemic and propaganda. Because of the nature of their origin, the acts are of the highest importance for the history of penal procedure under the Empire.[74]

On another tack, the large part played by sermons in Greek and Latin patristic literature offers, despite the limitations of the genre, a view of the audience which can be compared with that available from the oratory of the free *poleis* and cities of old. The spectrum of society thus revealed is in fact much wider.

[72] S. Mazzarino, in *XIe Congrès Intern. des Sciences Historiques* (Stockholm, 1960), Rapports II (1960), 35–54.

[73] H. Delehaye, *Les legendes hagiographiques* (Brussels, 1906); *Les passions des martyrs et les genres littéraires* (Brussels, 1921). On the use of this material: R. Aigran, *L'hagiographie, ses sources, ses méthodes, son histoire* (Paris, 1953).

[74] G. Lanata, *Gli Atti dei Martiri come documenti processuali* (Milan, 1973).

It is in the openness of Christian culture that the historical vision of Orosius belongs; he aimed deliberately to break completely with the traditional perspective of Classical history, bound to the culture and political attitudes of the upper classes. Whereas wars had always been the central subject-matter of Classical historians, Orosius intended by means of a negative evaluation of such wars to present a Christian view of history, theological and universalist, still centred on Rome but concerned with the destinies of the conquered.

The fact that they addressed themselves to an audience which was all-embracing and not necessarily educated meant that Christian authors had to have not only direct experience of the life of a Christian community, but also a real feeling for its problems; otherwise they stood no chance of being understood in practical terms, concerned as they were with moral and religious themes. Their writings thus allow one to recognise and reconstruct the realities of contemporary situations, even where problems are formulated in moral terms and the aim is to portray an ideal society – as it should be and not as it was.

The difficulties, however, should not be overestimated. For example in the works of St Ambrose, their fragmentary character, typical of the recording of a sermon, heightens the value of their direct testimony; the Classical cultural inheritance, which is important in his work, is outweighed by the vitality and sincerity of the whole context. The same point is relevant to the fact that much Latin patristic literature depends on earlier and contemporary Greek works, themselves dependent on Classical sources; the dependence may sometimes almost amount to translation, with errors, but we know from classical examples (one thinks of the Livian translation of Polybius) that politics and ideology may colour even a translation. The derivative nature of patristic literature, which might make one treat it as largely conventional, in fact allows it to reflect contemporary realities; the changes made to earlier versions and the references to matters of daily concern actually reveal the nature of social and economic conditions, where empty moralising might have taken over.[75]

We tend too often to consider the elements of the ancient literary tradition as all of the same kind (not, of course, in subject-matter) and to use them casually for our own historical purposes. The result is inevitably a blandly homogeneous treatment which eliminates what is specific to a work or an author. It is only an incomplete remedy to recover the ultimate source of a particular piece of information and to establish the priority of one source over another, thus enhancing its authority; we have not got beyond problems of subject-matter. In fact, ancient literary works belong to different cultural and social levels, they often form part of a rigidly defined literary genre, and are above all affected by the demands of the intended readership. The resulting diversity in form and content must be understood; its roots lie in enormous cultural variety and vastly disparate aims; these aims are in turn conditioned by social structures which are different from time to time, place to place, culture to culture.

In terms of method, therefore, before one attempts to evaluate critically the significance of any work or to use it for historical purposes, one must investigate the readership or audience for which it was intended, the aims of the author, and the means used to convey his thought and organise his text.

APPENDIX

Critical texts

The fullest collection is:
> *Bibliotheca Scriptorum Graecorum et Romanorum Teubneriana* (Leipzig)

[75] L.Ruggini, *Economia e società nell' 'Italia Annonaria'* (Milan, 1961); of methodological importance are the Introduction, 1–16 and Appendix IV (pp. 190–202): 'Il pensiero economico dei Padri della Chiesa a proposito dell'usura'.

Emilio Gabba

Further:

Scriptorum Classicorum Bibliotheca Oxoniensis (Oxford).

Collection G. Budé des Universités de France (Paris, Les Belles Lettres)

The Loeb Classical Library (London and Cambridge, Mass.).

Corpus Scriptorum Latinorum Paravianum (Turin)

Important late Imperial authors (Jordanes, Eutropius, Sidonius Apollinaris, Claudian, Ausonius, etc.) are published in:

'Auctores Antiquissimi' in *Monumenta Germaniae Historica* (Berlin)

Important texts, such as *Geographi Graeci Minores* or Ptolemy, are published by Firmin Didot (Paris), with facing Latin translation.

In the same series is C. Müller's:

Fragmenta Historicorum Graecorum I–V (Paris, 1841–1870)

F. Jacoby's new edition:

Die Fragmente der Griechischen Historiker (*FGrHist*) I (Berlin 1923, 1957²) to III c (Leiden 1958) with commentary, is incomplete.

The fragments of the Latin historians are in:

H. Peter, *Historicorum Romanorum Reliquiae* (Leipzig) I² (1914), II (1906).

The fragments of the Latin orators are in:

H. Malcovati, *Oratorum Romanorum Fragmenta*⁴ (Turin, 1976–9)

The texts of Christian authors are in:

J.-P. Migne, *Patrologia Graeca* (Paris, 1857–66) and *Patrologia Latina* (Paris, 1844–55)

Further:

Corpus Scriptorum Ecclesiasticorum Latinorum (Vienna)

Die griechischen christlichen Schriftsteller der ersten drei Jahrhunderte (Leipzig)

Corpus Christianorum, Series Latina (Turnhout)

Sources Chrétiennes (Paris)

Introductions and general works

H. Bengtson, *Einführung in die alte Geschichte*⁷ (Munich, 1975) = *Introduction to Ancient History* (transl. by R.I. Frank and F.D. Gilliam, Berkeley and Los Angeles, 1970)

G. Guggenbuhl and O. Weiss, *Quellen zur Geschichte des Altertums*³ (Zurich, 1964)

A. Rosenberg, *Einleitung und Quellenkunde zur römischen Geschichte* (Berlin, 1921)

C. Wachsmuth, *Einleitung in das Studium der alten Geschichte* (Leipzig, 1895)

Literature

Literary history

O. Bardenhewer, *Geschichte der altchristlichen Literatur* I–V (reprint, Darmstadt, 1962)

H. Bardon, *La littérature latine inconnue* I–II (Paris, 1952–6)

M. and A. Croiset, *Histoire de la littérature grecque* I–V[2] (Paris, 1896–1900)

P. de Labriolle, *Histoire de la littérature latine Chretienne* I–II[3] (Paris, 1947)

A. Harnack, *Die Chronologie der altchristlichen Literatur bis Eusebius* I–II (Leipzig, 1897–1904)

A. Harnack, *Geschichte der altchristlichen Literatur bis Eusebius* I–II (reprint, Leipzig, 1958)

E.J. Kenney and W.V. Clausen (eds.), *The Cambridge History of Classical Literature* II: *Latin Literature* (Cambridge, 1982)

A. Lesky, *Geschichte der griechischen Literatur*[2] (Bern and Munich, 1971)

H. Peter, *Die geschichtliche Literatur über die römische Kaiserzeit bis Theodosius I und ihre Quellen* I–II (Leipzig, 1897)

A. Puech, *Histoire de la littérature grecque Chrétienne* I–III (Paris, 1928–30)

A. Rostagni, *Storia della Letteratura Latina* I–III[3] (Turin, 1964)

M. Schanz, *Geschichte der römischen Literatur* I–II[4] revised by C. Hosius) (Munich, 1928–35), III[3] (1932), IV (1904)

F. Susemihl, *Geschichte der griechischen Literatur in der Alexandrinerzeit* I–II (Leipzig, 1891–2)

W. Schmid and O. Stählin, *Geschichte der griechischen Literatur* (Munich, I.1 (1929); I.2 (1934); I.3 (1940); I.4(1946); I.5(1948); II.1–2 (1920–4)

G. Williams, *Change and Decline: Roman Literature in the Early Empire* (Berkeley and Los Angeles, 1978)

Cultural history

G.J.D. Aalders, *Political Thought in Hellenistic Times* (Amsterdam, 1975)

G.W. Bowersock, *Greek Sophists in the Roman Empire* (Oxford, 1969)

M. Braun, *History and Romance in Graeco-Oriental Literature* (Oxford, 1938)

M.L. Clarke, *Higher Education in the Ancient World* (London, 1971)

H.–I. Marrou, *De la connaissance historique* (Paris, 1954)

H.–I. Marrou, *A History of Education in Antiquity* (Engl. trans., London and New York, 1956)

Emilio Gabba

J. Palm, *Rom, Römertum und Imperium in der griechischen Literatur der Kaiserzeit* (Lund, 1959)

M. Pavan, *La grecità classica da Tucicide ad Aristotele* (Rome, 1958)

E. Perry, *The Ancient Romances* (Berkeley and Los Angeles, 1967)

R. Pfeiffer, *History of Classical Scholarship* I–II (Oxford, 1968, 1976)

J.E. Sandys, *A History of Classical Scholarship* I–III (reprint, New York and London, 1967)

C. Schneider, *Kulturgeschichte des Hellenismus* I–II (Munich, 1967–9)

A. Stein, *Römische Inschriften in der Antiken Literatur* (Prague, 1931)

T. Steinby, *Romersk Publicistik* (Helsingfors, 1956)

M. Untersteiner, *Problemi di filologia filosofica* (Milan, 1980)

History of historiography

T.S. Brown, *The Greek Historians* (Lexington, Toronto and London, 1973)

J.B. Bury, *The Ancient Greek Historians* (1908; New York, 1958)

L. Canfora, 'Il "Ciclo" storico', *Belfagor* 26 (1971), 653–70

L. Canfora, *Totalità e selezione nella storiografia classica* (Bari, 1972).

L. Canfora, *Teorie e tecnica della storiografia classica* (Bari, 1974)

M. Dal Pra, *La storiografia filosofica antica* (Milan, 1950).

G. De Sanctis, *Studi di storia della storiografia greca* (Florence, 1951)

A. Dihle, *Studien zur griechischen Biographie* (Göttingen, 1956)

T.A. Dorey (ed.), *Latin Historians* (London, 1966)

T.A. Dorey (ed.), *Latin Biography* (London, 1967)

L. Ferrero, *Rerum Scriptor. Saggi sulla storiografia romana* (Trieste, 1962)

K. von Fritz, *Griechische Geschichtsschreibung* I. 1–2 (Berlin, 1967)

E. Gabba, 'True history and false history in classical antiquity', *JRS* 71 (1981), 50–62

B. Gentili and G. Cerri, *Le teorie del discorso storico nel pensiero greco e la storiografia romana arcaica* (Rome, 1975)

F. Hampl, *Geschichte als kritische Wissenschaft* I–III (Darmstadt, 1975–9)

E.A. Havelock, *Preface to Plato* (Cambridge, Mass., 1963)

Histoire et historiens dans l'Antiquité (Entretiens 4, Fondation Hardt, Geneva, 1958)

F. Jacoby, *Abhandlungen zur griechischen Geschichtschreibung* (Leiden, 1956)

F. Jacoby, *Atthis. The local chronicles of Ancient Athens* (Oxford, 1949)

Literature

M. Laistner, *The Greater Roman Historians* (Berkeley and Los Angeles, 1947)

A. La Penna, *Aspetti del pensiero storico latino* (Turin, 1978)

A. La Penna, *Fra teatro, poesia e politica romana* (Turin, 1979)

F. Leo, *Die griechische Biographie* (Leipzig, 1901)

S. Mazzarino, *Il pensiero storico classico* I–III (Bari, 1966)

Chr. Meier, 'Die Entstehung der Historie', in *Geschichte – Ereignis und Erzählung* (Munich, 1973), 251–305

G. Misch, *Geschichte der Autobiographie* (1907) = *A History of Autobiography in Antiquity* (London, 1950)

A. Momigliano, *Contributo alla storia degli studi classici (e del mondo antico)* I–VI (Rome, 1955–80)

A. Momigliano, *Studies in Historiography* (London, 1966)

A. Momigliano, *Essays in Ancient and Modern Historiography* (Oxford, 1977)

A. Momigliano, 'Storiografia Greca', *Rivista Storica Italiana* 87 (1975), 17–46 = 'Greek Historiography', *History and Theory* 17 (1978), 1–28

D. Musti (ed.), *La storiografia greca. Guida storica e critica* (Bari, 1979)

H. Peter, *Der Brief in der römischen Literatur* (Leipzig, 1901; reprint, 1965)

H. Peter, *Wahrheit und Kunst. Geschichtschreibung und Plagiat im klassischen Altertum* (Leipzig and Berlin, 1911)

Ed. Schwartz, *Griechische Geschichtsschreiber* (Leipzig, 1957)

C.G. Starr, *The Awakening of the Greek Historical Spirit* (New York, 1968)

K. Trudinger, *Studien zur Geschichte der griechisch-römischen Ethnographie* (Diss. Basel, 1918)

S. Ussher, *The Historians of Greece and Rome* (London, 1969)

P. Veyne, *Comment on écrit l'histoire* (Paris, 1971)

T.P. Wiseman, *Clio's Cosmetics. Three studies in Graeco-Roman literature* (Leicester, 1979)

T.P. Wiseman, 'Practice and theory in Roman historiography', *History* (1981), 375–93

CHAPTER 2

Epigraphy

INTRODUCTION

There can have been few major civilisations in which the incision of words on stone or metal for permanent display or record has played no part at all. But if the making and display of inscriptions is attested in many cultures, it was so distinctive a feature of Graeco-Roman civilisation that it deserves consideration as a major cultural phenomenon in its own right. As a consequence of this, the sheer volume of inscriptions from the ancient world, primarily but not only in Greek and Latin, gives epigraphy a central importance in the study of its history and culture, in a way which is not characteristic of historical approaches to most other periods or areas. Thus, it was to an epigrapher of the classical world that the editors of a post-war French encyclopaedia turned when they wanted to include a section on epigraphy as a historical discipline in general.[1]

The sheer profusion of epigraphic evidence – from tiny graffiti on walls or fragments of pottery, to stamps on jars, to the sepulchral inscriptions of innumerable individuals, to vast monumental inscriptions which may run to several hundred lines – creates its own problems. It would be a Herculean (and pointless) labour to work out even approximately how many Greek and Latin inscriptions have now been published; a guess of something over half a million might not be far out. Though many major projects for *corpora* of inscriptions have been undertaken – the great classics being the *Corpus Inscrip-*

---

[1] L.Robert, 'Épigraphie' in *L'histoire et ses méthodes* (*Encyclopédie de la Pléiade*, Paris, 1961), 453–97; German translation by H.Engelmann, *Die Epigraphik der klassischen Welt* (Bonn, 1970), with added notes by Robert.

tionum Latinarum and to a lesser extent *Inscriptiones Graecae* – none ever has been, or ever could be, completed without being already out of date. Even to offer an extended guide to the basic bibliography of classical epigraphy in general,[2] of Greek inscriptions[3] or of Latin ones,[4] is now a considerable enterprise which itself will be out of date immediately on publication. The most successful of epigraphic publications remain those great collections of the late nineteenth and early twentieth centuries which aimed to provide a very large representative *sample* of Greek or Latin inscriptions. W. Dittenberger's *Orientis Graeci Inscriptiones Selectae* I–II (1903–5) and *Sylloge Inscriptionum Graecarum* I–IV[3] (1915–24), R. Cagnat's *Inscriptiones Graecae ad Res Romanas Pertinentes* and H. Dessau's *Inscriptiones Latinae Selectae* I–III (1892–1916), remain the best places to begin the practice – which is of fundamental importance for understanding the ancient world and arriving at an original view of it – of reading inscriptions *in bulk*. Though we must always be conscious of how much inscriptions will *not* tell us – and a large part of this chapter will be concerned with precisely those limitations – it is still the case that inscriptions, read in bulk, provide the most direct access which we can have to the life, social structure, thought and values of the ancient world. Papyri and parchments, which may preserve public documents but also offer us thousands

[2] Note the valuable, and relatively recent, work of A. Calderini, *Epigrafia* (Turin, 1974), which would provide an excellent orientation in this field for anyone undertaking research in any area of Graeco-Roman history.

[3] The essay by Robert mentioned in n. 1 is almost entirely devoted to Greek epigraphy. More systematic surveys are given by G. Klaffenbach, *Griechische Epigraphik*[2] (Göttingen 1966), and G. Pfohl (ed.), *Das Studium der griechischen Epigraphik* (Darmstadt, 1977). Note also A. G. Woodhead, *The Study of Greek Inscriptions*[2] (Cambridge, 1981). The fullest survey of the types of material is M. Guarducci, *Epigrafia greca* I–IV (Rome, 1967–78), who reproduces and discusses a large number of texts, with illustrations.

[4] See I. Calabi Limentani, *Epigrafia Latina con un appendice bibliografica di Attilio Degrassi* (Milan, 1968), and E. Meyer, *Einführung in die lateinische Epigraphik* (Darmstadt, 1973). The classic work of R. Cagnat, *Cours d'épigraphie latine*[4] (Paris, 1914), has still not been replaced as an introduction to the subject. See now G. L. Susini, *Epigrafia romana* (Rome, 1982).

of examples of private, informal texts – letters, complaints, records of dreams, private financial accounts – are potentially even more revealing.[5] But the very special circumstances required for their preservation, which are consistently present only in the desert areas of Middle and Upper Egypt and in parts of the Near East – inevitably create a marked geographical bias in the evidence which they present.

For these reasons it is the reading of inscriptions, even more than of papyri, which will provide the essential direct acquaintance, the 'feel' for ancient society, without which the formulation of precise historical questions or hypotheses is an empty exercise, indeed cannot properly proceed at all. But as soon as a student does formulate any specific question, even in the vaguest outline, he or she will want to be able to trace all the relevant evidence. It is here that the difficulties begin, and some of them are fundamental. Firstly it is abundantly clear that only a very limited range of human activity and experience formed the subject-matter of inscribed material. Literature, archaeology, numismatics or papyrology may in certain cases provide an intelligible context which the inscriptions, in spite of the explicit character of the evidence they provide, do not. But epigraphy can never escape from the conundrum posed by all the vast, varied, but irremediably partial evidence surviving from the ancient world: how are we to construct an intelligible and not grossly misleading framework within which to interpret that fragmentary evidence which does happen to be left to us from antiquity?

That brings us to the second problem. What was originally inscribed was inevitably partial in what it chose to present to the contemporary reader; but what happens to have survived, happens to have been seen or excavated in the modern world, and happens subsequently to have been published – a consequence which may follow very belatedly or not at all – is infinitely more partial. In seeking to gather 'all the evidence' on a particular point we are at best summing up a minute sub-

---

[5] The standard, and very good, introduction to papyrology is E.G.Turner, *Greek Papyri* (revised edition, Oxford, 1980) with *idem*, *Greek Manuscripts of the Ancient World* (Oxford, 1971). Note also O.Montevecchi, *La papirologia* (Turin, 1973).

category of various infinitely receding larger categories. But can we do even that? Given the multiplicity of forms of 'publication', which include local antiquarian journals which never reach a wider market, it is in fact never possible to be certain that all the published evidence has been collected. But some approximation to this can be achieved by reading – and using the indexes of – the three major annual (or more or less annual) surveys of Greek and Latin epigraphy: the *Supplementum Epigraphicum Graecum* (*SEG*), published, with interruptions, since 1923, and designed to reproduce texts of new Greek inscriptions and note improvements in ones already known; *L'Année Épigraphique* (*AE*) published since 1888 and devoted to the reproduction of the texts of new Latin inscriptions and of Greek ones relevant to Roman history; and above all the *Bulletin Épigraphique* (*BE* or *Bull. Épig.*), a survey and analysis of Greek inscriptions, published in the *Revue des Études Grecques*. Since 1938 this last has been the work of Jeanne and Louis Robert, and it has been – and will remain – essential reading for anyone who wishes to understand Greek civilisation as it was in antiquity, above all in the post-classical period and in Asia Minor (present-day Turkey), the focus of the Roberts' own interests. To read the *Bull. Épig.* is probably the best way to gain a sense both of one's own overwhelming ignorance and of the excitement of exploring the vast, and ever-expanding mass of Greek which survives in inscriptions.[6]

Any reader of these publications would also gain a vivid impression of the immense geographical area over which Greek and Latin inscriptions are found, from Ai Khanum, which lies on the Oxus on the border of Afghanistan and the USSR, to Iran and the Persian Gulf, Mesopotamia, the Caucasus, the north coast of the Black Sea,[7] Romania, the

---

[6] An index to *Bull. Épig.* has now been published in various parts: *Index du Bulletin Épigraphique de J. et J. Robert, 1938–65*, I–III: *Les mots grecs* (Paris, 1972); *Les publications* (Paris, 1974); *Les mots français* (Paris, 1975); *Index du Bulletin Épigraphique de L. et L. Robert, 1966–73*, IV (Paris, 1979)

[7] For Ai Khanum see L.Robert, 'De Delphes à l'Oxus: Inscriptions grecques nouvelles de la Bactriane', *CRAI* (1968), 416; for the Black Sea region, note e.g. V.V.Struve, *Corpus Inscriptionum Regni Bosporani* (Leningrad, 1965).

whole of Europe within the Danube and Rhine, and North Africa from the Atlantic to Egypt. Egypt is also a conspicuous case of a phenomenon which by their very nature collections and surveys of Greek and Latin inscriptions tend to obscure; the inter-penetration of Graeco-Roman culture with a considerable range of other cultures. Many of the Greek inscriptions of Egypt come from temples and monuments of a specifically Egyptian character;[8] in Jewish funerary practice in Palestine, Hebrew, Aramaic and Greek texts are closely intermingled.[9] Similarly it is a fundamental (and to some extent neglected) fact about the 'Romanisation' of the Latin-speaking areas of N. Africa and the West, that neo-Punic texts, sometimes written in Latin characters, continued to be inscribed in N. Africa at least until the end of the second century AD,[10] and extended texts in neo-Punic appear in Sardinia until about the same time.[11] Palmyra, where the local branch of Aramaic was clearly the main language of ordinary speech, produces public inscriptions in either Greek or Palmyrene (heavily impregnated with Greek, and a few Latin, loan-words) or in parallel texts, throughout the three hundred years of its history.[12] The Semitic-language epigraphy of the Classical period, taken in all its branches from the western Mediterranean to Afghanistan, is a sufficiently important

[8] See the fully illustrated collections by A.Bernand: (1) (with E.Bernand), *Les inscriptions grecques et latines du Colosse de Memnon* (Paris, 1960); (2) *Les inscriptions grecques et latines de Philae* I-II (Paris, 1969); *De Koptos à Kosseir* (Leiden, 1972); (3) *Le Paneion d'El-Kanais: les inscriptions grecques* (Leiden, 1972); *Pan du désert* (Leiden, 1977); E.Bernand, *Recueil des inscriptions grecques du Fayoum* I (Leiden, 1975), II-III (Leiden, 1981).

[9] The documentary evidence for linguistic usage in Palestine (which also includes the well-known papyri and parchments from the Judaean desert and Qumran) is summed up in E.Schürer, *History of the Jewish People in the Age of Jesus Christ* II (Edinburgh, 1979), G.Vermes, F.Millar and M.Black (eds.), 20–8.

[10] See F.Millar, 'Local cultures in the Roman Empire: Libyan, Punic and Latin in Roman Africa', *JRS* 58 (1968), 126.

[11] E.g. M.G.Guzzo Amadasi, *Le iscrizioni fenicie e puniche delle colonie in Occidente* (Rome, 1967), p.133, no.8.

[12] For examples see J.B.Chabot, *Choix d'inscriptions de Palmyre* (Paris, 1922), and note M.G.Bertinelli Angeli, *Nomenclatura pubblica e sacra di Roma nelle epigrafi semitiche* (Genoa, 1970).

parallel phenomenon to Greek and Latin epigraphy to deserve a special emphasis here.[13] In this area too there is an excellent running survey, the 'Bulletin d'épigraphie semitique' published by J. Teixidor in the journal *Syria*.

THE GEOGRAPHY OF LANGUAGES

There is no need to catalogue here the substantial range of evidence – largely from inscriptions – for the multiplicity of languages used in the Graeco-Roman world; those attested in the Roman Empire are surveyed in a useful recent volume.[14] But it is worth emphasising how complex and interesting a world is revealed for instance by the late-Phrygian inscriptions of the Imperial period, all written in the Greek alphabet,[15] or the neo-Punic inscriptions from Africa written not only in the local variety of the Semitic alphabet but sometimes (as we have seen) in Latin characters, or in Greek ones.[16] By contrast the epigraphic remains of Celtic from France are all written in Latin or Greek characters, and no trace of a non-Classical script survives.[17] In this instance the very fact of composing a text for inscription must surely be regarded as a borrowing from Graeco-Roman culture.

Grossly inadequate as our often isolated fragments of inscriptional evidence are, they are often the best (or the only) evidence we have for the use of a language, or the contrasting uses of different languages, in a particular time and place. In western and central Europe, for instance, there

---

[13] The standard collection is *Corpus Inscriptionum Semiticarum* (*CIS*) (Paris, 1881–). Note also G.A.Cooke, *A Textbook of North-Semitic Inscriptions* (Oxford, 1903), and H.Donner and W.Röllig, *Kanaanäische und aramäische Inschriften*[3] I-III (Wiesbaden, 1973).

[14] G.Neumann, J.Untermann (eds.), *Die Sprachen im römischen Reich der Kaiserzeit* (Beihefte der Bonner Jahrbücher XL, 1980).

[15] O.Haas, *Die phrygischen Sprachdenkmäler* (Sofia, 1966).

[16] For this phenomenon see e.g. H.G.Horn and C.B.Rüger (eds.), *Die Numider* (Bonn, 1979), 107.

[17] For a relatively recent example see the discussion by K.H.Schmidt, 'The Gaulish inscription of Chamalières', *Bulletin of the Board of Celtic Studies* 29 (1981), 256.

is still nothing to suggest that any 'native' language was ever used in public documents in parallel with Latin, or indeed came into regular use in public inscribed documents separately from Latin. It does not of course follow that none was spoken, or even used in writing on perishable materials. However in Tripolitania in N. Africa, for instance, neo-Punic texts accompanied Latin ones on public inscriptions at least until the end of the first century AD. But the excellent volume of the *Inscriptions of Roman Tripolitania*, by J.M. Reynolds and J.B. Ward Perkins (1952), merely alludes to but does not print or discuss these parallel texts.

That this should be so is a product of both of the inevitable limitations of human knowledge, energy and skill, and of the costs of printing; the effort and expense of producing a volume of Latin and/or Greek inscriptions is great enough without the extra problems presented by other ancient languages and scripts. Yet it does deserve emphasis that this restriction, serious enough for our understanding of the local culture of Tripolitania, is a much more fundamental handicap when we come to the even richer mixture of cultures in the Near East, where we find a number of major documents inscribed from the beginning in parallel texts in two or more languages – and where the texts in different languages have tended to be published and discussed separately. This is the case even with the Rosetta stone from Egypt, a decree of the Egyptian priesthood passed in 196 BC, and reproduced in a Greek text and two Egyptian ones, written in hieroglyphic and demotic. The Greek text is available as Dittenberger, *Orientis Graeci Inscriptiones Selectae*, 90. But although, as is well known, it was the parallel texts which enabled Champollion to decipher the hieroglyphic script in the 1820s, the three versions have since then very rarely been discussed within the same covers.

Egypt is perhaps the most marked case where the skills necessary to study Greek inscriptions, papyri and ostraca (fragments of pottery with writing inked or scratched on them) on the one hand, and Egyptian ones on the other, have for understandable reasons been deployed as if in separate compartments. But it may be worth noting three relatively recent discoveries of major multi-lingual texts, which serve to show up both the present limitations of and the infinite possibilities of epigraphy in the Near East and central Asia.

(1) The trilingual inscription, in Aramaic, Lycian and Greek, from Xanthos in Lycia, almost certainly to be dated to 337/6 BC, that is, in the last years of the Persian Empire. The three texts, which concern the setting up of an altar and associated priesthood in the sanctuary of Leto at Xanthos, have had to be published by separate authors, if within the same volume, both in the initial publication and in the final report.[18]

(2) The two Greek inscriptions of the Indian king Asoka, of the mid third century BC. These are so far the only two Buddhist documents surviving in Greek. Both come from Kandahar. The first, published in 1958, has a parallel Aramaic text and is an invitation to the king's subjects to follow him in abstaining from meat.[19] The second was published in 1964 (Fig. 1).[20] In this case there is no parallel text in the epigraphic sense, but the inscription is a Greek version of the end of Edict XII and the beginning of Edict XIII of Asoka, already known from inscriptions of his put up elsewhere. The first contains moral precepts, and the second gives an account of the King's remorse and conversion after the

---

[18] For the initial publication see *CRAI* (1974), 82 (the Greek text); 115 (Lycian); 132 (Aramaic). The final report is *Fouilles de Xanthos* VI: *la stèle trilingue du Letoon* (Paris, 1979), 33ff. (the Greek inscription); 49ff. (Lycian); 129ff. (Aramaic). The correct date is that established by E.Badian, 'A document of Artaxerxes IV', in *Greece and the Eastern Mediterranean ... Studies presented to F.Schachermeyr*, ed. K.H.Kinzl (Berlin, 1977), 40.

[19] The Greek text is republished in *SEG* xx, 326, and, with a French translation, by J.Pouilloux, *Choix d'inscriptions grecques* (Paris, 1964), no.53, and both texts are reproduced and discussed by G.Pugliese Carratelli and G.Garbini in *A Bilingual Graeco-Aramaic Edict by Asóka* (Rome, 1964). Note also R.Thapar, *Asóka and the Decline of the Mauryas* (London, 1961).

[20] Published and discussed contemporaneously by D.Schlumberger, 'Une nouvelle inscription grecque d'Açoka', *CRAI* (1964), 1, and by E.Benveniste, 'Édits d'Asoka en traduction grecque', *Journal Asiatique* 252 (1964), 137.

1. Greek version of an edict of Asoka
(*CRAI* 1964, 140. Photographie d'estampage: M. Clair)

casualties and destruction brought about in a war which he fought in Kalinga. It does not seem that these truly remarkable documents have yet had their full impact on our conception either of the use of the Greek language in central Asia or of the nature of 'Hellenisation'.[21]

(3) The 'Res Gestae' of Shapor I. The record of the achievements of the early Sassanian king Shapor I (241–72) is carved on a stone wall at Naqsh-i-Rustam near Persepolis, and written in three languages, middle-Persian (the original text), Parthian and Greek. The complete Greek text, accompanied by the two Iranian versions in transcription, was published for the first time only in 1958.[22] It represents not only, in its second part, an immensely detailed account of the religious position and activities of an early Sassanian king but, in its first part, the only detailed account of a Roman war which we have from a non-Graeco-Roman source. More important, like the other major documents just mentioned – the Rosetta stone, the trilingual inscription from Xanthos and the edicts of Asoka – it gives some hint of the complexity of the mixture of cultures in these areas of Asia which were touched (at least) by Hellenisation. For any scholars who – individually or in collaboration – can deploy the varied linguistic skills required, there are whole areas whose social and cultural history in the Graeco-Roman period has hardly yet begun to be written. We have only to think of Egypt at almost any period, Hellenistic Phoenicia, Hellenistic Babylonia, with its combination of Greek and cuneiform documents,[23] Mesopotamia in the period of the Roman occupation, or Nabataea as a kingdom and as the Roman province of Arabia.

[21] Note however J.Harmatta, 'Zu den griechischen Inschriften des Asoka', *Acta Ant. Acad. Sc. Hung.* 14 (1966), 77.

[22] A.Maricq, "Res Gestae Divi Shaporis", *Syria* 35 (1958), 295; the Greek text is reproduced in *SEG* xx, 324. Note M.G.Bertinelli Angeli, 'In margine alle Res Gestae Divi Saporis', *Parola del Passato* 27 (1972), 40.

[23] Note e.g. M.Rostovtzeff, 'Seleucid Babylonia: Bullae and seals of clay with Greek inscriptions', *YCS* 3 (1932), 1; A.K.Grayson, *Assyrian and Babylonian Chronicles* (Locust Valley, 1975); G.J.P. McEwan, *Priest and Temple in Hellenistic Babylonia* (Wiesbaden, 1981). There is considerable further evidence in both languages.

It may be noted in passing, since this area is wholly beyond the competence of the author, that inscriptions are inevitably of the greatest importance for the study of the history of language – not only Greek and Latin but all the others used within the orbit of Graeco-Roman civilisation – as they are also for grammar, spelling, orthography and pronunciation. These subjects themselves have great historical significance. The sixteen hundred or so fifth-century BC ostraca from the Agora and Kerameikos of Athens so far published – and potentially the several thousand found in the Kerameikos in the 1960s and not yet published – give uniquely important evidence for the letter-forms, spelling and grammar used (in very varied ways) by ordinary Athenians of the Classical period. If and when these ostraca are published and properly studied they would in principle allow an attempt to reconstitute the text of (say) Aeschylus' *Persae* of 472, with the lettering and grammatical forms which would actually then have been in use. If that seems too far-fetched a possibility, it is still worth pointing out that the Athenian decree relating to Chalcis of (probably) the 440s remains the earliest documentarily attested piece of continuous Attic prose.[24] It would be agreeable to think that it is often introduced as such to students of Classics.

In the same way the vast body of Hellenistic inscriptions is the essential source for the evolution of the *koine* or common Greek language of the post-Alexander period (which did not exclude the preservation of dialect forms in some cities, for instance Doric in Rhodes or Cyrene), while the local inscriptions of Italy are the only basis for our knowledge of the various Italic tongues, and the gradual spread of Latin – itself a key element in the Romanisation of Italy.[25] Similarly, sur-

---

[24] *Syll.*[3] 64; *IG* I[2], 39; Meiggs and Lewis, *op.cit.* (n.25), no.52; now re-edited by D.M.Lewis in *IG* I[3] (1981), no.40. Photograph in B.D.Merritt, H.T.Wade-Gery and M.F.McGregor, *The Athenian Tribute Lists* II (Cambridge, Mass., 1949), pl.10.

[25] See eg. E.Pulgram, *The Tongues of Italy: Prehistory and history* (Cambridge, Mass., 1958); *idem, Italic, Latin, Italian, 600 BC–AD 1260: Texts and commentaries* (Heidelberg, 1978); E.Vetter, *Handbuch der italischen Dialekte* I (Heidelberg, 1953; P. Poccetti, *Nuovi documenti italici* (Pisa, 1979).

viving Latin inscriptions provide our only evidence of how Latin was written and spoken in Eastern Europe in the Roman Imperial period.[26] Whereas monumental inscriptions necessarily present a formalised language which may yield little trace of that used in ordinary life, graffiti on walls (best known of course at Pompeii) and pottery provide a means of access, comparable to that of the ostraca for the Greek of Classical Athens, to the grammatical forms and pronunciations actually used by ordinary people.[27] For the evolution of vulgar Latin, the third-century AD ostraca written by soldiers stationed at the frontier post of Bu Ngem in Tripolitania will be of exceptional importance.[28] Beyond that, in favourable circumstances, the graffiti of a town such as Pompeii (Fig. 2) may be extensive enough to allow an attempt to define the elements of a popular culture.[29]

All of this is simply to point out the obvious, that the inscriptions of the Classical world are first and foremost a body of texts, an ever-increasing mass of language, which inevitably outstrips all attempts at lexical or grammatical analysis. In one particular area of language, the history of nomenclature, the importance of inscriptions – above all because of their primarily local character – has long been obvious. A major conference was recently devoted to Latin onomastics,[30] and the *Lexicon of Greek Proper Names*, currently being prepared under the direction of P.M. Fraser, has required the efforts of a whole team of researchers and the use of a computer. From this it is quite clear that only work with a computer – and perhaps not even that – could enable lexicographical work on Latin, and especially Greek, to do any justice to the ever-growing volume of epigraphic material. The immense bulk of the computer-index to *CIL* VI, containing

[26] See H.Mihăescu, *La langue latine dans le sud-est de l'Europe* (Bucharest, 1978).

[27] See eg. V. Väänänen, *Le latin vulgaire des inscriptions pompéiennes*[3] (Berlin, 1966); *idem, Introduction au latin vulgaire*[2] (Paris, 1967).

[28] See the preliminary report by R.Marichal in *CRAI* (1979), 436.

[29] See M.Gigante, *Civiltà delle forme letterarie nell' antica Pompeii* (Naples, 1979).

[30] *L'onomastique latine*, Coll. Int. du CNRS, no.564 (1977).

2. A graffito from Pompeii showing a gladiatorial event
(from catalogue of Pompeii AD 79 exhibition, Royal Academy of
Arts, London)

the Latin inscriptions of Rome, gives some idea of the problems involved.

For any serious attempt at social or cultural history we normally require (as will be stressed again later) a substantial concentration of documents which can mutually illuminate each other. But it is precisely on the margins – at the geographical or temporal limits of a culture or civilisation – that the single document, however slight, may have a disproportionate importance. At the very least it may allow that form of reasoning which deploys a double negative – it will show that it is not the case that there are no examples of *x* from a particular time or place. That being so, the form of other arguments on larger issues will also be affected.

Let me take a final example from an area mentioned several times already, Afghanistan. Asoka had at least two proclamations inscribed in Greek at Kandahar. Could it be argued that he was just following contemporary royal fashion and had no real Greek-speaking public in the locality to address and convince? No, because P.M. Fraser has recently published a fragmentary Greek dedicatory epigram from a statue-base in Kandahar which dates to the first half of the third century and indicates that there was a sanctuary (*temenos*) there, and almost certainly shows that the place was a Greek city or settlement (and possibly even one of Alexander's foundations).[31] All that, with considerable consequences for our understanding of the area, can be revealed by four very fragmentary lines of Greek text.

If we move further west, a number of similar examples of marginal cases, where individual documents are of great importance, can be taken from the early history of Italy, which, because of new archaeological and epigraphical discoveries, has become one of the most interesting areas in the history of the ancient world. It is perhaps worth pointing out that the documents mentioned below, dating from between the late eighth century and around 500, are in four different languages, Greek, Latin, Etruscan and Punic.

(1) A very well-known example, 'Nestor's cup' from the eighth-century Greek settlement on the island of Pithecussae (Ischia) near Naples (Fig.3). The cup has this nickname because on its body are scratched three lines of verse in Greek, written from right to left and beginning 'Of Nestor I am, a cup pleasant to drink from'.[32] The cup and the graffito seem to belong towards the end of the eighth century. The consequences which can be drawn from these few lines are momentous. Firstly, this is among the earliest attested uses of the Greek alphabet. Secondly, while it has never been denied, even in the Classical period itself, that the Greek alphabet is a borrowing, with varied adaptations, from the 22-letter Phoenician/Hebrew alphabet, the consistent right-to-left writing here seems to indicate a particular closeness to the Phoenician source. That itself might not be correct (though evidence has been presented for a Phoenician presence on Ischia), for it has recently been argued that the earliest examples of Greek writing which we have (from the eighth century) reflect the Phoenician script not of that period but of some three centuries earlier.[33] The theory, based on letter-

---

[31] P. M. Fraser, 'The son of Aristonax at Kandahar', *Afghan Studies* 2 (1979), 9.

[32] See e.g. L.H.Jeffery, *Local Scripts of Archaic Greece* (Oxford, 1961), 235–6 and pl. 47; R.Meiggs and D.M.Lewis, *Greek Historical Inscriptions* (Oxford, 1969), no.1.

[33] J.Naveh, 'The Greek alphabet: New evidence', *Biblical Archaeologist* 43 (1980), 22.

3. Nestor's cup
(from A.Heubeck, *Schrift* (Archaeologia Homerica III.X),
Göttingen, 1979, fig. 41)

forms and other strictly palaeographical considerations, naturally has to contend with the fact (which could of course be altered by new discoveries at any moment) that there are no examples of Greek alphabetic writing before the eighth century. But in any case, if we look to the immediate context in Ischia, the double-negative form of argument is still relevant. It cannot be argued that all the Greek colonists on Ischia were illiterate, because at least one of them was literate. What is more, the graffito is in verse and appears to contain a literary allusion, if not to the *Iliad* at any rate to the content of a story incorporated in the *Iliad*. Moreover, since it is an undoubted fact that a version or adaptation of the Phoenician alphabet passed also to the Etruscans (who continued to write right-to-left), the graffito at least illustrates a possible channel through which these fundamentally important cultural transmissions may have passed.

(2) The 'Black Stone' (*lapis niger*) from the Forum in Rome. This famous stone contains an inscription, written vertically, in lines running alternately up and down, which is almost entirely unintelligible, but certainly in Latin. The

latest archaeological discussion of the *comitium* area of the Forum where the stone was found (and remains *in situ*) suggests that the construction dates to the sixth century BC. What is more, the presence of a fragment of Athenian Black-Figure pottery datable to *c.* 570–560 and containing a representation of Hephaestus strongly suggests that the monument should be identified with the Volcanal or shrine of Vulcan (= Hephaestus) which is known to have been situated in this area.[34] Since the identification cannot be certain, the argument is one of coherence, and cannot be conclusive. If it *is* correct, it naturally implies that the identification of the Greek Hephaestus and Vulcan was consciously made not later than the sixth century. But whether that is valid or not, the clear indications are that the inscription presents quite a complex Latin text of the regal period; it is thus one of a number of items of evidence for some degree of literacy *in Latin* (as opposed to Etruscan) in the Archaic period. The Rome of that period emerges as a relatively advanced community, a conclusion which is of some importance, even if it makes it all the more puzzling to understand why the close contacts with the Greek world which existed from the beginning took so long – until the third century BC – to engender a literary culture.

(3) The inscription of Sostratus from Gravisca. Another strikingly important item of evidence for Greek influence in Italy in the Archaic period is represented by the inscription discovered in 1970 at Gravisca, the port of Tarquinia in Etruria.[35] The inscription is on a stone anchor, dates to about 500 BC and runs 'I am of Aeginetan Apollo. Sostratus (son of) ... had me made'. It is difficult to exaggerate the importance of the discovery. Firstly, together with the other evidence from the sanctuary of Hera, it shows Greeks solidly estab-

[34] See F.Coarelli, 'Il Comizio dalle origini alla fine della Repubblica', *Parola del Passato* 32 (1977), 166; note the survey by T.J.Cornell, 'Rome and Latium Vetus, 1974–79', *Archaeological Reports for 1979–80* (1980), 71ff., on pp. 83–4.

[35] M.Torelli, 'Il santuario di Hera a Gravisca', *Parola del Passato* 26 (1971), 44; F.D.Harvey, 'Sostratos of Aegina', *Parola del Passato* 31 (1976), 206; J.Boardman, *The Greeks Overseas*³ (London, 1980), 206.

lished on the Etruscan coast in the late sixth century. Secondly, it would be carrying academic caution too far if we declined altogether to associate this Sostratus with the Sostratus mentioned in a passing aside in Herodotus (IV 152) as the man who made the largest trading profit ever known (among Greeks, as is surely implied). This Sostratus, or at the very least a relative, now acquires a firm location and approximate date (roughly contemporary with the foundation of the Roman Republic). Furthermore, a large number of Attic vases of this period from Etruria bear the stamp ΣO, which it is surely not too rash to associate with Sostratus. In that case we have an important indication of the character of Greek long-distance trade in the late Archaic period. The vases were manufactured in Athens, but carried to Etruria in substantial quantities by an Aeginetan trader, whose personality and profits were sufficiently well known to be alluded to by Herodotus more than half a century later. The *combination* of different types of evidence – a literary reference, a dedication *in situ* and marks on a large number of vases – is therefore certainly sufficient to re-open the question of long-distance trade in Archaic Greece as a significant activity, deliberately aimed at producing profits. Whether it would also suggest the existence of a *class* of traders is a different and much more complex question.

(4)   The gold leaves from Pyrgi. Pyrgi was one of the ports of the southern Etruscan city of Caere, and the three gold leaves, discovered in the excavation of a sanctuary there, apparently record a dedication made, probably early in the fifth century, by Thefarie Velianas, King of Caere. Their most immediate significance lies firstly in the fact that the dedication is to the Phoenician goddess Astarte and secondly that while two are in Etruscan the third is in Punic. Leaving aside the whole question of Phoenician/Punic influence and activity in the western Mediterranean in the Archaic period,[36] the leaves have a very precise relevance, as a marginal case, to the issue of the first Roman–Carthaginian treaty. Polybius (III

---

[36] See J.Heurgon, 'The inscriptions of Pyrgi', *JRS* 56 (1966), 1.

22) quotes this from an ancient and almost unintelligible document and dates it to the first pair of consuls in the Republic, who held office, according to him, twenty-eight years before Xerxes' invasion of Greece. The existence of these gold leaves, inscribed in Punic and Etruscan, probably a few decades later, will not, of course, serve to *prove* that there ever was such a treaty, or (still less), that Polybius' text, if genuine at all, is rightly dated to that period. But what it will do is to alter the terms of the argument, once again by the insertion of a double negative: it can *not* now be taken as a starting-point that the notion of written documents exchanged between Carthage and an Italian community in this area is an unacceptable anachronism.

PLACE AND DATE

The form of argument which relies on the fact that there is (at least) one epigraphic example of something from a particular time or place, thus destroying a possible negative generalisation, will often, of course, have a place in much better-attested periods also. For instance, the fact that even a few inscriptions in Etruscan should be discovered in the Republican province of Africa,[37] used on boundary-markers, opens up new perspectives relating to emigration from Italy and also to the use of the Etruscan language in secular, ordinary-life contexts. Or, alternatively, in a very crude and simple sense the discovery of a Latin military inscription (*CIL* III, 13430) recording a legion wintering at Leugaricio (Trenčin in Czechoslavakia, some eighty miles north of the Danube) and of another from the neighbourhood of Baku on the coast of the Caspian Sea indicating the presence of a legionary detachment (*AE* 1951, 263 – the easternmost Latin inscription so far discovered), serves to demonstrate the extension of a Roman military presence at least as far as these

---

[37] J.Heurgon, 'Inscriptions étrusques de Tunisie', *CRAI* (1969), 526; O.Carruba, 'Nuova lettura dell' inscrizione etrusca dei cippi di Tunisia', *Athenaeum* 54 (1976), 163.

places. It is precisely the fact that the vast majority of inscriptions come from contexts which can be located at least within reasonable limits, that gives them their very special significance both in contrast to and in combination with literary texts handed down in a manuscript tradition.

Many inscriptions can also be dated, either precisely – if they contain a date using a known system (e.g. the Seleucid era, Roman consuls or the titles of a Roman emperor) – or approximately, from considerations of archaeological context, style of monument, letter-forms of the inscription, use of formulae, nomenclature or language. But even formal, public inscriptions may sometimes be very difficult to place in a chronological context; and even greater problems may be presented, for instance, by private tomb-inscriptions from the Roman provinces.

EPIGRAPHY AS LITERATURE

The very close links and resemblances between Classical literature and Greek and Latin inscriptions, which can be considered and analysed as a sub-species of literary texts, have not, of course, escaped notice.[38] But it is relevant to suggest that for the Classically-trained student approaching Greek and Latin epigraphy one relevant stratagem might be to begin with one or more of those extended texts which can without any difficulty be seen as minor literary compositions; some of them are indeed prime specimens of narrative or rhetorical prose. A strictly literary analysis of methods of composition, introduction of themes, repetition and forms of explanation and justification addressed to the potential reader would be of exceptional value, for instance in relation to extended legislative inscriptions, particularly for example the long and complex inscriptions containing Roman laws which appear in the later second century BC.[39] Given the difficulty of

[38] Note for instance the compilation by R.Chevallier, *Épigraphie et littérature à Rome* (Faenza, 1972).

[39] For relevant analyses see D.Daube, *Forms of Roman Legislation* (Oxford, 1956); A.Watson, *Law Making in the Later Roman Republic* (Oxford, 1974). But see now A.N. Sherwin-White, 'The Lex Repetundarum', *JRS* 72 (1982), 18.

following the structure of these texts, it is not surprising that historical works devoted to this period show a distinct tendency to allude in passing to isolated aspects of them rather than treating them as what they are, by far the most important surviving products of the political processes of the period.

It may be worthwhile therefore to give a few examples of extended epigraphical texts which could be analysed as minor literary products, and which independently embody and reveal important aspects of the ideology or structure of the societies which produced them. I begin with two closely-related examples, both quite recently published, from early Hellenistic Greece, in that notable period when a real struggle, both ideological and military, was fought to preserve the traditional freedom of the Greek city against the claims of the rival monarchies.

(1)   Kallias of Sphettus. The inscription of 109 almost completely preserved lines honouring an Athenian named Kallias was voted in 270/69 BC and set up in the Agora.[40] The first part of the decree contains a highly allusive account, none the less giving many new specific details, of the revolt of Athens against Demetrius Poliorcetes in 287 or 286 BC and the role played in these events by Kallias, who (as the inscription reveals) was acting as the commander of a Ptolemaic garrison on Andros. The political and military background of the 280s is highly complex, and the chronological framework of the story is open to various different interpretations.[41] What matters in this context is the revelation of a new and quite extensive piece of early Hellenistic narrative prose; the ideology of liberation and attachment to democracy which informs the document throughout; by contrast with that, the dependence on Ptolemaic military assistance and the highly evolved diplomatic and ritual relations of

[40] T.L.Shear, *Kallias of Sphettos and the Revolt of Athens in 286 BC (Hesperia Supp. XVII, 1978).*
[41] See Chr. Habicht, *Untersuchungen zur politischen Geschichte Athens im 3. Jahrhundert v. Chr.* (Munich, 1979); M.J.Osborne, 'Kallias, Phaidros and the Revolt of Athens in 287 BC', *ZPE* 35 (1979), 181.

Athens with Alexandria; and the very full specification of the communal and ceremonial institutions of Athens which come into play in the allotment of appropriate honours to Kallias – who at the time of the document's composition was a Ptolemaic official on duty at Halicarnassus. No document could reveal more clearly the tensions and contradictions between the ideal of the freedom of the city-state and the power of the conflicting monarchies.

(2) Decree of the *Koinon* of the Greeks at Plataea in honour of Glaucon.[42] This beautiful and almost complete text of the mid third century BC was inscribed at Plataea by the common council (*Koinon*) of the Greeks in honour of Glaucon, the brother of the Athenian Chremonides, who had proposed in Athens in the 260s the alliance with Sparta and other states which led to the ultimately unsuccessful 'Chremonidean War' against Antigonus Gonatas. The inscription perfectly illustrates the use of Plataea as a symbolic rallying-point and the attachment to the ideal of freedom, and on the other hand the limitations imposed by the power-structure of the time, which meant that (as in the case of the previous inscription) aspirations to freedom from the rule of one major power inevitably meant being drawn into the diplomatic or military orbit of another. Rather than summarise or isolate particular features – which tends in any case to allow the all-important ceremonial, ritual and religious context to be obscured – I give a translation of the complete document:

At the time when Nicocleides son of Chaereas was priest and Archelaus son of Athenaeus was agonothete, decree of the Hellenes. Euboulus son of Panormostus the Boeotian spoke:
Since Glaucon son of Eteocles, the Athenian, when formerly he was dwelling in his native city, never ceased to show his goodwill either publicly to all the Hellenes or privately to those who visited

---

[42] R.Étienne, M.Piérart, 'Un décret du Koinon des Hellènes à Platées en l'honneur de Glaucon, fils d'Étéoclès, d'Athènes', *BCH* 99 (1975), 51; J.Pouilloux, 'Glaucon, fils d'Étéoclès d'Athènes', *Le monde grec: hommages à Claire Préaux* (Brussels, 1975), 376. This inscription is also translated in the excellent collection by M.M.Austin, *The Hellenistic World from Alexander to the Roman Conquest* (Cambridge, 1981), no.51.

the city, and afterwards when he held office at the court of King Ptolemy showed the same attitude, wishing to make clear the extent of his goodwill toward the Hellenes, and adorned the sanctuary with offerings and revenues which it is appropriate to reserve for Zeus the Liberator and the Harmony (*Homonoia*) of the Hellenes, and also enriched the sacrifices offered to Zeus the Liberator and to Harmony, as well as the contest which the Hellenes celebrate over the tombs of the heroes who fought against the barbarians for the liberty of the Hellenes – in order that all may be aware that the common council of the Hellenes returns to those, both living and dead, who honour the sanctuary of Zeus the Liberator, thanks appropriate to the benefits they have bestowed, it has been decided by the Hellenes to praise Glaucon and to offer precedence to him and his decendants in respect of any occasion when the athletic contests are being celebrated at Plataea, on the same basis as other benefactors, and that the ago-nothete should have this decree inscribed on a stone *stele* and dedicated beside the altar of Zeus the Liberator and Harmony, and that the Treasurer in charge of the sacred funds should make the expenditure for this purpose.

It hardly needs to be emphasised how complex are the administrative, religious and ceremonial institutions which provide the machinery and framework of the honours voted here. The significance of the ceremonials at the site of the battle of Plataea in 479, which were still carried out in Plutarch's time (*Life of Aristides* 21), is if anything increased by the fact that the decree was passed after the defeat of the Greeks in the Chremonidean War and the garrisoning of Athens by the forces of Antigonus Gonatas. The purpose of quoting the inscription here, however, is not to offer any detailed commentary, but simply to illustrate how individual inscriptions of sufficiently rich content, even ones which – like this – are quite short, can provide a focus of study through which the nature of a whole society or period could be analysed. Epigraphic texts of this sort can be taken (in a sense) individually and placed in a wider context in the same way as literary texts may be.

(3) The *Senatus Consultum* of 39 BC from Aphrodisias. This document of 95 long lines represents the fullest text of any *senatus consultum* so far published (Fig. 4). It is per-

4. The Senatus consultum from Aphrodisias
(from J. Reynolds, *Aphrodisias and Rome* (*JRS* Monograph 1, 1982), fig. 5)

haps the most important of the large dossier of inscriptions illustrating the relations of the Carian city of Aphrodisias with Rome recently published by Joyce Reynolds.[43] Without repeating the very detailed commentary given by Miss Reynolds, it is enough to say that the document both provides detailed evidence about, and raises many problems in relation to, a host of issues: the meeting-places of the Senate, its procedures and their documentation, Julius Caesar and his attachment to the cult of Venus/Aphrodite, the role of the Triumvirs in relation to Republican institutions, the nature of *asylia* and the privileges of 'free' cities. But the most complex and difficult question of all relates to the composition of the document as we have it. What exactly is it that the inscription is a record of? The proceedings of the Senate? The consul's (consuls'?) speech? A motion passed on his/their proposal? Why is the document, whose text is badly damaged in many places, marked by so many repetitions of the same subject-matter, which none the less do not exhibit exact verbal repetitions? And, in any case is the Greek text a complete translation of the Latin original or a set of extracts, or something more like a summary? What appears at first sight to be a documentary record soon turns out to show considerable ambiguities, not lessened by the fact that the actual inscription as we have it was inscribed more than two centuries later. Somewhere behind the actual physical object, the inscription carved in Greek in the early third century AD, lies a set of proposals passed in Latin by the Senate in Rome in 39 BC. How close we can come to the latter must depend in part on a detailed 'textual' and structural analysis, comparable to that applied to literary texts.

(4)   The 'Laudatio Turiae'. This famous inscription, containing an address by an unknown Roman to his unnamed deceased wife, recording her devotion to him and her services in the troubled period of the Triumvirate of Octavian, Antonius, Lepidus, has recently received renewed attention (Fig. 5).[44] If nothing else, it would deserve this attention as

[43] Joyce Reynolds, *Aphrodisias and Rome* (London, 1982), doc. 8.
[44] *ILS* 8393; M.Durry, *Éloge funèbre d'une matrone romaine* (Paris, 1950);

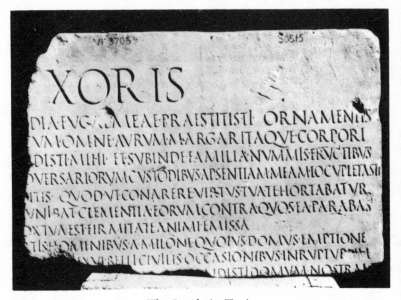

5. The Laudatio Turiae
(from E. Wistrand, *The So-called Laudatio Turiae* (Göteborg, 1976),
pl. 1)

one of the few pieces of narrative or rhetorical prose to
survive from the reign of Augustus, the most important era
of Latin poetry. Like the already famous Latin papyrus containing a few lines of the poetry of Cornelius Gallus,[45] it is
thus of prime importance as evidence for the style, grammar,
orthography and spelling in use in this period. It is also one of
the few extended biographical, or at any rate personal,
records of an individual, probably of equestrian rank, available to use from this period. The text offers not only reflections of historical events (the purchase of the house of Milo,
the proscriptions of 43, the husband's flight, the wife's pros-
tration before the feet of Lepidus to petition for his restoration), but evidence on inheritance and the handling of family

new edition with photographs by E. Wistrand, *The So-called Laudatio
Turiae* (Göteborg, 1976). As N. M. Horsfall demonstrated in a so far
unpublished paper given to the Oxford Philological Society, there is
much further epigraphic and interpretative work to be done on this text.

[45] R. D. Anderson, P. J. Parsons and R. G. M. Nisbet, 'Elegiacs by Gallus
from Quasr Ibrîm', *JRS* 69 (1979), 125, with pls. 4–6.

property, the conduct expected of wives and the importance of child-bearing to marriage. In other words, it is a central document for the values of Roman society. In this connection it may be significant that the surviving text, which is packed with expressions relating to moral duties and obligations, contains only a single passing reference to religious observance.

(5)   The *Tabula* of Banasa. The bronze tablet from Banasa in Morocco, finally published in 1971, is perhaps our finest documentary item of evidence for the archival procedures of the Roman emperors and for the limits and consequences of the granting of citizenship, as well as affording some glimpses of social structure in a marginal area of the empire.[46] In view of the almost complete state of the text and its exceptional character as a formal document, it seems worthwhile to reproduce it in full (omitting a few technical details):

(*c.* AD 168) Copy of a letter of our Emperors Antoninus and Verus, Augusti, to Coiiedius Maximus: we have read the *libellus* [petition] of Julianus the Zegrensian attached to your letter, and although the Roman citizenship is not normally granted by Imperial indulgentia to those tribesmen unless earned by the highest deserts, yet since you affirm that he is among the most prominent among those peoples of his and most loyal in his prompt obedience in our interests (and we do not think that many households from among the Zegrenses will be able to claim the same of their services), and since(?) we wish as many as possible to be aroused by the honour conferred by us on that house to emulate Julianus, we do not hesitate to give the Roman citizenship, without prejudice to the law of the tribe, to him, his wife Ziddina, and their children Julianus, Maximus, Maximinus, Diogenianus.

(AD 177) Copy of a letter of the Emperors Antoninus and Commodus, Augusti, to Vallius Maximianus: we have read the *libellus* of the chief of the tribes of the Zegrenses and have noted the favour with which he is regarded by your predecessor Epidius Quadratus, and also moved by the latter's testimonies, and the services and evi-

---

[46]   W.Seston, M.Euzennat, 'Un dossier de la chancellerie romaine, la *Tabula Banasitana*, étude de diplomatique', *CRAI* (1971), 468; A.N.Sherwin-White, 'The *Tabula* of Banasa and the *Constitutio Antoniniana*', *JRS* 63 (1973), 86; W.Williams, 'Formal and historical aspects of two new documents of Marcus Aurelius', *ZPE* 17 (1975), 37 on pp. 56–7; F.Millar, *The Emperor in the Roman World* (London, 1977), 130, 216, 223, 261–2, 473; U.Schillinger-Häfele, 'Der Urheber der Tafel von Banasa', *Chiron* 7 (1977), 323.

dence of his conduct which he himself puts forward, have given to his wife and children the Roman citizenship, without prejudice to the law of the tribe. In order that this may be recorded in our *commentarii* [records] find out what the age of each is and write to us.

Copied down and checked from the record [*commentarius*] of those given the Roman citizenship by the Divine Augustus [names of preceding emperors] . . . which the freedman Asclepiodotus produced, as it is written below:

In the consulship of Imperator Caesar L. Aurelius Commodus Aug. and M. Plautius Quintilius, on the day before the nones of July, at Rome [6 July 177].

Faggura, wife of Julianus, *princeps* of the tribe of the Zegrensians, age 22, Juliana, age 8, Maxima, age 4, Julianus, age 3, Diogenia, age 2, children of Julianus mentioned above:

At the request *per libellum* of Aurelius Julianus, princeps of the Zegrensians supported by Vallius Maximianus by letter [*suffragante. . . . per epistulam*], to these we have given the Roman citizenship, without prejudice to the law of the tribe, and without diminution of the *tributa* and *vectigalia* of the *populus* and the *fiscus*.

Carried out on the same day in the same place under the same consuls. Asclepiodotus, freedman: I have checked it:

Witnesses:

M. Gavius Squilla Gallicanus	(consul, 150)
M'. Acilius Glabrio	(consul, 152)
T. Sextius Lateranus	(consul, 154)
C. Septimius Severus	(consul, 160)
P. Julius Scapula Tertullus	(consul, 160/6)
T. Varius Clemens	(ex-*ab epistulis*)
M. Bassaeus Rufus	(ex-Praetorian Prefect)
P. Taruttienus Paternus	(Praetorian Prefect by 179)
Sex. [Tigidius Peren]nis	(probably Praetorian Prefect)
Q. Cervidius Scaevola	(lawyer, Prefect of *Vigiles*, 175)
Q. Larcius Euripianus	
T. Flavius Piso	(Prefect of the Corn Supply, 179)

Firstly the procedures recorded fall clearly within the wider category, fundamental to the nature of Imperial government, of petition-and-response. Secondly the document clearly illustrates one sub-category of this procedure, the way in which provincial governors might send on petitions from private individuals to the emperor, with a covering letter of recommendation. In this case the terminology used (*suffragante Vallio Maximiano per epistulam*) perfectly exemplifies G.E.M. de Ste Croix's justly famous demonstration – given long before this inscription was known – of how the meaning of words with the root 'suffrag-' shifted from votes by equals to petitions for favours addressed by intermediaries to superiors. In other words it is a clear example of how language was distorted by the impact of monarchy.[47] Thirdly, the right to grant the Roman citizenship was from the beginning one of the perquisites of the monarchic rule exercised by the Roman emperors. We had known already from Pliny's correspondence with Trajan (x 95; 105) that there were imperial *commentarii*, or archives, in which the names of the recipients of *beneficia* were entered; but not that there was a '*commentarius* of persons granted Roman citizenship' by all the emperors (other than subsequently unrecognised pretenders) back to Augustus himself. Nor, before the publication of this inscription, did we possess a single documentary text from these archives. The bulk of such an archive – in which, as the extract given implies, the individual entries were written up in remarkable detail – must have been very considerable. The document also confronts us with major unanswered questions as to the nature of archives on perishable materials, their organisation, location, form of storage and (?) transportability. For did they remain permanently in Rome or accompany the emperors on their increasingly frequent travels and campaigns? If not, in what sense could they be used by an emperor who might be a thousand miles away? The list of Imperial *amici*, first consulars in order of seniority and then the leading *equites*, also seems to give a perfect representation of the emperors' advisers as they were in 177. These distinguished gentlemen are listed as witnesses to a document which, seen from Rome, must have been of very minor local importance. If they really did attend in person to affix their seals that is quite a striking

[47] G.E.M. de Ste Croix, '"Suffragium": from vote to patronage', *British Journal of Sociology* 5 (1954), 33.

fact. But did they also discuss the *content* of Imperial written decisions and letters? If not, since so much of the emperor's work concerned the issue of written decisions in various forms, the significance of the role of advisers or *amici* must have been much less than often supposed.

The document also raises important questions about the citizenship itself, as it does about the nature of the *tributa et vectigalia populi et fisci*. But perhaps more significant is the fact that the bronze tablet, with all the information and problems which it presents to us, is only available firstly by the accident of survival (and bronze is for obvious reasons highly vulnerable) and of discovery, and secondly because it was originally in the interest of someone – presumably Julianus, the *princeps* of the Zegrenses – to have it inscribed and put up. It is the fundamental limitation and problem of epigraphy that in reading an inscription we are always reading what someone wished to tell not us but his contemporaries. The very notion of putting up an inscription in Latin will have been a cultural import which came to Banasa with the extension of Graeco-Roman culture. But the occasion would only arise firstly when some success, such as a favourable reply to a petition, had been secured, and secondly when there was some need to record this in a local context. None the less, in spite of all the problems of context and background, this is a beautifully explicit document which has almost infinite lessons to give us about the nature of the Roman Empire.

(6) The Tetrarchic Edict on Maximum Prices. The two Imperial letters in the *tabula* of Banasa are highly typical of the workings of Imperial government in the first three centuries in being *replies* to requests from interested parties. In the period of the Tetrarchy an important change seems to appear in the aspirations of government, the level of innovation which it sought and the degree of social and economic intervention at which it aimed.[48] This very distinctive phase, accompanied by major attempts at systematisation of the

---

[48] For a brief indication of the novelty and importance of the Tetrarchic edicts see Millar, *op.cit.* (n. 46), 257–8.

law,[49] was also marked by much more explicit and deliberate attempts to explain and justify Imperial decisions to the public. By far the most significant product of this development was the well-known edict on maximum prices, now known from a large number of fragments in the Greek East.[50] For our knowledge of its text we are (once again) bound to be dependent on whether in each province the choice was made to inscribe it on stone. So far, the fragments come from a quite restricted range of provinces, in the Greek-speaking part of the empire.[51] This is not the place to enter into any discussion of the products and services for which the edict lays down maximum prices, or of the perplexing problems of relative monetary and bullion values in this period, also the subject of another contemporary edict of which one fragment has been published.[52] What may be emphasised here is the vast preamble in which the emperors explain and justify their measures. As with the earlier documents mentioned, this could be considered first of all as a specimen of the official Latin prose of the early fourth century. Secondly, *whose* prose is it? The problem of the actual authorship of the

---

[49] See T.Honoré, '"Imperial" rescripts AD 193–305: authorship and authenticity', *JRS* 69 (1979), 51 on pp. 60–3; *idem, Emperors and Lawyers* (London, 1981), ch.4.

[50] For a full text as known to that date, with extensive commentary, see S.Lauffer, *Diokletians Preisedikt* (Berlin, 1971); note also M.Giacchero, *Edictum Diocletiani et Collegarum de Pretiis Rerum Venalium* (Genoa, 1974). Extensive epigraphic work on the texts, especially that from Aphrodisias, is however still in progress. See K.T.Erim and Joyce Reynolds, *JRS* 63 (1973), 99; J.Reynolds, *ZPE* 33 (1979), 46 (Aphrodisias); M.H.Crawford, J.M.Reynolds, *ZPE* 26 (1977), 125; 34 (1979), 163 (Aezani); *AE* (1977), 776–7 (Achaea).

[51] On the question of publication on stone and the importance of the role of the provincial governor, note M.H.Crawford and J.Reynolds, 'The publication of the Prices Edict: a new inscription from Aezani', *JRS* 65 (1975), 160. The geographical pattern there suggested is slightly extended by the publication of a new fragment from Odessus on the west coast of the Black Sea, see G.Mihailov, *Stele (Memorial to N.Kontoleon)* (Athens, 1980), 147.

[52] K.T.Erim, J.Reynolds, M.Crawford, 'Diocletian's currency reform: a new inscription', *JRS* 6 (1971), 171; see M.Crawford, 'Finance, coinage and money from the Severans to Constantine', *ANRW* II.2 (1975), 560 on pp. 578–81.

texts of all forms of imperial pronouncement, from speeches to *subscriptiones* (replies written under petitions given in by individuals or groups), is acute (and insoluble) in all periods, and is made all the more complex by the Tetrarchic system. What we have is at any rate a piece of extended propaganda and self-justification issued in the name of all four of the Augusti and Caesares. We can study it as a major expression of the new Imperial ideology, while recalling that the only contemporary observer from whom we have a surviving mention of it, Lactantius (*de mort. persec.* 7, 6–7), saw the edict as the work of Diocletian alone, and regarded it as a total failure.

With that we may leave this minute selection, inevitably quite unrepresentative, of that vast number of inscriptions (certainly far more numerous in Greek than in Latin) which can be read like – or even as – literary texts, and which have a sufficiently full and complex content for them to form a focus of study in themselves. That study itself, however, would have to consist of extended explorations of the wider context from which these documents come and to which they refer. In consequence, no clear line could or should be drawn between this approach and what must, obviously enough, be the normal one, the study of inscriptions in groups. The vital questions are, firstly, what types of groups and, secondly, what are the limits and nature of the questions which can be asked of them?

HANDLING INSCRIPTIONS IN BULK

Two preliminary points must be made. If the activity of increasing our knowledge and understanding of the past is valid at all, then every scrap of information, from a couple of letters scratched on a sherd onwards, potentially has a place in some wider framework of understanding. Hence comes the value of the apparently thankless task of producing reports and publications of endless archaeological and epigraphic finds, which at the moment do not seem to have any intelligible context or to make the slightest contribution to understanding. That may require several different levels or stages of work, not necessarily by the same person: a study of script and grammar in the Latin of a western province; an analysis of the linguistic patterns prevailing there; broader conclusions on the nature of 'Romanisation'. Or, just occasionally, someone with the energy and vision of a Rostovtzeff may be able to gather up a whole mass of disparate fragments of information and combine them to form an intelligible pattern.

But for the ordinary student of the ancient world who is not going to become an epigraphist himself, but who sees that the, published inscriptions provide both an extraordinarily privileged and immediate means of access to the life of antiquity and a (literally) inexhaustible mass of data, the choice of an area or theme, and the construction of questions which the inscriptions will actually answer, are all-important. There are, it is true, very few aspects of life which are referred to nowhere in the hundreds of thousands of surviving inscriptions. If it were a reasonable or adequate objective to catalogue isolated references to (say) agricultural production, the marketing of vegetables, the customs of non-urban communities, diet, childbirth or religious observances within the family, then that could always be done. But it does have to be accepted that whole areas of life will only appear tangentially, if at all, in the inscriptions, and that there are many areas, however desirable in themselves, where the inscriptions will not allow of any serious social history. One of these areas, for instance, is slavery. There are indeed important concentrations of documents, such as the manumission-inscriptions of Delphi or Thessaly, which are highly *relevant* to slavery and brilliantly illuminate its social framework from a very specific angle.[53] But an actual *history*

---

[53] For an interesting historical study of the manumission inscriptions from Delphi see K.Hopkins, *Conquerors and Slaves* (Cambridge, 1978), 133f.; for some Thessalian manumission documents see B.Helly, 'Actes d'affranchissements thessaliens', *BCH* 99 (1975), 199; and 'Lois sur les affranchissements dans les inscriptions thessaliennes', *Phoenix* 30 (1976), 143.

of slavery in any particular region cannot be written. Again, for almost all areas of economic life and activity inscriptions will provide the names of trades and occupations, regulations affecting markets or prices or the limits of the privileges enjoyed by the members of particular groups. But they will bring us very little nearer to an economic *history*. Similarly, the most detailed inscriptions which we have relating to agriculture, those concerned with Imperial estates in Africa,[54] resemble the inscriptions of Imperial mines in the Iberian peninsula[55] in being *regulations* which allude to many important aspects of economic and social life, but cannot by their nature take us further than that. These documents too would be best studied in the first instance as texts, in order to establish a clear view of their internal structure and purpose. But the limitation which faces us in collecting either isolated items of economic evidence (say on the names of trades or occupations, whether generally or in a particular place) or extended formal documents relating to economic life, is that we still cannot place this evidence within any worthwhile framework. We have no idea of how or where the produce of the emperor's estates in Africa was marketed or consumed, nor what happened to the silver from his mines in Spain.

This is not to say that ancient economic history should not be pursued – only that no one has so far escaped from the alternatives of having interesting ideas which do not relate to the evidence in a wholly satisfactory way, or collecting evidence which cannot in any real sense be interpreted. All serious work on ancient economic history using inscriptions would have to be conducted with the consciousness that all that can be achieved is preliminary collection and analysis of groups of relevant data.[56]

---

[54] These texts are reproduced eg. in *FIRA*[2] i, nos. 100–3; Tenney Frank (ed.), *Economic Survey of Ancient Rome* iv (Baltimore, 1938), 83–102.

[55] *FIRA*[2] i, nos. 104–5; translation and notes Tenney Frank (ed.), *Economic Survey of Ancient Rome* iii (Baltimore, 1937), 167–74.

[56] For instance the invaluable work of R. Duncan-Jones, *The Economy of the Roman Empire: quantitative studies*[2] (Cambridge, 1982), is more accurately characterised by the second than the first half of its title.

THE CASE OF THE GREEK CITY

Significant historical work with inscriptions, leading to results which are more than merely preliminary or indicative, must (I would suggest) satisfy two conditions: that there is a sufficient concentration of evidence either by locality, type or theme; and that it can be placed within some intelligible framework. Given the formality of nearly all types of inscription, and therefore the all too clearly defined and limited nature of what they are designed to say, the prospects of serious historical analysis are greatly improved if the inscriptions can be related to other evidence – literature above all, but also (in certain areas) papyri, and also coins, archaeo-logical evidence and studies of topography. Granted these conditions – i.e. granted that in many areas the concentration of evidence will be too thin to allow any coherent results – the study of the history, topography and institutions of parti-cular areas or cities will always be an avenue worth explor-ing. The work of Louis Robert, heavily emphasised at the beginning of this chapter, provides innumerable examples of studies of cities and areas in Asia Minor, using the evidence of inscriptions.[57] But we may note also, as examples, studies of the history and cults of Thasos,[58] of Cos[59] and of Gonnoi in Thessaly.[60] It is not an accident that all these are places in the Greek East, whose inscriptions tend both to be fuller and more revealing individually (i.e. to be, as suggested above, a minor form of literature in themselves), and to come in denser concentrations. Perhaps the only two towns in the Latin West of which real 'histories' can be written are Pom-peii and Ostia, both being cases where a relatively rich stock of inscriptions can be placed in an archaeological setting of

---

[57] For example L.Robert, *Études anatoliennes* (Paris, 1937); *La Carie* II (Paris, 1954) (by L. and J.Robert); *Villes d'Asie Mineure*[2] (Paris, 1962); *A travers l'Asie Mineure* (Paris, 1980).

[58] J.Pouilloux, C.Dunant, *Recherches sur l'histoire et les cultes de Thasos* I-II (Paris, 1954–8).

[59] S.M.Sherwin-White, *Ancient Cos: an historical study from the Dorian settle-ment to the Imperial period* (Göttingen, 1978).

[60] B.Helly, *Gonnoi* I-II (Amsterdam, 1973).

wholly exceptional character.[61] In the Greek East even a single sanctuary can produce a major series of inscriptions, allowing historical studies at various levels: so for instance the Asclepieion at Pergamum,[62] the great temple of Apollo at Didyma near Miletus,[63] or the sanctuary of Zeus at Labraunda in Caria.[64] An incomparably more extensive mass of inscriptions comes from the sanctuary of Apollo at Delphi.[65] The several hundred inscriptions of Delphi, stretching from the Classical to the Imperial period (for which there is an extensive series of Imperial letters concerned with the sanctuary) serve to create a not uncommon situation: that while we normally complain of a dearth of evidence for the history of the ancient world, here we find ourselves with *too* heavy a concentration of documents of very specialised types (accounts, dedications, letters) which, together with the vast archaeological remains, make a 'history' of Delphi in the ancient world an almost unimaginable task. We have such a history for part of the Hellenistic period;[66] but, for instance, no one has yet published a historical analysis of the role of Delphi in the Graeco-Roman world of the Empire. Much the same could be said of Delos,[67] where the pattern of the inscriptions is complicated by the island's special relationship

[61] For Ostia there is the classic study of R.Meiggs, *Roman Ostia*[2] (Oxford, 1973); for Pompeii no comparable work of synthesis exists. For work based on inscriptions and graffiti note the work of M.Gigante (n. 29 above) and Väänänen (n. 27 above). See also H.Castrén, *Ordo Populusque Pompeianus. Polity and society in Roman Pompeii* (Rome, 1975). The graffiti from Pompeii are collected in *CIL* IV and Supplements.

[62] Chr. Habicht, *Altertümer von Pergamon* VIII.3: *die Inschriften des Asklepieions* (Berlin, 1969), with an exemplary historical introduction.

[63] A.Rehm, *Didyma* II: *die Inschriften* (Berlin, 1958).

[64] J.Crampa, *Labraunda: Swedish Excavations and Researches* III.1–2; idem, *The Greek Inscriptions* (Lund, 1969–72).

[65] Volumes of inscriptions appear among the reports of the French excavations, *Fouilles de Delphes* III, in a series of separate fascicules divided by the architectural setting of the inscriptions and published at intervals since 1909.

[66] R.Flacelière, *Les Aitoliens à Delphes* (Paris, 1937); G.Daux, *Delphes au IIme et du Ier siècles* (Paris, 1936).

[67] The inscriptions are again published in the reports of the French excavations, *Inscriptions de Délos*, and so far run to 2,879 items. Note therefore G.Durrbach, *Choix d'inscriptions de Délos* I.1–2 (Paris, 1921–2).

to Athens and by its brief but very important role as a major international trading centre between 166 BC and the Mithridatic wars. It is, once again, as yet impossible to imagine serious historical work, using the epigraphic and archaeological evidence, which is not strictly divided, as such work has been so far, by periods or themes.[68] Here at least there has been a beginning of analytical historical writing.

But if we turn, to take only the most obvious example, to Ephesus, from where some 5,000 inscriptions, stretching from the sixth century BC to the sixth century AD, have recently been collected,[69] the evidence seems to call out for a historical study embracing topography and urban development, architecture, institutions, ceremonials and cults. It is curious, however, that the late antique and Byzantine period of Anatolian Greek cities (notably Ephesus itself) has been better studied recently than the Classical period.[70]

However, all these considerations pale into insignificance beside the fact that there is no serious analytical study of the one place where all the necessary conditions for a fully historical use of inscriptions are fulfilled, namely the most obvious of all, Classical Athens. Hellenistic Athens was the subject of a beautifully balanced, but now antiquated, history by W.S. Ferguson;[71] a new history, using the vast mass of new inscriptional material is awaited from Chr. Habicht.[72] But Classical Athens, of the fifth and fourth centuries, more than anywhere else in the ancient world, presents a concentration of literary, archaeological and very extensive epigraphical evidence which should allow a fully integrated historical treatment of a society and its evolution through time; and

---

[68] See e.g. P.Roussel, *Délos, colonie athénienne* (Paris, 1916); or the important recent work of Ph. Bruneau, *Recherches sur les cultes de Délos à l'époque hellénistique et à l'époque impériale* (Paris, 1970).

[69] In the series *Inschriften griechischer Städte Kleinasiens* and under the title *Die Inschriften von Ephesos* Ia (Bonn, 1979); II (Bonn, 1979); III–VI (Bonn, 1980; VII, 1–2 (Bonn, 1981).

[70] See C.Foss, *Byzantine and Turkish Sardis* (Cambridge, Mass., 1976); *Ephesos after antiquity: a late antique, Byzantine and Turkish city* (Cambridge, Mass., 1979).

[71] W.S.Ferguson, *Hellenistic Athens. An historical essay* (London, 1911).

[72] Note the preliminary study of the early period mentioned in n.41 above.

here, alone among all ancient cities, the evidence of public inscriptions can be set against the background of a detailed contemporary analysis of the working of the constitution, the Aristotelian *Athenaion Politeia*.[73] As yet, to take only a few examples of those aspects to which the inscriptions are most relevant, we have detailed studies of the Treasurers,[74] an excellent account of the working of the council,[75] studies of the political geography of Attica[76] or a very full prosopography of the richer Athenians and their families.[77] The combination of literary and epigraphic evidence also makes possible a very full understanding of Athenian festivals.[78] Without multiplying further examples, it is enough to pose the question, in concluding this section, as to why Classical Athens has attracted no major historical study.

A strictly geographical concentration of inscriptions, such as lies relatively unexploited not only in the individual areas and cities mentioned but also in a host of others, is not the only type of concentration which would allow serious study. Few would now dare to attempt a synthetic view of the functioning of 'the Greek city' over many centuries in the manner of that great historian, A.H.M. Jones, even if his work remains essential reading for all students of the Greek world.[79] But there remain major themes where substantial series of documents are available, stretching over wide areas in time and space. One example is the major subject of the formal, diplomatic, military and financial relations between

---

[73] Note the massive recent commentary on this work by P.J.Rhodes, *A Commentary on the Aristotelian Athenaion Politeia* (Oxford, 1981).

[74] W.S.Ferguson, *The Treasurers of Athena* (Cambridge, Mass., 1932).

[75] P.J.Rhodes, *The Athenian Boule* (Oxford, 1972). Cf. B.D. Merritt and J.S.Traill, *The Athenian Agora* xv, *Inscriptions: the Athenian councillors* (Princeton, 1974).

[76] J.S.Traill, *The Political Organisation of Attica: a study of the demes, trittyes and phylae and their representation in the Athenian Council* (*Hesperia* Supp. XIV, 1975).

[77] J.K.Davies, *Athenian Propertied Families, 600–300 BC* (Oxford, 1971).

[78] See L.Deubner, *Attische Feste* (Berlin, 1932); A.W.Pickard-Cambridge, *The Dramatic Festivals of Athens*², rev. J.Gould and D.M.Lewis (Oxford 1968); H.W.Parke, *Festivals of the Athenians* (London, 1977).

[79] *The Greek City from Alexander to Justinian* (Oxford, 1940).

Greek cities and Hellenistic kings, involving for instance the evolution of royal cults,[80] the form and content of royal letters to cities,[81] the prosopography of royal emissaries and office-holders,[82] or the forms of control and exploitation in the overseas possessions of the Ptolemies.[83] Subjects such as these can be effectively studied for two reasons. Firstly, because, in spite of diversities over time and space, it is reasonable to start from the hypothesis that the Hellenistic monarchies were functioning systems, in which each item of evidence will make some contribution to the understanding of the whole.[84] Secondly we are dealing with explicit documents which not only name and locate offices and functions, but also reveal at least some elements of the values pertaining to the system. The honorific or cult inscriptions for kings, the texts of decrees honouring men who protected a city's rights against royal encroachment, or the letters of the kings themselves, will all reveal at least the formal public values accepted in Hellenistic society. But behind the diplomatic history of the relations of city and monarch, which has many elements of continuity stretching from the fourth century BC to the late Roman Empire, and whose primary documents could (once again) be seen as constituting a minor branch of literature with its own themes and variations, lies the major historical theme of the vitality of the Greek cities and the vigour with which they competed with each other and demanded acceptance of their claims from the successive monarchs under whose rule they fell.

This activity in itself is only a product of the communal,

---

[80] Chr. Habicht, *Gottmenschentum und griechische Städte*[2] (Munich, 1970).

[81] The collection by C.B. Welles, *Royal Correspondence in the Hellenistic Era* (New Haven, 1934), could now be greatly extended, for instance by the third-century letters from Labraunda (see n. 64).

[82] E. Olshausen, *Prosopographie der hellenistischen Königsgesandten* I: *von Triparadeisos bis Pydna* (Louvain, 1974).

[83] R.S. Bagnall, *The Administration of the Ptolemaic Possessions outside Egypt* (Leiden, 1976).

[84] Note the classic, if perhaps too schematic, study of E. Bikerman, *Institutions des Séleucides* (Paris, 1938), and D. Musti, 'Lo stato dei Seleucidi', *Studi Classici e Orientali* 15 (1966), 61–200.

political and ceremonial life of the Greek cities, which can be studied not only (as above) locality by locality, but also thematically. Here again there are strict limits on what the formal, public inscriptions available to us will reveal. We cannot hope to gain more than passing hints of the overall social composition of a Greek city, of its economic life or of the relations of town and country. Indeed the inscribed documents will hardly mention the peasant villages of the countryside except when a king makes a grant of some of them to a favourite. The inscriptions will rarely even make clear the sources of the surplus wealth which evidently did pass into the hands of the upper classes of the cities. What they will do is to illustrate public expectations as to the semi-voluntary deployment of that wealth on building, the provision of shows or food, offerings and sacrifices or embassies to a king – in short the system of 'euergetisme' whose importance in the early Hellenistic city was recently adumbrated by Paul Veyne.[85] These values and expectations – and the specific roles performed – can legitimately be compared across a whole range of cities. Simply by way of example, I offer a translation of one of these honorific decrees, which comes from Erythrae and probably dates to the 330s, just before the opening of the Hellenistic period proper:[86]

It was voted by the Council and People on the proposal of the Prytaneis, Generals and Auditors. Since Phanes, son of Mnesitheus, is a good man and both shows every willingness in being constantly well disposed towards the People of Erythrae and has contributed money without interest both towards the sending away of the soldiers and the razing of the acropolis, it has seemed right to the Council to crown Phanes son of Mnesitheus with a gold crown worth fifty Philippic staters, and to proclaim this at the Dionysia. Zenodotus the agonothete is to see to the proclamation. He [Phanes] should be granted maintenance in the *prytaneion*. This decree is to be inscribed on two *stelai*, of which one is to be placed

---

[85] P. Veyne, *Le pain et le cirque: sociologie historique d'un pluralisme politique* (Paris, 1976), ch. 2.

[86] H. Engelmann and R. Merkelbach, *Die Inschriften von Erythrai und Klazomenai* I (Bonn, 1972), no. 21.

in the sanctuary of Athena and one in the sanctuary of Heracles, so that all may know that the People knows how to return appropriate thanks for the benefits [*euergetemata*] conferred on it.

It was precisely this perfectly conscious and explicit convention of the repayment of concrete benefits (in this case, it seems, simply bribing a Persian, or perhaps early Hellenistic, garrison to go away) with honours and ceremonial rights and the immortalisation of these on stone in appropriate places, which was the source of so many of the tens of thousands of public inscriptions surviving from the Greek cities. Taken individually, they may often do no more than allude to elements of social, economic and religious life; the use of a particular currency, the observance of festivals, the role of city officials, public maintenance for them and a variety of honorands in the *prytaneion*, or the existence of certain important sanctuaries. Taken collectively, they may allow the exploration of a vast, but not infinite, range of questions about ancient Greek society and its institutions; and all the more so if considered along with literary, numismatic and archaeological evidence.[87] Given the volume and complexity of the epigraphic evidence and the various strategies available for approaching it – whether (as above) on a local basis, or by studying vocabulary, concepts and ideologies, or by isolating particular institutions – there is almost infinite scope for exploring what the inscriptions do tell us, whether explicitly in what they report or implicitly in the fundamental structures of the values and assumptions which they embody. In the vast mass of the inscriptions of the Greek cities and sanctuaries, above all in Asia Minor, which stretch from the fourth century BC to the third century AD, we can for once perhaps afford not to worry too much about the many areas of social and economic life to which they will only allude (or which they will pass over altogether) until we have explored more fully how much they do convey.

---

[87] For a relevant recent example see S.G.Miller, *The Prytaneion: its function and architectural form* (Berkeley, 1978).

In one particular area the (relatively) unexplored possibilities are obvious, namely the religious life of the cities. Naturally there has been a vast range of studies of particular aspects, including collections of the sacred regulations from Greek cities.[88] But the standard modern work on Greek religion is not alone in its tendency, when it reaches the Hellenistic and Roman period, to concentrate on the general and the abstract, on 'ruler-cult', philosophy, oriental cults, monotheistic tendencies or astrology.[89] In other words the tendency is to select out those aspects which seem to represent religious systems logically comparable to Christianity. To do so is to fail to do any real justice to the complex cult and ceremonial institutions of the communal life of the Greek cities.[90] For any enquiry into this area the inscriptions are central, not only for the vast range of customs and institutions on which they contain information, but also for the religious concepts, values and distinctions which they explicitly and implicitly express.[91]

For reasons which it would be very interesting – if exceedingly difficult – to explore, the voting and putting up of monumental inscriptions, though still known, ceased to be so distinctive a feature of Greek city life after the third century AD.[92] The spread of Christianity and the increasing dominance, and (apparently) increasing demands, of the Roman state and its representatives were clearly all of some

---

[88] F. Sokolowski, *Lois sacrées de l'Asie Mineure* (Paris, 1955); *Lois sacrées des cités grecques: Supplément* (Paris, 1962); *Lois sacrées des cités grecques* (Paris, 1969).

[89] M.P. Nilsson, *Geschichte der griechischen Religion* II: *die hellenistische und römische Zeit*[2] (Munich, 1961).

[90] For a serious, if still too brief, attempt to represent the communal religious institutions of the ancient world in their local contexts see R. MacMullen, *Paganism in the Roman Empire* (New Haven, 1981).

[91] For a valuable analysis of the vocabulary of sacrifice as directed towards the Roman emperors see S.R.F. Price, 'Between man and God: sacrifice in the Roman Imperial cult', *JRS* 70 (1980), 28.

[92] The volume of the late Roman and Byzantine inscriptions of Aphrodisias in Caria, currently being prepared by Charlotte Roueché, will be the most extensive series of Greek city inscriptions of this period so far published.

relevance here. We may however note, in leaving this area, a perfect example, from an inscription, of the transference into the role of bishop of the values of secular city life. The inscription comes from Laodicea Combusta in Phrygia and dates to the crucial turning-point, the reign of Constantine.[93]

I, M. Julius Eugenius, son of Cyrillus Celer of Kouessos, town-councillor, having served on the governor's staff in Pisidia and having married Flavia Iulia Flaviane, daughter of Gaius Nestorianus, a senator, and having served honourably in the meantime, when an order went out under Maximinus that the Christians should sacrifice and not be allowed to resign the service, endured very many torments and succeeded in leaving the service under the governor Diogenes while keeping the Christian faith. After staying in Laodicea for a short time I was by the will of the all-powerful God installed as bishop. For twenty-five years I administered my bishopric with much honour, built the whole church from the foundations, and also all the surrounding ornamentation, consisting of porticoes and tetraporticoes and paintings and mosaics and a fountain and gateway, and fitted it all with dressed stone, and in a word with everything. Being about to depart from human life, I have made for myself a plinth and tomb, on which I have had the foregoing inscribed to the glory of the church and my family.

THE LATIN WORLD

Turning away from the central areas of Greek culture, it is worth noting that the region of which the most complete and thoroughly-edited collection of Greek inscriptions has been made is present-day Bulgaria.[94] But when we come to the Latin-speaking world it must be stressed that although in many areas inscriptions are of prime importance – sometimes as limiting cases in the way discussed above – they rarely rise to either the complexity of content or the density of concentration found in the inscriptions of the Greek cities. In the history of Rome for example, though, as we saw above, public inscriptions had begun even in the regal period,

[93] *Monumenta Asiae Minoris Antiqua* I, 170.
[94] G. Mihailov, *Inscriptiones Graecae in Bulgaria Repertae* I (Sofia, 1956; rev. 1970); II (Sofia, 1958); III.1 (Sofia, 1961); III.2 (Sofia, 1964); IV (Sofia 1966).

neither the inscribing of laws or regulations nor the presentation on inscriptions of individual careers became a major feature until quite late in the Republic. The career-inscription, giving a man's public offices in great detail, is a distinctive phenomenon of the Imperial period, discussed below. None the less the Republican inscriptions of Rome and Italy are prime documents for the history of the Latin language, as they are also for its orthography and spelling, and must therefore be studied on the stones or at any rate with the aid of photographs.[95] The relatively few extensive texts embodying laws or decrees of the Senate begin in the second century BC and have been collected and discussed many times.[96] There is still room, however, for treatments of these texts which do not aim so much at either restoration of lost sections (often involving prolonged and fruitless arguments about line-lengths) or reconstructions of their political context and purpose, as at using them as evidence for the history of language and (as mentioned above, p. 99) at understanding their composition as texts. Even more profound ambiguities attend the question of what can be considered a companion group of texts, the so-called 'municipal laws' of the late Republic. We owe to the late M.W. Frederiksen a fundamental discussion of the nature of these documents. Are they in fact 'laws', generated in some way from the centre of power in Rome? How and from what sources was each text as we have it put together? When, by whom, and for what

---

[95] The main Latin inscriptions of the Republic, except for the laws and *senatus consulta*, are collected by A. Degrassi, *Inscriptiones Latinae Liberae Reipublicae* I (Florence, 1957; rev. 1965); II (Florence, 1963); *Inscriptiones Latinae Liberae Reipublicae; Imagines* (Berlin, 1965), with excellent photographs. It is unfortunate that not all the earliest inscriptions, i.e. those of the regal period (e.g. the Lapis Niger, see p. 94–5 above), are included. For texts and linguistic discoveries (but no photographs) see the excellent Loeb volume of B.H.Warmington, *Remains of Old Latin* IV: *Archaic Inscriptions* (Cambridge, Mass., 1940). The time has arrived, with many new discoveries, for a new edition of this work.

[96] E.g. I.Bruns, *Fontes Iuris Romani Antiqui*[7] (1907); S.Riccobono, *Fontes Iuris Romani Anteiustinianae*[2] (1941). The most detailed discussion of any one Republican law is K. Johannsen, *Die lex agraria des Jahres 111 v.Chr.: Text und Kommentar* (Diss. Munich, 1971).

reason was it inscribed?[97] Not all of the questions which were thus so effectually opened up have yet been answered. It will not seem paradoxical, in view of what has been said above, that a significant proportion of the most detailed, clear and explicit Republican documents is in fact drawn from the repertoire of the epigraphy of the Greek cities and is thus available to us only in Greek translation.[98] The inter-play between Greek and Latin as the vehicles of official prose, in both the Republican and the Imperial periods, thus becomes a major historical subject in its own right.[99] The volume of these texts (and the difficulty of the problems associated with them) has been considerably increased by the publication in 1974 of several extensive new sections, found at Cnidus, of the Roman 'pirate-law' of *c.* 100 BC.[100] As noted above (p. 103) the important new series of Republican documents in Greek from Aphrodisias also brings extensive further evidence, and further problems. But, the major individual documents apart, there are only limited categories of inscriptions which are important for the history of the Republic. One such category, which is best considered as being even closer to literature than most others, is the historical (or pseudo-historical) inscriptions put up in Rome and representing one aspect of the Augustan revival: the lists (*fasti*) of the pairs of consuls since the beginning of the Republic and of the *triumphatores*; and also the *elogia* recording the achieve-

[97] M.W.Frederiksen, 'The Republican municipal laws: errors and drafts', *JRS* 55 (1965), 183.

[98] See R.K.Sherk, *Roman Documents from the Greek East: Senatus consulta and epistulae to the Age of Augustus* (Baltimore, 1969).

[99] Note two fundamental older works, P.Viereck, *Sermo Graecus* (Diss. Göttingen, 1888); L.Hahn, *Rom und Romanismus im griechisch-römischen Osten* (Leipzig, 1906). See now H.J.Mason, *Greek Terms for Roman Institutions: a lexicon and analysis* (Toronto, 1974); M.Kaimio, *The Romans and the Greek Language* (Helsinki, 1979); E.Garcia Domingo, *Latinismos en la Koine* (Burgos, 1979).

[100] M.Hassall, M.Crawford and J.Reynolds, 'Rome and the eastern provinces at the end of the second century BC', *JRS* 64 (1974), 195. For subsequent discussions see the survey by J.Reynolds, M.Beard, R.Duncan-Jones and C.Roueché, 'Roman inscriptions, 1975–80', *JRS* 71 (1981), 123.

ments of the great military commanders of the Republic, which were designed to accompany the statues of these men put up in the Forum of Augustus.[101] As contemporary products, direct documentary parallels to the literary works of Vergil and Livy, these are of great interest. As 'documentary' attestations of alleged historical facts their status cannot be any higher than that of the literary sources of the same period.

The epigraphic record of the Roman Republic in the provinces is still sparse, except – as always – in the Greek East,[102] and it is perhaps only in the rapidly developing epigraphic material of Italy, which can be followed in the annual survey 'Rivista di epigrafia italica', published since 1973 in *Studi Etruschi*, that it is beginning to be possible to trace major themes (cf. also p. 90 above).·

It is one of the most marked features of the culture of the Imperial period that this situation alters progressively. In the East, as mentioned above, the mass of city inscriptions continues as before, closely associated, above all in the second century AD, with very extensive public building. From the first century AD onwards the same is true of Latin-speaking North Africa, contrasting sharply with the almost total absence of epigraphic record from the first one-and-a-half centuries of Roman rule there. It is obvious that in a general way the putting up of inscriptions was a quite important facet of the city life which was characteristic of the Graeco-Roman world, and therefore spread steadily along with urbanisation. Thus we have a substantial harvest of inscriptions also from the Mediterranean coast of Spain and from the south (Baetica/Andalusia), and progressively less until we reach the north-west, which seems hardly to have been touched by Graeco-Roman patterns of life at all. Gaul too, while some

---

[101] Collected and edited in A. Degrassi, *Inscriptiones Italiae* XIII. 1: *Fasti consulares et triumphales* (Rome, 1947); XIII. 3: *Elogia* (Rome, 1937).

[102] Note e.g. K. Tuchelt, *Frühe Denkmäler Roms in Kleinasien: Beiträge zur archäologischen Überlieferung aus der Zeit der Republik und des Augustus* I: *Roma und Promagistrate* (Tübingen, 1979); R. Mellor, ΘΕΑ 'ΡΩΜΗ: *The worship of the goddess Roma in the Greek world* (Göttingen, 1975).

Latin inscriptions are found in all regions, produces relatively
few, and only a very short list of extended documents of
individual importance: the best known are the famous bronze
tablet from Lyon with the text of the Emperor Claudius'
speech on the admission of Gallic nobles to the Senate,[103] and
a complex document of the 230s honouring one Sennius
Sollemnis.[104] But from Britain, whose civil and military
inscriptions have been collected and edited with exceptionally lavish care,[105] to Dalmatia and the middle Danube,
the scattered Latin inscriptions, often slight and insignificant
in themselves, are the primary evidence for the spread of
Roman civilisation, the Latin language and the institutions of
the self-governing town. They also provide evidence (for
example) for nomenclature, occupations and the observation
of the cults of local or imported deities. But it is important to
stress once again that the historical value of relatively scattered inscriptions can only be indicative or illustrative. Valid
negative conclusions can almost never be drawn from such
evidence; in France in particular the fact of continuous occupation of urban sites in the intervening centuries means that
no negative conclusions, or even statistical inferences can
ever be drawn from what happens to survive. The double-
negative form of argument (see p. 92 above) can, however,
be validly used. If (for instance) even a few persons used
Latin to scratch imprecations on lead tablets deposited in
Gloucestershire,[106] it follows that it cannot be argued that
Latin was in use in Britain only in official or military contexts.

Even more than in the Greek East there is much that we
can never hope to learn from the epigraphy of the Latin West.
None the less it is a historical fact of the greatest importance
that the Roman period saw the spread of forms of city or

[103] *CIL* XIII, 1668; *ILS* 212.
[104] CIL XIII, 3162; H.G.Pflaum, *Le Marbre de Thorigny* (Paris, 1948).
[105] See R.G.Collingwood and R.P.Wright, *Roman Inscriptions of Britain* I:
Inscriptions on stone (Oxford, 1965).
[106] M.W.C.Hassall, R.S.O.Tomlin, *Britannia* 10 (1979), 341–4. Note the
publication by the same authors of four of a find of over forty lead
tablets from Bath, *Britannia* 12 (1981), 370–6.

communal self-government, invariably using Latin; in consequence it is possible to collect and analyse the surviving texts of municipal decrees.[107] The most vivid evidence for local self-government comes from the two well-known *leges* (charters?) of Domitian's reign from Malaca and Salpensa in Spain. These two documents, which preserve extensive extracts from the constitutional codes of the two *municipia*, suffer from a lack of comparative material, and leave unanswered fundamental questions about the authorship or legal source of the codes (delivered by the emperor or the governor of Tarraconensis or generated locally?), the degree of innovation intended (since both places had magistrates in office already) and the relation of the production of these codes to the two towns' status as *municipia* – a term whose definition is controversial – and to their possession of 'Latin rights'.[108] The two texts, which have not been re-studied in detail for some time, would deserve an epigraphical and historical re-examination. At the moment, granted that we know that there were many Punic towns in the western Mediterranean (of which Malaca had been one, according to the geographer Strabo), which must also in their Punic phase have had 'constitutions', and that we can find also communities, like the Vanacini in Corsica,[109] with the institutions of local self-government but without either of the specifically Roman statuses of *municipium* or *colonia*, the whole question of the 'Romanisation' of communal institutions in the West remains in a state of conceptual confusion.

However, it is precisely in the Roman Empire that the detailed study of the formal types of information which inscriptions are designed to reveal has been most successfully pursued. The genre of the honorific inscription, immortalising the record of a man's offices, statuses and (sometimes)

---

[107] R.K.Sherk, *Municipal Decrees of the Roman West* (Buffalo, 1970). The number of texts found by Sherk (65) is strikingly small.

[108] For some heretical views on these questions see F.Millar, *op.cit.* (n. 46), 394–410, 485–6 and App. IV.

[109] *CIL* x, 8038; F.F.Abbott, A.C.Johnson, *Municipal Administration in the Roman Empire* (Princeton, 1926), no. 59.

benefactions, continued to be very common in the East, and also spread to the West. On the one hand the carefully graded *cursus* or 'career' laid down for Roman senators in the Republic and expanded by a large number of new functions under the Empire, comes to be illustrated by literally hundreds, perhaps thousands, of inscriptions giving the offices held by individuals. On the other hand the honorific inscriptions from towns in Italy and the provinces, both Greek- and Latin-speaking, reveal the major historical development that people from many (though not all) of these places served as 'equestrian' officers in the Roman army, or rose higher into the so-called 'equestrian civil service' which developed in the first century and a half of the Empire. This relative openness of access to Roman offices is a very significant aspect of the political character of the Empire. A nexus thus developed between office-holding and 'euergetisme' (see p. 118 above) in small towns, service as an officer in the Roman army, posts as an equestrian civil official, the rank of senator and even the position of emperor. The link between local institutions, the imperial service and the patronage of the emperor is nowhere better illustrated than in the Latin inscription of Q. Domitius Marsianus (Fig. 6), put up in his home town, Bulla Regia in the province of Africa, in the 170s AD:[110]

To Q. Domitius Marsianus, son of Lucius, tribe Quirina, procurator of Augustus of the patrimonium of the province of Narbonensis, procurator of Augustus for the iron mines, procurator in Gaul for receiving the census declarations of the province of Belgica throughout the districts of the Tungri and Frisavones and of Germania Inferior and of the Batavi, *praefectus militum*, adlected into the *decuriae* by the Emperors M. Aurelius Antoninus and L. Aurelius Verus, Caesares. When the Town Council had voted to put up an equestrian statue of him at public expense, his brother L. Domitius Fabianus erected it at his own expense, thus sparing expenditure on the part of the city.

Copy of the *codicilli* [letter of appointment]:

Caesar Antoninus Augustus to his own Domitius Marsianus greetings. Having long since been eager to promote you to the splendour of a ducenariate procuratorship, I am now making use of the

[110] *AE* (1962), 183; cf. H.G.Pflaum in *Bonner Jahrbücher* 171 (1971), 349.

6. An inscription honouring Domitius Marsianus
(from *Fasti Archaeologici* 13 (1958), pl.26, no.78)

opportunity which presents itself. Succeed therefore to Marius Pudens with an expectation of my unfailing favour so long as you retain the conscious possession of probity, diligence and experience. Farewell my Marsianus, dearest to me.

The inscription comes in fact from the base of the equestrian statue (which has not survived) which stood in Bulla Regia to record for his fellow-citizens the favour which Marsianus had earned in the Imperial service. His brother Fabianus, if not actually a member of the city council (as he probably was), was at least a well-off resident of the town. The inscription thus offers a very clear example of the roots in local communal life which are a primary characteristic of those who entered the Imperial service. But there is a catch here which typifies the limits of what epigraphical evidence can tell us. For in a very large number of cases we owe our knowledge of the careers, and indeed of the existence, of these men precisely to the fact that a local community had some motive to commemorate them on an inscription. If there were men who rose in the Imperial service but retained no local roots, and neither kept a family connection nor served as town councillors or annual officials nor held priesthoods nor acted as a *patronus* of the town, the chances of their being recorded on inscriptions will have been greatly reduced.

A rather similar limitation affects Imperial letters, of which one sub-category, the Imperial letter of appointment addressed to a member of the senatorial or equestrian order, is best represented by Aurelius' letter in this inscription. No one ever recorded in an inscription an Imperial letter informing him that he could *not* have a particular post; and similarly cities never put up inscriptions displaying Imperial letters rejecting requests or informing them that they had lost a dispute with a neighbouring city. We have a small number of documentary texts of such letters only because cities involved in disputes sometimes inscribed unfavourable letters or replies addressed to their neighbours, which were therefore implicitly or explicitly favourable to themselves.[111]

[111] For this category of letter see Millar, *op.cit.* (n. 46), 431f.; 436f.; 438f.;

None the less the genre of the Imperial letter, together with the more informal type of Imperial reply known as a *subscriptio*, is represented by several hundred documentary texts in both Latin and Greek, preserved on inscriptions and papyri and in legal and literary sources, and is therefore both a sub-literary type, which deserves study in its own right, and a prime source for the nature of the Roman Empire as a system.

The Marsianus inscription is unusually rich in both giving the text of the Imperial letter and retailing the circumstances of the erection of the statue (which will not have been wholly unlike the famous one of Marcus Aurelius from the Capitol). More commonly, such inscriptions concentrate on the successive steps of the man's career – often in reverse chronological order to bring the most important posts to the beginning. In spite of the many severe limitations on what these inscriptions *can* by their nature tell us – limitations frequently not recognised in modern work, as we shall see – there is no question of the scale and importance of the information which, by retailing equestrian and senatorial careers, they have revealed about the workings of the Empire. The two editions of the *Prosopographia Imperii Romani* (1897–8 and 1933 onwards, so far up to L) bear witness to the vast store of information from this and other sources which has now been reduced to intelligible order.[112] Given the steady flow of new inscriptions, the technical work of compiling lists of the holders of particular offices, recording the earliest or latest appearance of a particular office, following the rise of successive generations of a family and so forth, can continue indefinitely. There are also a number of broad and indisputable historical conclusions which arise from this mater-

J.Reynolds, 'Hadrian, Antoninus and the Cyrenaican cities', *JRS* 68 (1978), 111; *Aphrodisias and Rome* (London, 1982), docs. 10, 13, 14.

[112] Note also the supplementary collection by B.Thomasson, *Senatores Procuratoresque Romani* (Göteborg, 1975), collecting and analysing careers documented, or more fully documented, since the appearance of the relevant volumes of *PIR*[2].

ial. Firstly, an equestrian 'career' following a succession of posts in (at least) roughly graded orders of seniority and prestige did evolve in the course of the first century and a half.[113] Secondly, entry to equestrian posts and the Senate was gained by men from many (but, so far as the inscriptions can tell us, not all) provincial areas. Thirdly, the career of Marsianus, which took him solely to the region of Gaul, seems to have been exceptional, in that both equestrian and senatorial careers generally show a marked absence of geographical specialisation. If we take the usual characteristics of the succession of posts followed as our evidence, then in this respect the Empire seems to have been an integrated system, which showed no tendency to regional compartmentalisation.

Our difficulties arise as soon as we step outside the confines of the formal evidence actually presented to us by those inscriptions which happened to be created in the ancient world and happen to have been preserved and to have been published in the modern era. Is our picture of the geographical areas from which *equites* and senators came simply dictated by the accident of what happened to be inscribed? Or could we reasonably relate the communal investment in monumental inscriptions to the social conditions which would allow at least some families in a local community to rise into the equestrian service and the Senate – and thus regard them as parallel products of socio-economic conditions which were present in some places and not in others? Or again, even if such varying regional patterns really existed and are significant to us, were they of any conscious significance at the time? Marcus does not imply that it was of any importance to him that Marsianus came from Bulla Regia, or from the province of Africa. It is we who impose the categories of 'the African contribution to the Imperial service' or suppose (for instance) that Hadrian might have favoured Italians as opposed to provincials in appointments to the senatorial office of *praefectus aerarii Saturni*. But

---

[113] Note the classic analysis of these careers by the late H.G.Pflaum, *Les carrières procuratoriennes équestres* I–III (Paris, 1960–1), with the review by F.Millar, *JRS* 53 (1963), 194–200.

even if we can be sure of the identification of men's local origins (as we can with Marsianus, but often cannot), we have no clear indications that such categories had any relevance at all to the appointments made by emperors. These and similar ambiguities, both statistical and conceptual, haunt – and have so far almost entirely vitiated – all attempts to go beyond the formal records which the inscriptions present, to conclusions involving choices, values and intentions.[114]

The same ambiguities attend all attempts to interpret the succession of posts previously held by a man as the basis of his specific claims (in terms of relevant experience or quali-fications) to a more senior post. But the fact that a list of posts is the only evidence which we happen to have does not mean that we should be confident that it provides a sufficient explanation, or any explanation at all. We can never know the relevance of personal qualities (including quiescence and lack of dangerous ambitions), family background, the influence of intermediaries or simply the fact of having been available and of the right seniority at the right time. It may be indicative that Aurelius' letter – one of the rare items of evidence which even alludes to the motives of Imperial choice – implies that the promotion was a personal favour, dependent on the personal moral and social qualities of the recipient. Personal patronage may or may not have been an important factor; but what is clear is that the formal evidence of the inscriptions fully demonstrates a pattern of variety rather than concentration of 'relevant experience' in the case (say) of Prefects of Egypt[115] and in general fails to show consistent patterns of promotion in equestrian careers.[116] The same difficulties of interpretation attend senatorial careers. Were men picked for their abilities? If they rose rapidly – i.e. gained the consulate early or had few

---

[114] For demonstration of the dangers inherent in such attempts see the review of a number of recent prosopographical works by G.P.Burton in *JRS* 70 (1980), 203–9.

[115] See the demonstration by P.A.Brunt, 'The administrators of Roman Egypt', *JRS* 65 (1975), 124.

[116] See R.P.Saller, 'Promotion and patronage in equestrian careers', *JRS* 70 (1980), 44; *idem, Personal Patronage in the Early Empire* (Cambridge, 1982).

intermediate posts – is that a sign of the recognition of their abilities? But, if so, their background 'experience' when they reached the major military posts will have been less, not greater.[117] Or (again) did men rise by virtue of their social background, connections or personal charms? But in any case the whole area may be one of conceptual confusion, for we may be imposing irrelevant and anachronistic categories on the business of holding public office, which may have been a prize to be won and exploited, a recognition of wealth and social status, or a burden to be avoided. All that is clear is that the genre of the monumental inscription, formally listing a man's successive offices, is a very distinctive feature of the society and culture of the High Empire. It would well deserve study as such, in particular because it is not, to anything like the same degree, characteristic of either the preceding or the following period.

It is worth the emphasis given here partly because it is a specific instance of the wider phenomenon of the place of inscriptions in the culture of the ancient world, and partly because it offers a particularly clear example both of the extensive information which inscriptions can make available when treated collectively and of the dangers which lurk everywhere as soon as we go beyond the formal analysis and arrangement of that information and attempt wider historical and social judgements. To take only one example, there is no harm in pursuing the much-practised genre of assembling the names, dates and careers of those who held office in a particular province.[118] Such a study will always be useful as a work of reference. But as soon as we ask – and attempt to answer from the career inscriptions – (say) what sort of men the emperor sent to Britain and on what principles his selection was based, we enter issues which touch on the values of the entire society, and which we can solve, if at all, only by the consideration of all the other evidence.

---

[117] See B. Campbell, 'Who were the "Viri Militares"?', *JRS* 65 (1975), 11.
[118] For the most recent example see A. R. Birley, *The Fasti of Roman Britain* (Oxford, 1981).

Very similar problems would emerge if we were to look in detail at the vast epigraphic (and papyrological) documentation now available for the structure and working of the Roman army in the High Empire. A significant proportion of the evidence owes its existence to the same very important element in Imperial culture, the honorific inscription. It is this genre of inscription, for instance, which provides our only substantial body of evidence for what was evidently a highly important class of office-holders whose rank came just below – and overlapped with – that of *equites*, namely the centurions and 'first centurions' who might rise from the ranks or might be directly commissioned, and might proceed further in a form of career known only from inscriptions, to important equestrian civil positions. The framework of a significant element in the Roman state is thus revealed – but, equally, basic questions about functions, social background and criteria for promotion must remain unanswered.[119]

This survey of the inscriptions from the Graeco-Roman world and their uses to the historian cannot do justice to the sheer volume of the surviving examples or to their infinite variety of type and scale; probably the most common single type of inscription from the Latin West, for instance, is the brief tomb-inscription of a private individual who held no public office. It is, of course, this genre which has lasted most successfully into the modern world and continues to have a place in contemporary culture. The ancient tomb-inscription, for instance, like the modern, very commonly mentioned the person's age at death. So, granted the enormous number of such inscriptions, do we for once dispose of a valid body of statistical data, illuminating the fundamentally important question of the expectation of life in the ancient world? The answer appears to be no, for the graphs thus produced are both impossible in their overall patterns and tend to show a marked

---

[119] See B. Dobson, 'The significance of the centurion and "primipilaris" in the Roman army and administration', *ANRW* II.1 (1975), 392; *Die Primipilares. Entwicklung und Bedeutung, Laufbahnen und Persönlichkeiten eines römischen Offiziersranges* (Cologne, 1978).

concentration on ages of death which are multiples of five. In other words, what the epitaphs reveal is not an objective sample of ages at death but a pattern produced by choices as to who was commemorated; they also cast light on wider social issues such as the level of literacy.[120]

But it is the formal monumental inscription – containing a law, communal decision, letter from a superior, regulation of cult practices, accounts of a temple or vote of honours – which is the most distinctive and historically important product of the role in ancient culture of the inscribing of words on stone or bronze. The motives for the inscription of particular documents are quite often made explicit in the documents themselves (as above, p. 119) without our thereby being enabled to understand the very marked prevalence of the public inscription in ancient society as a whole, or what deductions we should draw from this evidence about the extent of popular literacy. All that is clear is that each and every public inscription is the result of a deliberate choice, whether motivated by the need to proclaim rules or privileges in permanent form or to give equally permanent expression to the highly competitive value-systems of most ancient communities. This explicit and formal character is both the great strength and the limitation of the inscriptions as historical evidence. But whatever caution must be observed in drawing conclusions from them, the ever-growing mass of inscriptions in Greek and Latin, and also in other languages, from the ancient world still represents a major cultural phenomenon in itself[121]. Some branches of it also can and should be considered as minor (but in bulk very extensive) literary genres, which provide a whole range of deliberately composed prose and verse to set against the remains of ancient literature surviving in the manuscript tradition. But the extent of the latter, however inexhaustible its interest, can only increase marginally, largely through the

---

[120] See most recently R.P.Duncan-Jones, 'Age-rounding, illiteracy and social differentiation in the Roman Empire', *Chiron* 7 (1977), 333.

[121] Compare the valuable recent essay by R. MacMullen, 'The epigraphic habit in the Roman Empire', *AJPh* 103 (1982), 233.

publication of papyrus fragments. It is epigraphy which provides our most direct access to ancient society and culture, and which shows every sign of being able to add indefinitely to the stock of available texts. It thus represents the best guarantee we have that our understanding of the ancient world need never be static.

CHAPTER 3

Archaeology

Nowhere are the distinctive assets and liabilities of archaeology as a source shown up so conspicuously as in Greek and Roman history. While the decisive theoretical battles of archaeology have long been fought out on other fields and between bigger battalions, it is in the closer encounters of Classical archaeology that the more continuous attrition of empirical testing takes place. The experience has not had much influence on wider archaeological thought, but it has revealed certain assets on the part of archaeological evidence in an historical context: four of these, which I would single out as the most important, are its independence, its directness, its experimental character, and its unlimited potential for future extension. None of these qualities should be understood as implying objectivity. In so far as the ideal of total objectivity can be pursued at all, it is no more at the command of the archaeologist than of the historian. Less widely acknowledged, but in the long run just as important, are the peculiar liabilities of archaeological evidence. It is impossible simply to give a list of these; a great part of the discussion in this chapter arises from their existence. But one can say at the outset that archaeological evidence particularly lends itself to misunderstanding of one form or another: occasionally, to misunderstanding by the archaeologist of the identity of what he himself has discovered; much more often, to his misunderstanding of the *meaning* of his own and others' discoveries; equally frequently, to misunderstanding by historians of what is the scope of permissible inference from archaeological data in general or from a particular discovery. To these and other failures of understanding and communication, we must turn presently.

Anthony Snodgrass

First, however, the assets. The 'independence' of archaeological evidence consists in the fact that the hypotheses and arguments of the archaeologist are part of a great nexus of general archaeological theory and practice, which is something entirely independent of historical theory, if only because it has evolved partly from the findings of archaeologists working on fields that are not historically documented. To give a simple example: in 1904 G.E. Fox argued that a suite of rooms in the Roman villa at Chedworth in Gloucestershire had served as a *fullonica*, an establishment for the fulling of cloth.[1] The references to the British textile industry in documentary sources such as Diocletian's Price Edict and the *Notitia Dignitatum* provided a natural incentive for this interpretation; but it was also based on the analogy of actual fulling-installations such as that found at Pompeii, and especially on representations in wall-paintings of fulling operations. Because the establishment was manifestly too large for the needs of one villa and therefore argued a commercial purpose, Fox's observations were widely taken up in general accounts of the rural economy of Roman Britain. It was not until two generations later that I.A. Richmond re-examined this part of the site at Chedworth.[2] By close study of the stratigraphy he was able to show that the supposedly complementary parts of the *fullonica* had not after all been contemporary with each other in construction and use, while his great knowledge of bath-installations in other Romano-British buildings helped him to perceive the true explanation, that these rooms belonged to successive re-arrangements of the villa's bath-suite. This kind of experience, though often in a less clear-cut form, is by no means uncommon in archaeology: even when the rightness of the new explanation is less than demonstrable, the doubts cast on the old one can be salutary. Part of the significance of this particular illustration is that Fox's reasoning was probably in

[1] 'Notes on some probable traces of Roman fulling in Britain', *Archaeologia* 59.2 (1904), 207–32.
[2] 'The Roman villa at Chedworth', *Transactions of the Bristol and Gloucester Archaeological Society* 78 (1959), 5–23.

part *a priori*, and based on the natural desire to match the material remains with the historical and iconographical sources; it stood to be corrected by the purely archaeological arguments (characteristically empirical in their basis) of Richmond. It is often, and in my opinion rightly, argued that archaeology has the same ultimate aims as history. But the two disciplines use different techniques and different data. It is also true that, just as there are aspects of history for which archaeology cannot be used, so there are fields of archaeology which lie beyond the reach of historical evidence.

In speaking of the 'directness' of archaeological evidence, I am partly drawing a contrast with the quality of some of the other evidence used in ancient history, which is not always acknowledged by its practitioners. Ancient historians use the word 'source' with a latitude which most students of later periods would repudiate: Herodotus is a 'source' for the history of Saïte Egypt (*c.* 664–525 BC), Thucydides for the conspiracy of the Tyrannicides, Tacitus for the reign of Tiberius, and Plutarch for the life of Themistocles. One weakness of this usage is that it leaves one without a distinctive term for the documents or other contemporary records from which these much later writers derived their accounts and which may in some cases still survive. It is this very circumstance which gives archaeological evidence some of its value in ancient studies: the excavated physical remains, at least at the moment of their discovery, do bring us closer to some kind of historical reality than we are ever likely to get through any other medium. They represent what somebody once did, not what some contemporary or later writer says that they did. But this moment soon passes: the material cannot be given a truly historical meaning until it has been subjected to a series of processes, all in one sense or another very hazardous. In many cases, these include removal from its immediate physical environment (which is itself presently destroyed), cleaning, identification, verbal description, dating, establishment of geographical origin, drawing, photography, conservation, preliminary and final publication. The possibility of human error hangs over every stage.

By the end, the true facts may become as distorted, obliterated, even forgotten, as in any written account of past events. Indeed, at a trivial level an excavation report *is* a piece of written history, a point underlined in the last twenty years by the case of Sir Arthur Evans' account of his own excavations at Knossos which has at times been handled in a way reminiscent of the treatment given to, say, Rameses II's account of the Battle of Kadesh. But the fact remains that the starting-point of an excavation report is often eye-witness observation, and always contemporary documentation of some kind. That is an asset not to be despised.

The experimental quality of archaeology is closely linked with the fourth and final factor that we shall consider in a moment – the supply of fresh archaeological evidence. It is this which enables archaeology to proceed, at times, by the kind of experimentation which is more often associated with the natural sciences. The archaeologist can form hypotheses, ranging from straightforward historical propositions ('The Vikings reached North America') to complex models of human behaviour, and then test them by searching for evidence that is entirely new, either because it lies undiscovered beneath the ground or because it has never before been applied to this particular end. Or he can pose open-ended questions or problems ('Did the peasants of the ancient Mediterranean world live predominantly on their land or in towns?') and similarly search for the evidence that will provide an answer. The historian working only with non-archaeological sources cannot normally use this procedure, least of all in ancient history, because discoveries of new documentary material, though not as rare as is widely believed, are almost entirely unpredictable. Archaeology can also on occasion operate in a more literally experimental way, by producing replicas of ancient structures, artefacts and processes and then testing them in action.

That the soil of Greece and Italy should still, after more than a century of intensive exploitation, be producing archaeological material in apparently endless quantity is always a source of surprise to laymen. There is a natural tendency to suspect that little of this material is of real significance. The suspicion is justified in one sense only: there is little chance that any future discovery will have quite the breadth of impact that was produced, for example, by the bringing of the Elgin Marbles to London or the discovery of the great Bronze Age civilisations of the Aegean. But this is largely because we are better informed today. There have been discoveries in the past decade, and there will be many more in the future, which would have dumbfounded educated people everywhere if they had occurred a century or two earlier (as they could well have done); on the modern world, their impact is more muted. It is, on the other hand, a complete mistake to imagine that we are by now well supplied with evidence on all important aspects of ancient history, as a few almost random examples will show: how many Republican villas in Italy have been excavated? how many Messenian sanctuaries, Spartan cemeteries or Boeotian town-sites? how many Classical village-settlements from the countryside of Attica? how many Bronze Age settlement-sites in Arcadia? how many Greek colonies on the Mediterranean coasts west of Sicily? The answer to each question is to be reckoned, if at all, on the fingers of one hand. Yet today the rate of work is increasing, to an almost alarming degree. Many excavations are occasioned by modern building-operations, but many others are not. In the unoccupied zone of the island of Cyprus alone, there were fourteen foreign and six Cypriot expeditions excavating in 1978; 120 excavations of Roman sites in Britain are to be expected in a normal year. Clearly there is going to be, for the foreseeable future, a colossal influx of new archaeological evidence for ancient history. To the obvious question, through what medium this evidence is to be communicated to historians and to the world at large, the only answer is by excavation reports, monographs and syntheses, of which the first two must be written by professional archaeologists and even the third requires someone expert enough to pick out the significant details mentioned in. passing by a summary or provisional account. Ideally this work should be given priority over that of actual excavation; in practice it will lag far behind. Yet the means of communication are more highly developed today than in the days when one had to travel to hear the excavator's oral account of his newest discoveries. If only a portion of the seed falls on good ground, there will still be a crop for historians to harvest.

Next, a word about definitions. There are those who would include inscriptions and coins as a part of the archaeological evidence, but this seems to me to be valid only in the unimportant sense that they too are often found by excavation: once discovered, their interpretation proceeds by techniques quite separate from those of the archaeologist, and that is why they are treated elsewhere in this volume. On the other hand, there is a field of essentially archaeological activity, of swift and comparatively recent growth, which is often overlooked: field survey and other field-work not involving excavation. There are several areas where this has already proved itself potentially or actually a more fruitful source of evidence than the excavation of sites. There is also the growth, more recent still, of the use of the techniques of the physical sciences, which has made some important contributions to Classical archaeology. Yet among the public and even among some professional scholars working in other fields, the impression remains that archaeology *is* excavation. This is about as accurate as saying that medicine is surgery. The earlier remarks (see p. 139) about the stages in the communication of archaeological results were intended to show how illusory, in one aspect, this belief is; but beyond that there is a kind of collective misapprehension that, at least sub-consciously, pervades the belief of many people, archaeologists included. It could perhaps be called the positivist fallacy of archaeology. It holds that archaeological prominence and historical importance are much the same thing; that the observable phenomena are by definition the significant phenomena.

One cure for the illusion is first-hand experience. Twenty-five years ago, T.J. Dunbabin in his lectures 'The Greeks and their Eastern Neighbours' argued that the serious historian of early Greece 'must be prepared to forget that he is an historian and to study archaeology for its own sake'; the best prescription was to work on an excavation or study intensively an object or class of objects.[3] He was right, though some of his readers at the time must have found this hope more pious than realistic. It seems less so today, and there are now many ancient historians who by following this prescription have acquired as clear a grasp of the archaeological realities as many archaeologists have. But for most people it will always remain true that 'historical' statements about the remains are more interesting than archaeological ones; this is why propositions that are not merely false but, on closer analysis, devoid of actual meaning ('Stonehenge was built by the Druids'; 'This is the tub in which Telemachus took the bath described in the *Odyssey*'), still retain some of their hold. One can only trust that this tendency will weaken with the passage of time; and that there will not always be disappointment at the discovery that the Curia in Rome, besides being restored, preserves the form of a period 300 years after Cicero, or that the walls of Phyle are of a building-style which makes it impossible to associate them with the famous events of 403 BC.

The illusion can also be cured by reflection. On an urban site, for example, the most fully preserved architectural phase will belong, other things being equal, not to the period of greatest historical importance, but to the latest period when the site had any economic importance at all. Among the portable archaeological finds, many potentially significant classes of material will be absent because of their perishability or intrinsic value; by contrast, broken pottery, lacking these qualities, will have a quantitative predominance which is out of all proportion to its historical significance. In rejecting a fallacy of this kind, one is tempted as often to go to the opposite extreme and say that the truth about archaeology is the reverse: that the function of archaeology has been not to

[3] *The Greeks and their Eastern Neighbours* (Society for the Promotion of Hellenic Studies, Supplementary Paper VIII, 1957), 15.

buttress the historical account nor even to supplement it, but to undermine it. Certainly there is no shortage of examples in which the result of excavation appears at first sight to have been exactly that. Take, for instance, the statements of Herodotus about the Greeks in Egypt during the reign of the Pharaoh Amasis (569–525 BC).[4] He says (II 178) that Amasis 'gave' the Greeks the city of Naucratis to settle in; that Greek trade was concentrated at Naucratis to the exclusion of other sites (II 179); and that Amasis withdrew a settlement of Greek mercenaries, established nearly a century earlier at a place called Stratopeda on the eastern frontier of Egypt (II 154), and brought them to Memphis to act as his own bodyguard. What does archaeology suggest? The excavation of Naucratis from 1884 onwards provided conclusive evidence that Greeks were permanently settled there well before the reign of Amasis. There are inscriptions in Greek and an unmistakeably Greek temple in the Ionic order as well as much pottery ranging from the late seventh century BC down to Amasis' period. Greek pottery belonging to the time of Amasis has, however, also been discovered at a number of Egyptian sites outside Naucratis, making it hard to accept the picture of the concentration of trade from Greece, or at least to associate it with this Pharaoh. At Tel Defenneh a major settlement of Greek mercenaries, in the general area of 'Stratopeda' if not identical with it, was also partially excavated and provided no evidence, either for establishment a century earlier than Amasis or for abandonment in his reign; on the contrary, its Greek pottery-finds began if anything later than those from Naucratis and were positively concentrated in his reign. A very similar pattern was found at Memphis, to which the mercenaries were supposed to have been withdrawn; occupation by mercenaries seems to have covered much the same period at the two sites. Thus matters remained for many years, until in 1978 Dr E.D. Oren reported the discovery of a dozen further sites with evidence (including burials) for the

[4] Discussed by M.M. Austin in *Greece and Egypt in the Archaic Age* (Cambridge Philological Society, Supplementary Volume II, 1970).

settlements of Greeks in the north-eastern Delta, the vicinity of 'Stratopeda'.[5] Again, the pottery-finds cover much of the sixth century BC (including Amasis' reign); furthermore one of these sites is heavily fortified and makes as plausible a candidate for identification with 'Stratopeda' as does Tel Defenneh. The archaeological evidence thus tells a coherent story: a community of Greeks was settled at Naucratis from before 600 BC; presently, with all the air of a planned movement, groups of Greeks, probably mercenaries, were very widely stationed at strategic points on the eastern frontier of Egypt, and at Memphis; meanwhile, items of Greek trade were occasionally finding their way to yet other places in Egypt. The subsequent accession of Amasis has no detectable impact on conditions at Naucratis, nor does it lead to the withdrawal of the mercenaries from any of the frontier posts so far found; still less does it bring a curtailment of the distribution of Greek finds on other Egyptian sites.

Has the evidence of excavation therefore destroyed the credit of Herodotus' account? Not really, I would argue. On the questions of detail, it is perfectly possible that even now the particular site called 'Stratopeda' has not been located, that the Greek pottery at places outside Naucratis was traded by non-Greek middlemen, and (though this is the hardest obstacle to overcome) that Herodotus' phrase about 'giving the Greeks Naucratis' was intended to cover some purely institutional change of the kind that leaves no material trace. But it also seems to me that, at a more theoretical level, the claim that Herodotus' account has been falsified by archaeology is a relapse into another variant of the 'positivist fallacy'. It assumes that archaeology and history are operating in essentially the same order of historical reality; that archaeological observations are made, so to speak, in the same language as historical statements. In fact the overlap between the two is small and occurs, in the main, only in those cases where the activities of a significant part of the

---

[5] In *Greece and Italy in the Classical World* (Acta of the XIth International Congress of Classical Archaeology, London, 1978) (1979), 199.

community are directly influenced by contemporary historical events. Historical events of this kind seldom occur, as can be confirmed by consulting, say, criminal records or proceedings of private societies during periods of political and military crisis; much of life goes on unchanged. Thus it is with the evidence from Egypt that we have been considering. The archaeological evidence has displayed exactly the qualities – directness, potential for expansion and above all independence – which we attributed to it earlier. In so doing, it has revealed Herodotus' account as being a very inadequate summary of the history of the Greek presence in Egypt in these years; on the use of Greek mercenaries, for example, any future account of the episode will probably give at least as much prominence to the archaeological findings as to Herodotus' statements. But it has not destroyed the entire credibility of Herodotus' account, because it is not in the nature of archaeological evidence to do so. What it has rather done is to cast doubt on the chosen *emphasis* of the historian's version. It is this subtler kind of contradiction which W.H. Auden had in mind when he wrote:

> From Archaeology
> one moral, at least, may be drawn,
> to wit, that all
>
> our school text-books lie.
> What they call History
> is nothing to vaunt of,
>
> being made, as it is,
> by the criminal in us:
> goodness is timeless.
> ('Archaeology', in *Thank you, fog*; London, 1974)

To attempt to make any corresponding statement about the limits of the historian's inferences would be presumptuous, and perhaps impossible. It is enough to say that the more broadly the ancient historian interprets the scope of his subject, the more likely he is to find archaeological evidence helpful to him. This is best illustrated by taking

examples of different historical approaches, as I shall now try
to do, and showing how archaeological evidence can be used
or misused in the service of history. The ancient historian
has, perhaps paradoxically, an advantage here in that the
quality of his documentary evidence has never been good
enough for him to subscribe to the old, naïve notion of
history as the mere recording of past events, or to aim at the
goal of pure objective description. Such notions, though long
since abandoned by professional historians, continue to survive in some outsiders' views of history. The absurdity of
total description as a goal for the historian can be illustrated
by a recent use of it, taken (as it had to be) not from history
but from historical fiction, where as a narrative device it
serves a different purpose:

> The rearmost shell of this salvo exploded seventy-one feet from
> Löwenherz's port engine. The theoretical lethal radius of an
> exploding 10.5 cm. shell was fifty feet. This one fragmented into
> 4,573 pieces of which twelve weighed over one ounce, 1,525
> weighed between one ounce and a fiftieth of an ounce, and 3,036
> were fragments of less than a fiftieth of an ounce. Twenty-eight
> fragments hit Löwenherz's Junkers. Four pieces penetrated the port
> motor . . . (Len Deighton, *Bomber* (1978), 434)

It is as well that the recording, in this way, of every particle
of relevant information is not within the powers of the historian, and of the ancient historian least of all. Interpretation,
vital in any study of the past, is the life-blood of ancient
history. Perhaps less readily, ancient historians have learned
from those working in later periods that cultural, social and
economic history, local history, demography, historical
geography, the history of science, the history of ideas, and
other sub-disciplines can be fruitfully pursued for antiquity as
well. Whether or not this is pure gain for ancient history as a
whole, it is certainly beneficial for the collaboration of historian and archaeologist, as already hinted.

A corresponding breadth of approach is also, however,
required of the Classical archaeologist. The traditional art-
historical bias of the subject, from this point of view, needs
to be shifted. For a long time, the subject has remained

imbued with that spirit in which Lord Charlemont wrote two centuries ago: 'We have reason to believe that the World is still in Possession of a Portion at least of those Masterpieces which have been the Admiration of all Antiquity; and we cannot but flatter ourselves that we have had the Glory of being the Discoverers of this inestimable Treasure . . .'.

However, this must not be taken to imply an elimination of art history, which makes a central contribution to our understanding of cultural history as a whole. 'When time gives historians the perspective to judge our age,' writes a despairing commentator on twentieth-century Britain, 'they may epitomise its barbarism not in our violence, intolerance and irrationality, but in the suicide of western art.' (Paul Johnson, *The offshore islanders* (1972), 584). If that is indeed their conclusion, it will be reached only after much art-historical and archaeological research of the kind which has long been devoted to antiquity. (A quite different but interesting point is that the same research may lead them to a very different view from that of the contemporary commentator.) But alongside the art of a civilisation, there are many other aspects of its material culture whose significance we can instantly recognise in a present-day case and about which, in the case of the past, we can therefore reasonably ask archaeology to inform us. With some of these, long the object of research in non-Classical fields, Classical archaeologists have only recently begun to concern themselves seriously: animal husbandry, agriculture, diet and pathology, and industrial techniques of various kinds, especially metallurgy – to name only a few. The process is analogous to the one taking place in ancient history. But the important thing is that it is happening at all. It is a real pleasure to be able to write, in concluding this section, that the prospects for future collaboration between ancient historians and archaeologists are becoming more favourable every year, and that this is already giving new vitality to both disciplines.

We may now consider one by one the different aspects of ancient historical research to which archaeological evidence may be applicable.

CHRONOLOGY

Traditionally, this aspect has played the dominant role in the handling of archaeological evidence for historical purposes, and for this reason it may be taken first. For the dating of events in periods too early to be covered by written records, or in regions on the fringe of the literate Classical world, archaeology has a long-recognised utility. It is also in the chronological field that the more recently available scientific techniques have been most prominently employed. Many of these last have too wide a margin of potential error to be useful in a period as well documented as that of Classical antiquity but, as we shall see, there is an exception in the case of dendrochronology.

For much of the period between 750 BC and AD 600, a chronological framework covering certain of the finer wares of Greek and Roman pottery is now generally agreed among archaeologists.[6] As the years pass, the framework is subjected to repeated tests (though with decreasing frequency) as new finds occur in historically dated contexts. Over the last generation or more, it has usually passed these tests with no more than minor inaccuracies being revealed, which suggests that within this period it cannot be very far wrong. It is a matter of opinion what degree of precision the framework possesses as a result of this, but in the best-studied periods an error of more than fifteen or twenty years would now be surprising. The deficiencies of the framework are that the finer wares in question cover only a tiny fraction of the pottery in production at any one time, are geographically uneven in their distribution and are not uninterruptedly consecutive in time. This means that many excavations in ancient Mediterranean sites are largely or entirely deprived of the help that these diagnostic wares can give; the chronology has instead to be established at the first or second remove, by using other wares or objects altogether, which have been

[6] For convenient discussions, see R.M.Cook, *Greek Painted Pottery*[2] (1972), ch. 11; J.W.Hayes, *Late Roman Pottery* (1972), *passim*; F.Oswald and T.Davies Pryce, *An Introduction to the Study of Terra Sigillata* (1920), ch. 3.

found elsewhere in association with the more closely dated series and acquire a looser and more indirect dating from them. But there is a deeper underlying weakness about the framework which affects it at many points: we can see this as soon as we ask the question, how was the framework established in the first place?

The answer is that with a few negligible exceptions (such as the Panathenaic prize amphorae in fourth- and third-century Athens which are inscribed with the name of the annual magistrate, or the funerary urns from Ptolemaic Egypt marked with regnal years), each fixed point has been derived either from the discovery of pottery in a context believed to be associated with a dated event in history or, less often, from its association with more closely dated objects such as coins. But a message of this chapter has been that archaeological material and historical events are hard to bring together, because they represent different facets of human existence. Thus, for example, there is an easily intelligible process, well known to archaeologists, whereby a deposit of material becomes 'sealed', that is cut off from later intrusions either by having a continuous layer of soil superimposed on it, or through concealment in a grave. It is usually possible to detect whether anyone has subsequently dug through the stratum, or robbed or re-used the grave. The process of sealing will thus provide a lower chronological limit, a *terminus ante quem*, for all the material in the deposit. But how often is such a sealing process even plausibly, let alone demonstrably, associated with a dated historical event? The commonest circumstance is the destruction of a settlement, especially helpful when it is followed by total abandonment. But first, the possibility of other unrecorded destructions, accidental or otherwise, has to be excluded; then there remains the problem of the extent of most settlement-sites. If the sealed deposit in effect covers several acres, it is of course the latest material in any part of this deposit which provides the fixed dating-point. The difficulty in pinning down this latest material, even in relative terms, is exemplified by several instances in prehistory. What stage in the pottery-sequence had been reached when the palatial site at Knossos was destroyed? 'The end of Late Minoan II', said Sir Arthur Evans; 'Late Minoan III A 1', said others who had accepted his stratigraphy but refined his pottery-classification; 'the beginning of Late Minoan III A 2', say yet others, a generation later, to make no mention of those who reject Evans' scheme of stratification altogether. A similar process of scrutiny and downward revision seems to have begun with the Mycenaean pottery from Tell el Amarna in Egypt, a settlement not destroyed but abandoned after a brief occupation. Much the same has also been attempted for the pottery from the settlement on Thera, destroyed by volcanic disturbances a century or more earlier.[7] In these cases there was no close link with any dated historical event; the aim was the more modest one of establishing which material could be used to date the sealing of the deposit. Closer examination leads to new refinements of typology and some of these may reveal the presence of supposedly later features. Then either the scheme of relative chronology has to be adjusted, or the whole typological sequence is revised so that the chronology can be kept. All this tends to undermine confidence.

The same method can be used, often with better results, with graves or communal burials which have a known date. Here the process of 'sealing' is less equivocal and the problems caused by the quantity of material scarcely arise. Once again, it is in Aegean prehistory that there is the greatest dependence on this method, when Minoan and Mycenaean pottery has been found in Egyptian tombs which can be dated to the reign of a specific Pharaoh. The main danger lies in the fact that the pottery has by definition been imported over quite long distances, comprises only a small fraction of the grave-goods in any one burial, and may have been highly prized; it may therefore have been made appreciably

[7] See for example M.R.Popham, *The Destruction of the Palace at Knossos* (Göteborg, 1970); V.Hankey and P.M.Warren, 'The absolute chronology of the Aegean Late Bronze Age', *BICS* 21 (1974), 142–52; several papers in C.Doumas and H.C.Puchelt (eds.), *Thera and the Aegean World* I (1978).

earlier than the date of the tomb in which it is found. Archaeologists sometimes resort too readily to this 'heirloom' explanation, but enough unquestionable instances have occurred to show that it must apply at times in antiquity. But in historical times, such dated burials are in any case not common; they have mainly occurred in the form of communal graves associated with important battles, such as Marathon (490 BC), Delion (424) or Chaeronea (338), or the grave of the Lacedaemonians killed in 403 BC, which was discovered in 1930 in the Athenian Kerameikos.[8] Apart from lingering doubts over the identity of these tombs (as with the 'tumulus of the Plataeans' at Marathon, below, page 166), these finds on the whole offer the best dating evidence for ancient pottery of any period; the circumstances make the use of heirlooms relatively unlikely.

Less satisfactory is the dating evidence gained from the foundation of a dated settlement. Here the element of 'sealing' is absent; it is merely a question of pursuing excavation over a wide area of the site until one is satisfied that some of the earliest deposits have been found, or the graves of the earliest settlers identified. The risk is the same as that of extensive destruction-levels, only in reverse; further examination may at any time reveal deposits earlier than the earliest that were previously known, and on which chronological equations have already been based. The conclusions must therefore remain provisional. Some examples of this process, by now notorious among specialists, have occurred on Greek colonial sites in Sicily, notably Megara Hyblaea and Selinus; Thucydides (VI 4, 2) offers credible foundation-dates (728 and 628 BC respectively in these particular cases), and excavations had progressed far enough for the earliest pottery at each site to be provisionally identified; an absolute chronology for early Greek pottery was established which leaned heavily on these and a few other such fixed points; then re-examination of the material at both sites

[8] See F.Willemsen 'Zu den Lakedämoniergräbern im Kerameikos', *Athenische Mitteilungen* 92 (1977), 117–57.

revealed stylistic phases hitherto undetected and apparently earlier.

Yet the very fact that the chronology of Greek painted pottery is based on this range of different kinds of evidence gives it a cumulative strength which is lacking in any single category. When inferences based on destruction-dates in one area agree with those based on foundation-dates in another, it is reasonable to conclude that both are approximately correct. So far this question has been discussed in terms of Greek painted wares which, with their rapid and logical development and their wealth of iconographical detail, establish a more or less adequate framework for the years between *c.* 750 and 300 BC. For about a century and a half after that we have a series of dated Hellenistic deposits, but they are more thinly distributed and affect a narrower range of wares. There then ensues a hiatus before the process is resumed, first by the Italian and then by the provincial *terra sigillata*. In most important respects this fills the same role as the Greek pottery but with rather more precision. Attribution to individual craftsmen, instead of resting on stylistic observation supplemented by occasional signatures, is assured by the frequent occurrence of potters' stamps; dating contexts are often potentially more accurate thanks to the fuller documentation of Roman military history and the narrower dating-range of Roman Imperial coins. From the accession of Augustus to the end of Trajan's principate we have a series of military sites in Gaul, Germany and Britain whose occupation is historically attested and was often brief, which have been scientifically excavated and which have produced *terra sigillata* in adequate quantities. When this evidence falls away in the later Empire there remains the evidence of provincial cemeteries where pottery is associated with Imperial coins, extending to after AD 400. Occasional correlations for other Roman wares are possible later still: there are deposits containing 'Late Roman C' ware which are dated by a great earthquake at Antioch on the Orontes in AD 526; the Slav invasions in the late sixth century of our era, and those of the Persians and Arabs in the earlier seventh, offer at least the possibility of further fixed points in the ceramic series.[9]

For the traditional methods of determining chronology, pottery is the only class of archaeological material which stands comparison with coins and inscriptions; at times it is more accurately datable than either. In default of any of these, other materials must be used – sculpture, architecture, terracottas, metalwork – but on closer examination these usually prove to depend ultimately on the original three sources of dating evidence; they thus offer chronological information of the same type, but less direct and accurate. For the historical period, the very different method of dating by techniques based on the physical properties of objects – radiocarbon, thermo-luminescence, thermo-remanent magnetism – provide even less precision and are therefore seldom of use except in the detection of modern fakes. But in recent years, such great advances have been made with dendrochronological dating that one day it can be expected to bring about, in ancient history, a minor but significant sequel to the undoubted revolution that it is creating in prehistoric chronologies. In prehistory, this has been achieved mainly through its use in conjunction with the radiocarbon technique, to correct and refine the less reliable but more widely available evidence which the latter offers. In ancient history, its contribution will be more direct, by confronting the archaeological dates which have been derived, by the traditional means that we have been reviewing, from historical events. The prospect is rather stimulating.

Dendrochronology involves the slow and painstaking build-up of a tree-ring sequence over a long period, as is suggested by the fact that it was already being pioneered in the early years of this century by the American astronomer A.E. Douglass. It was no accident that it first evolved in the New World, where exceptionally long-lived species like the sequoia and the bristlecone-pine are available. In Europe, where few trees live to a great age, this technique was

---

[9] See Roman references in n.6 above.

developed through B. Huber's studies in the years from 1938 onwards, and had to proceed by laborious compilation through the establishment of 'overlaps' between relatively short sequences, each within a restricted geographical area. The preservation of substantial pieces of timber in archaeological contexts, on which the application of dendrochronology depends, is best favoured by the more temperate climate-zones of Europe. A 'master' tree-ring chronology, extending back thousands of years, could thus be built up for northern and western Europe. From the viewpoint of history, some of the most valuable early results were achieved in regions only briefly in touch with the Mediterranean civilisations, where archaeological contexts existed which were already approximately datable. One thinks especially of the work of E. Hollstein and H. Cüppers on Roman bridge-timbers from the Rhineland, which was helped by the fact that approximate historical dates existed for some of the structures; of these, that of AD 310 for a bridge at Cologne was the most precise. This gave a fixed point which, by reversing the normal application of dendrochronological dates, itself 'anchored' a useful early sequence covering as much as 1,060 years. In the Mediterranean world, no epoch of Classical history can yet be covered by such absolutely-dated sequences, but even when there is a 'floating' sequence available the results can be both illuminating and startling, as has been shown recently by P.I. Kuniholm's work at Gordion.[10] He has used the 806-year floating sequence earlier derived from the timbers in the burial-chamber of the Great Tumulus at Gordion, known to have been constructed in the earlier Iron Age and approximately dated to the late eighth century BC by cross-links with Assyrian types of vessel portrayed on reliefs at Khorsabad. Other timbers, both from Gordion and from other sites on the Anatolian plateau, could thus be dated relatively to the construction of the Great Tumulus; but it

---

[10] P.I.Kuniholm, *Dendrochronology at Gordion* (dissertation University of Pennsylvania, 1977, available in microfilm), *passim*; especially pages 45–53.

was within the tumulus itself that the main surprise was encountered.

The tomb-chamber is in the form of a cabin composed of squared timber beams, from which a few tree-rings might therefore have been trimmed; but the cabin was enclosed in a loose outer casing of unsquared logs (some of these found with traces of their bark attached) held in place by rubble backing. The whole was then covered by a gigantic mound of earth. What Kuniholm has found is that the latest preserved tree-ring on the timbers of the inner chamber conforms to reasonable expectations: it is very close in date to those of two other monuments whose finds are of similar date, 'Tumulus P' and 'Tumulus Koerte III'. All three should date to the late eighth century BC, and their latest tree-rings range from the 612th to the 623rd years of the 'floating' Gordion sequence, the Great Tumulus timber being the latest within this very narrow spread. The epoch when the trees were felled and the three tombs constructed can therefore be reasonably equated with these years of the tree-ring sequence. But when the logs of the *outer* casing of Great Tumulus (unsquared) were examined, no less than three of them proved to have the very same year for their final ring and it was the 806th year of the 'floating' sequence – 183 years later than the last year found in the inner tomb. So far there is no insuperable difficulty: the 183 outermost rings of the carefully squared timbers of the inner chamber could simply have been removed by the carpenters. But then Kuniholm finds that, in the whole area of the settlement and cemeteries of Gordion, only one monument produced a tree-ring later than the 806th year of the outer structure of the Great Tumulus. Most were very substantially earlier, even when the tree-rings were associated with Persian buildings in the city, dated archaeologically to the *sixth* century BC. The range for these and other 'late' buildings was from the 303rd to the 727th years of the sequence, with just one outlier from the 853rd year.

Most archaeologists would conclude that there is but one sensible interpretation of these facts: that the 806th year of the sequence represents the approximate date of the Great Tumulus and that the earlier tree-ring dates are explained by the trimming off of the outermost rings. But this will mean that, with one exception, every single structure so far tested at Gordion was composed of timbers which had either been drastically trimmed, or were being re-used after centuries had elapsed, and were thus very aged. There will also be the coincidence that three of these structures, at roughly the same date in the late eighth century, had almost the same number of rings removed so as to leave on the surface a ring of rather before 900 BC. There is also a third difficulty not yet mentioned: some of these same timbers had also been used for radio-carbon tests and the results, allowing for any conceivable adjustment, still came out as substantially later than the venerable dates which we have been inferring for the surviving beams. For these reasons, Kuniholm himself is more drawn to the only other possible alternative: that it is the *623rd* year which marks the approximate date of the construction of the tomb. The radiocarbon dates will then fit nicely, and the other Gordion timbers will be about 183 years less 'aged' than we had thought, several of them coming fairly close to the archaeological date of their associated structures. But there is now a serious new objection: the outer chamber of the tomb, and consequently the whole superimposed tumulus, will have to belong to the mid sixth century BC; the inner chamber with its precious contents will have stood unprotected yet unplundered through an era of well-attested violence and unrest in the city's history; and, one might add, Professor R.S. Young who excavated the tumulus with great skill in 1957 will have missed a major discrepancy, of about 183 years, in the two stages of its construction.

Both alternatives thus bristle with difficulties, and there seems to be no third possibility. When one of the first applications of a new and precise dating technique to a documented historical context produces such results as these, the way seems open to all sorts of sceptical and disparaging conclusions, either about the validity of the traditional dating methods or about the accuracy of the new one. Personally I would conclude, not without some agonising, that it is after all the *former* of the two alternative interpretations which involves the less intractable problems. A somewhat later date than the late eighth century for the Tumulus (and thus for the 806th year of the sequence) is archaeologically possible and would marginally ease the problems. The other interpretation, by contrast, seems to me acceptable only if combined with some further and totally hypothetical assumption – for instance, that a temporary (and no doubt smaller) earth tumulus had protected the inner tomb during the unstable epoch between its two stages of construction.

POLITICAL AND INSTITUTIONAL HISTORY

This might seem the very last aspect of history on which archaeology could be expected to throw light. It is, of course, true that a political system is itself an elusive thing in material terms; only in rare cases like that of Classical Athens, where we have a wealth of historical and topographical documentation, and the help of epigraphy into the bargain, has it proved possible to match the architectural remains to an already-known political structure. In different circumstances, where the details of the political system are not a given element, attempts have sometimes been made to reconstruct such a system from almost exclusively material evidence, as for example in the Minoan city at Mallia; or from evidence partly of this kind, as on certain Archaic sites; but inevitably they have attracted controversy. In general, our understanding of the political development of prehistoric and even of proto-historic societies (that of the Etruscans for instance) remains flimsy in the extreme. What hope then is there of turning archaeological evidence to profitable use in such a field?

It is obvious that, here as elsewhere, the more broadly archaeological research and political history are defined, the greater the possibilities for using the one as a source for the other. What is more debatable is the claim that this collaboration has already produced results which could not have been achieved otherwise, and which are important, even central, to the understanding of ancient political history. But it is, after all, essentially a political act to found a settlement in the first place; thereafter, the introduction of urban development and planning, the establishment of official cults, the allocation of land, the devolution of power to local centres, the organisation of the army, the formation of alliances and the extension of territory are all elements of political history. And for each of these activities archaeological evidence is available for use, if not necessarily in the ways in which it has traditionally been applied. Sometimes experience has taught us that certain of the more obvious archaeological criteria do not have the significance that they have been thought to possess; equally, our understanding of some statements in historical sources has had to be modified from the literal or anachronistic interpretation of them which had prevailed previously. In the foundation of settlements, for example, it has become clear that fortification is a criterion of very variable significance. From reading ancient sources which mostly date from a mature period in the growth of the ancient states, one is left with the impression that fortification-walls surrounding the settlement-area were a normal feature of any well-equipped city; such indeed they had become, but things had not always been so. Many fortifications on colonial or provincial sites have been proved to date from a century or more after the original foundation; that is, when a cross-section has been taken through the wall, the pottery underlying the very earliest structure has proved to date from at least a century after the earliest pottery found elsewhere on the site. This is as widely true of Greek and Phoenician colonies in Sicily (where some excavators have shown a reluctance to accept it) as it is of Roman towns in central and northern Gaul and Britain. In the homelands of Greece and Italy, town-walls were if anything even slower to appear: it is doubtful whether either Athens or Rome was walled by 500 BC. This throws an interesting light on the simultaneous advance of civilisation and insecurity.

Archaeology has also provided one of the explanations, at least in the Archaic period, for the delay in the fortification of cities: that previously there had been nothing which merited fortifying. Here again, there had been a tendency to take in a literal sense the statements of Classical writers which incorporated terms like *polis* and *synoikismos*; ambiguous though both these words were known to be, scholars still envisaged an urban settlement ('polis') as the invariable product of the union of settlements under one capital ('synoecism') when they read these passages. There had of course to have been an earlier stage in urban growth, and there was a *locus classicus* to illustrate it: the repeated phrase of Thucydides in his account of early Greece (1 5, 1; 10, 2), to describe the form of the primitive city composed of villages (*kata kōmas oikoumenē*). The revelation has been that this kind of 'city' persisted so late, at least in the non-colonial areas. For urbanisation in its true sense, the great age appears to have been the first half of the sixth century BC; Thucydides, whether he realised it or not, was describing an era scarcely more remote from his times than Regency London is from ours.

On other political questions, a wider range of archaeological techniques can be brought to bear. At several periods of ancient history, notably in Archaic Greece and late Republican and early Imperial Rome, there were few more burning issues than that of the allocation of land. To find any extant physical traces of this process was a forbidding task: that substantial areas of the ancient agricultural landscape have been recovered is one of the great triumphs of aerial photography, whose techniques were pioneered in the 1920s but developed with a new rigour and insight through military experience in World War II. The best-known achievement has been the recognition of large tracts of land in the Po valley, in Apulia and in Tunisia, with smaller nuclei in other areas such as southern Gaul and Greece, which had been centuriated – that is, divided up into carefully-surveyed rectangular plots in the manner employed by the Romans when allocating land to retired veterans. Already this has changed and enlarged our understanding of the circumstances in which centuriation was applied. At the same time, physical evidence has been recovered for other types of landdivision used by the Romans and, on occasion, by the Greeks

before them. Outstanding work was done by Père A. Poide-
bard on the Syrian *limes*, by Colonel J. Baradez in Algeria, by
R.G. Goodchild in Tripolitania and in Roman Britain by a
whole series of pioneers, most recently Professor J.K.S. St
Joseph. For an earlier age, D. Adamasteanu has made
remarkable discoveries, using air-photographs, as to the
Archaic land-apportionment in the territory of the Greek
colony of Metapontum; nor should John Bradford's study of
Classical fields and terracing in Attica be forgotten.[11]

A growing recognition of the political importance of religious cults has been a feature of recent historical work, and
this is another field to which archaeology can contribute.
Indeed, archaeological evidence is so obviously germane to
the study of cult that in this case the appropriate note to
sound is one of warning. It is unfortunate that the excavation
of sanctuaries, that time-honoured area of Mediterranean
archaeological activity, proceeded too far too soon; for in fact
it presents peculiarly complex problems of stratification and
association. Isolated classes of artefacts have been published
superbly – Adolf Furtwängler's volume of 1895 on the
Olympia bronzes is still a shining example today;[12] individual
sacred buildings, even when very fragmentary, have been
measured, analysed and reconstructed on paper with great
skill; but the historical interpretation of the sites as a whole
has lagged far behind. We still have only a hazy notion of
how a major sanctuary actually worked, the aspect about
which written sources tell us least. Again, to understand the
political significance of a cult, it is necessary to be able to
identify the deity to which a sanctuary is dedicated and, in
Greece at least, there is a long list of instances where this has
proved impossible, even where temples are preserved. As a
result, there are potentially valuable bodies of documentary
and epigraphic evidence which cannot be related to the physical remains. Particular difficulties surround the question of

[11] For earlier references, see J.Bradford, *Ancient Landscapes* (1957); also
D.Adamasteanu, 'Le suddivisioni di terra nel Metapontino' in *Problèmes
de la terre en Grèce ancienne*, ed. M.I.Finley (The Hague, 1973), 49–61.
[12] *Olympia* IV: *die Bronzen* (Berlin, 1895).

chronology: the better-preserved buildings can be dated with reasonable accuracy, but many sanctuaries show a long antecedent period of dedications with no accompanying structures. How were the early dedications housed? When and why were they jettisoned like so much rubbish, as excavation has proved them often to have been? Above all why, in the case of many major Greek sanctuaries, do dedications of the Archaic period predominate so heavily over those of later periods? These are some of the questions which archaeology has failed not only to answer but usually even to ask.

One other area of political activity calls for special treatment because, unlike those discussed so far, it has long been seen as a promising area for applying archaeological evidence – perhaps unjustifiably so. This is the whole field of inter-state relations, from diplomatic and commercial links to wars, conquests and, in cases where there is no documentary evidence, relationships of a colonial nature. Once again, it is mainly the Greek world that is involved, if only because the superior documentation of Roman history removes many areas of doubt. The favourite basis for such interpretations is of course the Greek pottery-styles, which offer a standing temptation because of the uniquely precise determination of their geographical and chronological positions. There are two levels of objection to this practice, of which the first and much the less important is that this determination may not be so precise, particularly in geographical terms, as it has been claimed to be. In recent years there has been a small but disquieting series of findings, based on scientific tests of one kind or another (usually trace element analysis) as to the provenance of Greek regional wares. While in most cases this has confirmed the views previously held of the associations of particular *decorative styles* with particular regions, it is otherwise with the questions of *fabric*. It has revealed that decorative styles could be, and were, imitated closely enough to pass the test of ordinary visual inspection and be accepted as the 'real thing'; only fabric-analysis has shown that a different centre of production, possibly hundreds of miles away from the originating region, is involved.[13] In simple terms, the result is that numerous 'imported' pots are now revealed as locally-made, and that suspicion therefore falls on many other cases where no such tests have yet been applied. Of course, the imitation of the artefacts of another community may be just as important, in historical terms, as the importation of them, and neither is necessarily susceptible to explanation in terms of political influence.

Far more substantial, however, are the objections to applying the evidence of pottery to such ends in the first place. The question of the commercial significance of pottery is not directly relevant here except in the comparative sense, that any doubt which hangs over this aspect applies, *a fortiori*, to the question of its political significance. If, as most archaeologists now accept, the production and circulation of pottery reflected the policy of the state hardly at all, then clearly we must be very cautious indeed in using it to interpret inter-state relations. If Region A exports a large quantity of pottery to Region B, or exercises obvious influence over the styles employed there, the inference that there is some political influence over Region B may still be quite unjustified. It may reflect nothing more than the fact that Region B was short of suitable potter's clay deposits, or that Region A had an acknowledged pre-eminence in that particular industry. We are back once more in the shadow of the 'positivist fallacy': pottery is nearly always the most plentiful and sometimes the only material evidence available – if we cannot use it, where else can we turn? One answer is that in fact there usually are other categories of evidence available, only they have not yet been studied with the same thoroughness as pottery, so that their implications are less clear. With sculpture, terracottas, architectural detail, roof-tiles, grave-types,

[13] For four recent instances, see G.Vallet and F.Villard, *Mégara Hyblaea* II: *la céramique archaïque* (1964); J.P.Morel, 'L'expansion phocéenne en Occident' (*BCH* 81 (1957), 853–96), on 'Aeolic grey bucchero' at Massalia and elsewhere; M.Farnsworth, I.Perlman and F.Asaro, 'Corinth and Corfu: a neutron activation study of their pottery', *AJA* 81 (1977), 455–68; M.Coja and P.Dupont, *Histria* V: *les ateliers céramiques* (Bucharest and Paris, 1979).

weapons or bronze dress-accessories, understanding of regional style is progressing steadily: one day it may be possible to use these as indications of external contact and, if so, several of them could have greater historical significance than pottery. Yet the example of present-day experience, as often in archaeology, is a standing warning against using artefacts as indicators of political relationships.

Political relations, however, are merely a function of political *entities*. Archaeologists outside the Classical field have become increasingly uneasy about the validity and application of the whole concept of 'cultures', that is geographical assemblages based on similarity of artefact-types. Here they would do well to consider the evidence, both for and against, offered by the results obtained in Classical lands; and we in turn should consider how far this concept is tacitly applied in the ancient Mediterranean world, and what material evidence is used. I believe that here the potential for archaeological evidence may offer grounds for optimism. For example, one of the most fundamental and most neglected facts of Greek and of Italian history is the persistence, right down to our own times, of certain regional divisions of culture, material and otherwise. These divisions cannot have their origins in the period when the Greek states of the historical era were in the process of formation, first because the regions are in many cases larger than the individual historical states, secondly because they are perceptibly earlier than the latter. For Greece, the Late Bronze Age is the very latest period by which the regional divisions must have taken shape, since they can already then be recognised in terms of material culture. It is true that prehistoric archaeologists have consciously looked for these divisions on the analogy of those existing in historical times; but the fact remains that they have found them. 'Boeotian', 'Attic', 'Messenian' are identifiable archaeological categories, at least by the later phases of the Bronze Age. It is possible that the boundaries of such regions coincided with those of the Mycenaean kingdoms, but that is a hotly disputed question and not essential to the argument. What is not debated is that by the early historical period, five hundred years later, these divisions have acquired a political (and incidentally a linguistic) significance. In Greece, some of the regions embrace the territories of a number of smaller states, largely independent of each other but owing a wider allegiance to their region, sometimes by means of a formal league (Achaea, Arcadia, Boeotia); some house unitary states of an 'ethnic' nature even in historical times (Locris, Acarnania, Aetolia). In one case (Attica) a whole region has coalesced into a single city-state, while in another (Laconia and Messenia) two such regions are forcibly amalgamated. By about 700 BC, they are all in some sense political entities, and they may have been so earlier; the fact remains that they are first detectable as archaeological group-ings, linked by similarities of burial-customs and of pottery-style and fabric. In other words, they are archaeo-logical 'cultures'. It is encouraging that M. Pallottino has recently used similar evidence from Italy to reach much the same conclusion there: that the ethnic and linguistic structure of ancient Italy, as we know it from later historical sources, must have been established at this same early date.[14] There may be lessons here for both archaeologist and historian.

MILITARY HISTORY

The contribution of archaeology here is more predictable, in form and in importance; yet its value is not exactly what it is often imagined as being. The most obvious and substantial physical relics, namely fortification-works, can certainly at times be related to historical accounts of wars, or else extend them. But when it comes to the topography of individual campaigns and battles, the historian often turns to archae-ology in vain. It is worth pausing a moment to consider why this should be so. The fundamental discrepancy between archaeology and 'event-orientated' history is and will always

[14] 'Problemi attuali della protostoria Italiana nel quadro dello sviluppo del mondo classico', in *Greece and Italy in the Classical World* (above, n.5), 57–71, especially 60–4.

be their very different time-scales. In ancient warfare, a campaign of huge scale and significance, like the Persian invasion of Greece in 480/79 BC, could be prepared and carried out virtually without leaving any permanent and positive (as distinct from destructive) physical trace. This is partly because of its short duration, partly because of incidental factors like the relatively backward development of ancient siege-craft. As a result, excavation has not much light to throw on the great wars of the ancient world; a destruction-level here, a monument there, a communal grave elsewhere, are the most that can be produced. An apparent exception arose with the discovery in 1970 of the 'tumulus of the Plataeans' at Marathon; its precise location was so unexpected and hard to reconcile with any natural interpretation of the ancient sources for the battle that it seemed that archaeology was re-writing a famous chapter in history. Yet by 1977 the identification of the tumulus was already being seriously questioned, mainly on archaeological grounds.[15] The episode in my view reflects not just problems of a particular kind, but the general nature of archaeological evidence: it seldom speaks the language of historical events.

That a lasting contribution has been made by archaeology to ancient military history is in part the result of incidental historical factors whose effects are detectable by excavation; and in part, yet again, through the extension of archaeological techniques far beyond excavation. Because the ancients, at certain periods, practised burial with arms; because they regularly dedicated military spoils at sanctuaries; above all, because they introduced the human figure as the dominant element in their art and were especially addicted to military subjects – these are the prime reasons why so much light can be thrown on their military development. Such evidence is obviously appropriate not to events but to processes: it enables us to build up a background of technical, tactical and even organisational development,

[15] See P.G.Themelis, 'Marathon', *Arkhaiologikon Deltion* 29 (1974), A (1977), 226–44, 297–8.

against which the known campaigns can then be set. Its value lies in the fact that this background was largely impossible to reconstruct from documentary evidence.

But a contribution of a much more specific kind has been possible (as with land-systems) through the development of archaeological air survey and, to a lesser extent, of field-work on the ground as well. A classic instance is that of the history of Roman military operations in northern Britain. As long ago as 1747, in the aftermath of the Battle of Culloden, a young lieutenant of engineers (the future Major-General William Roy) was appointed to army mapping duties in Scotland and indefatigably planned and recorded the Roman military installations which he found. Thus began the process of filling out by archaeological observation the exiguous documentary sources for these operations. The activities of Agricola between AD 79 and 84 seemed to provide the best opportunities. In 1918, excavation at Camelon produced the first positive material indications of Agricola's presence in Scotland; the picture was soon extended. Then in the years from 1945 on, J.K.S. St Joseph developed to a new degree of refinement the recognition of military sites from the air. A number of permanent forts, hitherto unknown, were discovered; in several cases excavation later proved them to be of Agricolan date. Much more numerous, however, were the temporary marching-camps found; here the main contribution of excavation was to relate series of overlapping camps on the same site, thus building up a relative sequence; a typology was constructed in which camps of different size and plan could be assigned to different periods. When the camps occur further north than Strathtay, historical evidence confines their possible date to the two alternatives of Agricola's and Septimius Severus' campaigns. In this way, not only have Agricola's steps been traced at least as far north as Banffshire, but in the process the course of Severus' expeditions of AD 208 and 209 have been even more fully reconstructed.[16] This is a remarkable achievement, and one which

[16] Well summarised by J.K.S.St Joseph, 'Types and dates of temporary

it may prove possible to replicate in some of the less built-up regions around the Mediterranean. It also provides a good instance of a problem (an unusually specific one in this case) which was posed by historians, or at least by the study of history, and was left for archaeologists to try to answer. This is often the best procedure for advancing the co-operation of the two disciplines; problems posed by the archaeologists themselves have a habit of not being historically very significant and, to be still more candid, much archaeology has never been directed at the solution of problems at all. These observations are particularly relevant to the next section.

ECONOMIC AND SOCIAL HISTORY

There is a sense in which every archaeological find ever made contributes to economic and social history; but it is not a very helpful sense. To expect historians to monitor the entire output of excavation in Classical lands would, as we have said, be preposterous. A better procedure is for archaeologists to provide, in their excavation reports and monographs, a primary treatment of the more relevant finds that is oriented towards economic and social history, and for the help of like-minded historians (as suggested above, page 143) to be enlisted in this study. Archaeologists, even if not disposed to explore the economic implications themselves, can make it far easier for others to do so by improving their communications: that is, by not even claiming to pursue the will-o'-the-wisp of total objectivity in presenting the 'facts', but acknowledging the interpretative nature of all archaeological reporting; by describing, in excavation reports, their stratification in terms intelligible to those unfamiliar with excavation; by cataloguing their finds by function rather than by the material of which they are made; by grouping together deposits which belong together, rather than

camps in Scotland', *JRS* 63 (1973), 228–33; see also 'The camp at Durno and Mons Graupius', *Britannia* 9 (1978), 271–87.

abstracting, from *all* the deposits, each class of finds in turn. Several of these suggestions are taken from an article by Mrs S.C. Humphreys which has become something of a classic since it was first published in 1967.[17] For the archaeologist writing a monograph on a particular category of archaeological evidence, one can only urge that his treatment (and as a reflection of this, his title) be in some degree aimed at those students in other fields who, if they only know it, will be able to extract valuable information from his book.

But these are only the first steps; there is still a long way to go. Younger archaeologists, with whom the primary initiative lies, are showing (at least in the English-speaking countries) a strong tendency to work in those prehistoric and proto-historic fields where the problem of mastering the ancient sources hardly arises. To some extent this gap is being filled by the increasing familiarity with archaeological method on the part of the younger ancient historians. This should take care of some immediate needs, and there is, after all, a certain unreality about making specific programmatic demands for the future development of a discipline. It is more fruitful to ask for a change in attitudes, and here the signs are already more favourable. In the past, whereas it was universally recognised that the essence of historical enquiry was the search for explanations and causes, the same was not seen to be so clearly true of archaeology; in fact, many archaeologists acted as if it were not. Today Classical archaeologists (and not only those of the younger generation) are more often asking themselves the questions 'why?' and 'how?'. Pottery studies provide a good example. After generations of study of the stylistic development of Greek pottery by art-historical methods, the moment was felt to be ripe, in the period between the two World Wars, to harness this material to far-reaching economic arguments. This episode continued strongly into the 1950s and is not yet entirely over. But in the last generation a third approach has grown

[17] 'Archaeology and the social and economic history of Classical Greece', *Parola del Passato* 116 (1967), 374–400 (also printed in *Anthropology and the Greeks* (1978), ch. 4).

up which is in every sense critical of the other two. The pottery industry has been studied as an industrial phenomenon, not just as a sort of artists' collective. In the process, some absolute estimate of its scale has been reached. As a result of this in turn, the economic significance of pottery exchanges has been scrutinised; many earlier conclusions about trade, economic policy and even political influence (cf. pages 162–4) have been undermined.[18]

These recent developments have probably been influenced by the changes of emphasis in ancient history, whereby social and economic problems have come more to the forefront and increased attention has been paid to the methods of anthropology. Certainly there were audible criticisms of the earlier approaches from historians and anthropologists. For example, the shape of a pot, instead of being seen as the result of factors in the personality of an individual craftsman, is now more often looked at in terms of its function, both literal and social; its decoration, similarly, being designed for a market of some kind, is scrutinised for other influences besides the purely artistic ones; its geographical origins and the distribution of its type are less often taken as evidence for the operation of an undifferentiated 'trade', but are looked at in a more sophisticated way which takes account of the exact context (whether the type is found, for example, only in graves, or as dedications at sanctuaries, in Greek or in non-Greek settlements, in regular association with other wares, in strictly contemporary or also in later contexts, in a restricted social milieu; and so on).

All this is part of a wider and essentially beneficial phenomenon: the realisation, on the part of the archaeologist, of the distinctive contribution that he can make to social and economic history. It is no exaggeration to say that in the past Classical archaeologists were often unaware of the potential value of their own findings in this respect. Purely 'archaeo-

---

[18] See particularly R.M.Cook's article 'Die Bedeutung der bemalten Keramik', *JdI* 74 (1959), 114–23, on general principles; for a specific example, F.Villard, *La céramique grecque de Marseille* (Paris, 1960), 72–161.

logical' data such as the relative chronology of mosaic pavements in Romano-British villas, or the discontinuation of burial with arms in Archaic Greece, once they were put into the hands of historians, have proved rich sources of historical inference. It has been a similar story with much wider principles like that of the quantification of data. For a hundred years and more, Classical archaeologists have been handling bodies of material which are of sufficient size to be susceptible of quantification, and even to form statistically significant samples: the numbers of temples belonging to successive phases of architectural development, the numbers of pots from a given site or from the output of a given workshop, the numbers of grave-goods from the successive phases of a cemetery, the incidence of different types of statue (at any rate in the Archaic era) or of carved grave-stelai (in Classical Athens) – the potential of many such groups of data, long since available, is now at last being exploited.

Quantification is also an essential feature of the technique of archaeological survey which, more clearly here than in any other aspect of history, has an almost unlimited contribution to make. By recording systematically the traces of all settlements of all periods in a given region (or, more realistically, in a sample of a given region), survey work can provide, ready-made, the data for demographic studies and, less directly, material for the study of environmental change, agricultural practices, land-holdings, market organisation, communications and a dozen other aspects of local history. Solutions range from one-man surveys of small political and geographical units (such as islands) to large centralised projects like the *Forma Italiae* series, produced by the Unione Accademica Nazionale, which already comprises over twenty volumes covering thousands of square kilometres of the Italian landscape. Another distinctive asset of survey is that, in its nature, it is more likely to throw light on rural as opposed to urban settlement, whereas the bias of the documentary sources is in the opposite direction, emanating as it does from the ancient city and reflecting in the main its workings and tastes. By survey, the archaeologist can amass more relevant information for the economic development of a region than he can by excavating a single site, however rich; particularly when one reflects that nearly all excavations, too, are confined to a sample of the site. Excavation, being slower and more labour-intensive, is also more costly in proportion to its results. As so often, the initiative in this field has in the first instance lain outside Classical lands and, when introduced to Greece, Italy and the Mediterranean, has tended to concentrate on areas and periods where documentation is thin or non-existent. But as well as being a substitute for historical documents, survey results can supplement them in a very substantial way, as has been made clear when expeditions have included in their coverage, or even been centred on, historical communities.

Consider, for example, a question already posed hypothetically (above, page 140): where did the peasants of the ancient world actually live? For Roman Italy, a well-reasoned answer has now been put forward by P.D.A. Garnsey, drawing on the detailed results of field-survey expeditions in southern Etruria, Molise and northern Apulia: an answer not the less interesting because it runs counter to some of the best-known statements of the ancient literary sources for this question.[19] In brief, he finds that the traditional picture of a landscape largely depopulated of a free peasantry by later Republican times, of agriculturalists concentrated in towns, and of the progressive extension of slave labour on rural estates, cannot be entirely reconciled with the results of field survey. One final effect of archaeological survey whose value will be most widely appreciated is that it, and it alone, can produce an accurate large-scale historical map, at any rate of a small region. All Classical archaeologists and most other Classicists have at some time felt the acute shortage of such maps; now, at last, some are taking the initiative to remedy that lack.

[19] 'Where did Italian peasants live?', *Proceedings of Cambridge Philological Society* 205 (1979), 1–25.

Archaeology

Under this perhaps amorphous heading I group those aspects of history on which Classical archaeology, as traditionally practised, could reasonably be expected to throw most light. The time-honoured study of works of art, their content, their place in the historical development, their relationship with other contemporary art (including literature) would appear to be nothing if not a contribution to cultural history. Yet once again one must acknowledge that the results have been disappointing from this point of view, and once again the cause is a familiar one. Just as Classical archaeologists have been unaffected by some of the recent changes in archaeological theory and practice, so they have stood apart, for a much longer period and with less obvious reason, from developments in the approach of the art historian in non-Classical fields. The whole notion of the *function* of art, the appreciation that the visual arts are directly shaped by the society for which they are practised, and that they therefore directly reflect the nature of that society – these are not deeply engrained in archaeological thinking. Here too, the question 'why?' is not very often asked. Instead, a good part of the energies of Classical art historians (and thus of the whole activity of Classical archaeology) is taken up with the largely descriptive discipline of classification: that is, the locating of works of art, with increasing accuracy and detail, in a framework of chronological and geographical categories, if possible extending to attribution to individual artists and workshops. This is an essential preliminary to art history, but would not elsewhere be regarded as art history itself. Not only does it not bring much illumination to the broader field of cultural history if it stops there; but as far as Greek art is concerned, it does not do so for traditional political history either, for the particular reason that Greek art happens to have extraordinarily little directly historical content. The result is, yet again, a tendency towards the isolation of the discipline of ancient art history; it may be no coincidence that the formative years of the subject coincided with the birth of the doctrine of 'art for art's sake'.

Yet the art of the ancient world provides real scope for the writing of cultural history: it survives in relatively large quantities; there is a by no means negligible body of ancient literature devoted to it; and the fact that the status of the artist in antiquity had a lower place in the social hierarchy than it has today, so far from forming a serious obstacle, can actually be turned to advantage when we are using art as a medium for examining society as a whole. It means that the artist was continually the object of external pressures – social, religious and professional – to a degree which is hard for us to picture with our accepted notions of the independent artist and his free inspiration. It means that he can occasionally show the ordinary man's reaction to those pressures, in a way that few ancient writers could afford to do, even when they were equipped to: one thinks particularly of the vase-painter, whose product was not of great intrinsic value and not often directly commissioned by the patron; and who could introduce with impunity caricature scenes, vernacular versions of myths or a generally 'debunking' style to his work. It means, therefore, that he can fill an important gap in our understanding of ancient societies.

But there are more difficulties here than meet the eye. The language of Greek and Roman art is usually thought of as direct, widely intelligible and not in need of the detailed interpretation and careful translation without which the works of ancient literature cannot be communicated to the world. In fact, both stand in the same danger of being misunderstood, but for different reasons: with literature, the risk is that of our being misled by error in interpretation; with works of art, it is that we do not see the need for an interpretation at all. There are books in plenty to describe, classify and date them; to explain their subjects; but not, usually, to explain the works themselves. In some cases, this is because our knowledge is too limited to provide such an explanation; the result is that the spectator becomes habituated to not being given one. This is true of sculpture above all. Yet there can hardly have been a single piece of large-scale Greek or Roman sculpture which did not have a meaning, religious or

secular; which did not carry an intelligible message to contemporaries. Sometimes we must confess outright that the
message is lost to us, at least for the time being: until it can be
established, for example, whether the famous bronze statue
from Artemision represents Zeus, or Poseidon, or not a deity
at all, our understanding of this work is essentially defective.
Similarly, to know whether the head no.437 in the National
Museum at Athens does or does not represent Julius Caesar is
critical to our understanding both of the work and of the
subject. Sometimes we are offered a whole choice of interpretations, most or all of which must be false, as for example
with the mid fifth-century BC relief known as the 'Mourning
Athena', which is thereby placed almost on a par with an
undeciphered text. Sometimes a long-accepted interpretation
of a familiar monument is suddenly called into question, as
has happened recently with no less a work than the Parthenon frieze; if it does *not* represent the Panathenaic procession,
then there is no end to the false suppositions which, consciously or unconsciously, have been based on the belief that
it does.[20] Faced with hazards of this kind, it is not surprising
that many Classical archaeologists prefer to stick to the relatively secure ground of artistic evaluation and classification.

Yet when more enterprising approaches have been tried,
they have usually proved fruitful, often by advancing our
knowledge and understanding and almost always in intellectual stimulation. In certain areas of ancient art history, the
achievement stands beyond dispute, but is often forgotten:
for instance, in the interpretation of mythical scenes, especially on vases. As long ago as 1880, Carl Robert began a
series of painstaking iconographic studies, culminating in the
great work of his old age, *Archäologische Hermeneutik*, a classic
account of the means adopted by Greek artists to convey a
mythological narrative. This has been, in its main outlines,
so universally accepted ever since that it is seldom acknowledged any longer; indeed, only in recent years has there been

[20] See F.Chamoux, 'L'Athéna mélancolique', *BCH* 81 (1957), 141–59;
J.Boardman, 'The Parthenon frieze: another view', in *Festschrift für Frank
Brommer* (Mainz, 1977), 39–49.

a revival of discussion of the whole question with which Robert was dealing.[21] Yet what could be more fundamental, both to the art history of this and many subsequent periods, and to the broader interpretation of Greek myth? The successive solutions which artists found to these problems of narrative are vital steps in the intellectual development of their times. In particular, the discovery in Archaic Greece of a means of representing a whole myth by one single 'closed' composition makes extremely interesting comparisons, first with the narrative methods employed by early Greek poets; then with the contrasting means used by Greek artists of the Classical period to portray myth; and finally with the essentially Roman device of 'continuous narrative', which Robert's contemporary Franz Wickhoff had expounded in 1895, and which prevailed in Western art for some fifteen centuries.[22] This is the very stuff of cultural history.

Portraiture is a medium which in its nature brings art very close to history. Most studies of it have nevertheless treated ancient portraits as isolated art-objects and (since the majority of surviving examples are in the form of sculpture) as illustrations of a particular stage in the development of the sculptor's art. To do this is to side-step the really important (and, I would argue, the really interesting) questions about portraiture in the ancient world: such as, why was it scarcely existent in Archaic society? Why, when athletic portrait-statues of living subjects had long since been tolerated, were other kinds of private portrait apparently only acceptable when they were posthumous? (I am of course assuming that the degree of individual characterisation that made a portrait

---

[21] See especially N.Himmelmann-Wildschütz, 'Erzählung und Figur in der archaischen Kunst', *Abhandlungen der Akademie der Wissenschaften und der Literatur* (*Geistes-und Sozialwissenschaftliche Klasse*) (Mainz, 1967), 73–100; P.G.P.Meyboom, 'Some observations on narration in Greek art', *Mededelingen van het Nederlands Instituut te Rome* 40 (1978), 55–82; and, more elementary, J.E.Henle, *Greek Myths: a Vase-Painter's Notebook* (Bloomington and London, 1973).

[22] Wilhelm Ritter von Härtel and F.Wickhoff, *Die Wiener Genesis* (Vienna, 1895); Wickhoff's contribution was translated and edited by Mrs S.A. Strong as *Roman Art* (1900).

recognisable as such, even when of an unknown subject, was approximately the same for contemporaries as it is for us two millennia later). How, when the demand for personal portraiture eventually became irresistible, did the portrait manage to take over such a central place in the social transactions of the Hellenistic age? It might be possible to give answers to all these questions in purely artistic terms, but the answers would certainly be inadequate and probably wrong as well. Here as in some other respects, historians of Roman art, less preoccupied than the Hellenists with the sheer quality of the works and confronted with a more overtly political message, have progressed rather further in their understanding.

To give a simple illustration of one of the problems: consider our own reactions, on the one hand when we encounter a portrait in an exhibition devoted to a single artist or theme; and on the other hand, when we enter a portrait gallery – perhaps a sculptural one like the 'Walhalla' erected by King Ludwig I of Bavaria on the banks of the Danube near Regensburg. In the first case, we are interested in the style of the artist, the way in which he adapted it to the portrait, the common features of his portraits generally; in the second, we are more concerned with the subjects, their place in history, the principles on which they have been chosen and the purpose of the gallery generally. At Walhalla, where the vast majority of the busts were carved in a homogeneous style between 1807 and 1842, it is only when we are brought up short by the starkness of the features of Bruckner, Stifter and Strauss (carved respectively in 1937, 1954 and 1973) that artistic considerations suddenly become uppermost. In our study of Greek portraits (though again this is less true of Roman), we adopt exclusively the former, 'exhibition' type of approach; yet the evidence shows that Greek contemporaries invariably encountered the portrait in the latter, 'gallery' type of context; a reading of Pausanias shows that this was still true in the second century AD. The appearance of Dieter Metzler's *Porträt und Gesellschaft* in 1971 was therefore a welcome innovation, and a similar approach to a broader range of sculpture has now been adopted in the closing chapter of Andrew Stewart's *Attika* (1979).[23]

One advantage of this type of research is. that it is not necessary to be an archaeologist to carry it out with distinction. Other Classical scholars who have familiarised themselves thoroughly with the evidence, and who possess the courage of their convictions in matters artistic, have produced masterly treatments of cultural questions in which much of the primary evidence is archaeological. Again one tends to think first of religion, where in the last two generations the work of men like M.P. Nilsson and A.B. Cook has set a standard for future approaches by showing the indispensability of the archaeological material.[24] As a result, there are deities, such as Artemis in the Greek pantheon, for whose early evolution and for many of the details of whose cults archaeology has provided as much evidence as all the surviving written sources. Excavated sites, such as the Sanctuary of the Great Gods on Samothrace, have brought to light a range of religious practices previously quite unsuspected, several of them pre-Greek in origin but absorbed into the ritual of the sanctuary. But there are numerous other fields for this kind of activity as well. An excellent example was given recently by Sir Kenneth Dover's study *Greek homosexuality* (1978). For centuries scholars have been more or less uneasily aware of the prevalence in Greek imagination of homosexual love; but until the widely different categories of evidence could be brought together, as they are in Dover's book, it was impossible to evaluate the phenomenon properly. Now we have an indication of the date from which overt homosexual practices became acceptable to Greek society; of the differential standards that were adopted in judging different acts within

---

[23] D. Metzler, *Porträt und Gesellschaft: über die Entstehung der griechischen Porträts in der Klassik* (Münster, 1971); A. Stewart, *Attika: studies in Athenian sculpture of the Hellenistic age* (Society for the Promotion of Hellenic Studies, Supplementary Paper XIV, 1979).

[24] See especially M.P.Nilsson, *Geschichte der griechischen Religion* I-II (Munich, 1941–50); A.B.Cook, *Zeus* I-III (1914–40).

homosexual behaviour generally; of the geographical unevenness in our evidence and the undoubted local variations in attitudes; and of much else. Most of this would have been impossible without the detailed study of the 500-odd vase-paintings listed in Dover's text.

But this is only one notable recent example. There are several other areas of cultural life where the artistic and archaeological evidence has proved itself indispensable long since, and is nowadays handled with due respect. Among the most obvious are ancient music and musical instruments, poetic recitation, theatre-production, athletics, domestic entertainment, education and reading, marriages and funerals, racial attitudes and the role of women. It would be true to say that our knowledge and judgement of many of these aspects of ancient life has been radically modified from that of earlier generations, since this broadening of approach took place.

By treating its subject in terms of the various branches of *historical* studies, this account has left many specific aspects of archaeological evidence out of consideration. One of these aspects, the archaeology of graves, deserves a few words in its own right, since it does not fall squarely within any of the categories used here. The prominence of grave-excavation in Mediterranean archaeology can be expected to continue, even if in the future excavation is increasingly confined to rescue operations arising from urban building and the construction of roads and pipe-lines. One great asset of cemeteries is that they consist of easily quantifiable units: throughout much of Classical history, single burial was practised, so that each grave represents a single act of interment and its grave-goods form a single closed deposit. A cemetery whose graves cover several generations may give a cross-section of a society more representative of the range of prosperity, as well as being chronologically wider, than will an excavated settlement of the same date, where most of the finds and architecture will belong to the final stages, and where the discovery of the full range of housing of all levels of society will be, at best, a costly and long-drawn-out process; or indeed than a sanctuary-deposit, in which most links of personal ownership are lost. Yet there are several obscure variables in funerary studies; above all, that of the relation between social hierarchy and funerary hierarchy, between a society's wealth and the wealth and elaboration of its graves. This makes it an urgent task to develop a more systematic approach to grave-archaeology; we need some kind of theory of funerary sociology and indeed funerary ideology. Fortunately there are signs that this need is now appreciated: an international colloquium on the latter topic was held in Naples in December 1977.[25]

Several of the larger published cemeteries of the Greek and Roman world have also been made the subject of valuable syntheses and statistical analyses. Predictably, these have concentrated on the earlier periods when therè is less competition from other, more historically-oriented classes of evidence. The cist-tombs of the Early Bronze Age in the Cyclades, for example, were analysed in some detail by A.C. Renfrew in 1972; the size of the sample was large enough to justify the use of a computer. The graves of the important Early Iron Age cemetery in the Kerameikos at Athens were studied through the medium of their metalwork by H. Müller-Karpe in 1962, and through that of their stratigraphy and pottery by R. Hachmann in 1963. A broader study of the burials of the same period in the Argolid was published by R. Hägg in 1974, while J.B. Ward-Perkins and others have contributed comparable studies of the graves of the large Quattro Fontanili cemetery at Veii in Etruria. Surveys of the whole field of burial customs have been undertaken, for Greece by D. Kurtz and J. Boardman in 1971, for Rome by J.M.C. Toynbee (1971) and in a very useful collection of papers edited by R. Reece in 1977.[26] Excavators of cemeteries

---

[25] *L'idéologie funéraire dans le monde antique*, Cambridge, 1982.

[26] D.Kurtz and J.Boardman, *Greek Burial Customs* (1971); J.M.C. Toynbee, *Death and Burial in the Roman World* (1971); R.Reece (ed.), *Burial in the Roman World* (Council for British Archaeology Research Report XXII, 1977).

are themselves beginning to incorporate statistical studies of their material in the primary publication. But there are many fresh fields of synthesis to be conquered: among the most obvious (and the most formidable) are the hundreds of graves now recorded from Classical Athens and Rome.

Alongside these broader studies, the discoveries of exceptional individual burials continue to make contributions to archaeological knowledge. Even here, the conclusions have often been more problematic than one would expect from the relatively simple process of interment on a single occasion: as witness the instances from Marathon, from Gordion and from the Egyptian tombs containing Minoan and Mycenaean pottery which have been mentioned earlier. It is fitting to end with the most celebrated recent find, the royal tomb at Vergina in Macedonia which was opened in November 1977 and which its discoverer, Professor M. Andronikos, tentatively identifies as that of Philip II.[27] If his identification proves right, this alone will contribute a certain amount of evidence that will be useful to historians of the period. But a greater value attaches to the inferences which will stand irrespective of the correctness of the identification. To begin with, we now have, thanks to this impressive discovery, a new and almost certain localisation for the site of Aigeae, mentioned in several ancient sources as the place of burial of the Macedonian kings, but hitherto placed by most modern scholars some distance to the north, at Edessa; this will affect many questions of ancient topography. We have for the first time a standard of Macedonian royal burial by which to judge other rich tombs. We have much new information on the military equipment of the era. We have a whole new chapter in the history of Greek tomb-paintings, a fragmentary field but one which throws unique and contemporary light on the whole lost achievement of Greek free painting. It will be years before the wealth of potential knowledge yielded by this one discovery can be exploited to the full, and this process will outlast the dazzlement of the intrinsic wealth of the finds.

[27] 'The tombs at the Great Tumulus of Vergina', in *Greece and Italy in the Classical World* (above, n. 5), 39–56.

Anthony Snodgrass

The recurrent message of this chapter has been that, for the full value of archaeology's contribution to ancient history to be realised, the same qualities need to be shown by scholars in both disciplines: understanding of the different problems that confront each side in the pursuit of a common aim, and of the even more clearly different status of the evidence that each side has to offer; and above all, breadth of approach in interpreting the whole nature of historical enquiry.

APPENDIX

It may be helpful to give here, in addition to the works cited in the footnotes, some examples of books which successfully apply archaeological evidence to some period or theme of ancient history.

On the questions of the *theory and method* of the application of archaeological evidence to ancient history, there is a fundamental difficulty, alluded to in the opening sentences of the chapter: that most works on archaeological theory studiously avoid making more than passing refences to Classical archaeology. This is even true of Bruce Trigger's *Time and Traditions: essays in archaeological interpretation* (Edinburgh, 1978), even though most classicists will derive substantial benefit from his chapter 2 in particular. One corner of the Classical world which does sometimes come into consideration is Roman Britain, and for this field (and by implication for other historical cultures) there is real enlightenment to be gained from I.A.Hodder and C.Orton's *Spatial Analysis in Archaeology* (Cambridge, 1976).

On *chronology*, although there are several thorough treatments of the non-archaeological evidence (see most recently A.E.Samuel, *Greek and Roman Chronology: Calendars and years in Classical antiquity (Handbuch der Altertumswissenschaft* I, 7) (Munich 1969), there is no work which systematically integrates the material evidence with this. R.W.Ehrich (ed.), *Chronologies in Old World Archaeology* (Chicago, 1965) is characteristic in leaving its readers to discover that the chronologies end in *c.* 2000 BC. One can only refer the reader to the works cited in notes 6–10 · above, dealing with particular aspects.

Political and institutional history

One may single out a few basically historical works for their perceptive use of archaeological material, notably W.G.Forrest's

Archaeology

The Emergence of Greek Democracy (London, 1966) and, on a regional level, P. A. Cartledge's *Sparta and Lakonia: a regional history* (London, 1979).

Economic and social history

Here the field is much richer. One way of achieving the necessary range of expertise is by collaborative works, and an outstanding example of these is M.I.Finley (ed.), *Problèmes de la terre en Grèce ancienne* (Paris/The Hague, 1973). Notable recent studies and monographs include: C.G.Starr, *The Economic and Social Growth of Early Greece* (New York, 1977); A.Burford, *The Greek Temple-builders at Epidauros* (Liverpool, 1969) and *Craftsmen in Greek and Roman Society*, (London, 1972); L.A.Moritz, *Grain-mills and Flour in Classical Antiquity* (Oxford, 1958); G.E.Rickman, *Roman Granaries and Store Buildings* (Cambridge, 1971).

Military history

Here again, collaboration has produced some of the most fruitful results in J.-P.Vernant (ed.), *Problèmes de la guerre en Grèce ancienne*, and J.-P.Brisson (ed.), *Problèmes de la guerre à Rome* (Paris/The Hague, 1968 and 1969 respectively). But see also P.A.L. Greenhalgh, *Early Greek Warfare: horsemen and chariots in Archaic Greece* (Cambridge, 1973); J.S. Morrison and R.T.Williams, *Greek Oared Ships, 900–322 B.C.* (Cambridge, 1968); W.K.Pritchett, *Ancient Greek Military Practices* I, and *The Greek State at War* II–III (Berkeley/Los Angeles, 1971, 1974 and 1979); J. K. Anderson, *Military Theory and Practice in the Age of Xenophon* (Berkeley Los Angeles/London, 1970).

Cultural history

A welcome move here is the 'Fontana History of the Ancient World' series, in which there have appeared so far: R.M.Ogilvie, *Early Rome and the Etruscans* (1976); J.K.Davies, *Democracy and Classical Greece* (1978); M.H.Crawford, *Republican Rome* (1978); O.Murray, *Early Greece* (1980); and F.W.Walbank *The Hellenistic World* (1981); and C. M. Wells, *The Roman Empire* (1984). One work of art history certainly deserves mention here because of its unusual breadth of approach: Martin Robertson's *A History of Greek Art* (Cambridge, 1975).

In a separate class are the books written by archaeologists on periods accounted fully historical: R.M.Cook's *The Greeks till Alexander* (London, 1962); John Boardman's *The Greeks Overseas*

Anthony Snodgrass

(revised ed., London, 1980); F.Chamoux' *The Civilisation of Greece* (London, 1965); A.W.Johnston's *The Emergence of Greece* (Oxford, 1976); and my *Archaic Greece* (London, 1980) all come under this heading on the Greek side, while the obvious Roman counterpart is the 'History of the Provinces of the Roman Empire' series, in which have appeared *S. S. Frere, Britannia*; J. J. Wilkes, *Dalmatia*; A. Mocsy, *Pannonia and Upper Moesia*; G. Alföldy, *Noricum* (London, 1967, 1969, 1974 and 1974).

CHAPTER 4

Numismatics

INTRODUCTION

A coin is defined, traditionally and correctly, as a piece of metal of a determined standard issued by a competent authority; in other words, coins of a particular issue must have approximately the same weight and fineness in order to be usable and they must also bear the mark of a specific authority. A Roman who picked up a denarius of the Roman Empire or a Greek who picked up a tetradrachm of Syracuse (Fig. 7) knew that they were produced by the Roman or Syracusan state and contained a certain quantity of silver. In order to convey this information a Greek or Roman coin usually bears a legend and a type or types; an obvious example is the earliest denarius of the Roman Republic (Fig. 8), which bears the legend ROMA, thereby indicating that it was produced by the Roman state, and the mark of value X to indicate that it was worth ten bronze asses, the bronze as being then the basic unit of reckoning. The official character of the coin is reinforced by its types, Head of Roma/Dioscuri (protector deities of Rome).

Coinage was probably invented in Western Asia Minor

7. Tetradrachm of Syracuse
(courtesy of the Department of Coins and Medals, British Museum)

185

8. Early Roman Republican denarius
(courtesy of the Department of Coins and Medals, British Museum)

around 600 BC. The ancient world had, of course, long been familiar with the notion of precious metal passing by weight, and the step of preparing beforehand pieces of metal guaranteed as being of a certain weight was perhaps taken in order to make it possible to count out, rather than weigh out, the pay of mercenaries (for the way in which coins were struck see p. 207). The use of coinage spread rapidly in the Greek world, perhaps largely because a Greek *polis* saw the possession of its own coinage as an important element of its autonomous administration.

The earliest coinages were of electrum, a naturally occurring mixture of gold and silver. But pure silver rapidly became the standard coinage metal of the Greek world, joined in due course by bronze and other copper alloys for small change and pure gold for large denominations. Some Classical Greek coinages, notably that of Athens, were substantial; but they were small compared with the coinages of Alexander and his successors, these in turn being small compared with the coinage of Rome.

The production of coinage had begun at Rome around 300 BC, and as Rome conquered the Mediterranean the use of her coinage gradually spread. By the time of Augustus, the denarius was in use throughout the Mediterranean world, except in Egypt, where Augustus perpetuated the coinage system of the Ptolemies. The volume of the denarius coinage was naturally enormous.

Where coinage existed, it played a significant role in economic activity and, given the primitive nature of ancient banking systems, it was regularly transported in large quantities, hoarded and lost. The chance discovery of coins buried with the intention of recovery, but never recovered in antiquity, provides the principal source of the ancient gold and silver coins in existence today.

Such coins are naturally a potential source of great importance for the history of the ancient world. Neither their use nor the evaluation of this use is particularly difficult. Yet historians who would never accept without demur the dating of an inscription proposed by an epigraphist tend both to follow uncritically the latest numismatic manual where it is necessary to cite a coin and to ignore the diversity of numismatic evidence. I hope to show that such approaches are unjustified.

The questions to ask are – of what does a particular coinage consist, what is its date, where was it produced, what can it tell us, how does one interpret this information? Similar techniques are relevant to many of these questions, and in trying to answer them one needs to remember two things: what one may call the rules of numismatic evidence and also the historical context. For numismatics is not an autonomous subject – it is part of history, and work on coinage is best done by people who are primarily historians or archaeologists, who use coinage to help solve the problems which relate to their interests, whether in financial administration, the fiscal needs of a state, units of reckoning, monetary usages, interpretation of types, art history or the dating of archaeological levels.

What is offered here, however, is neither a history of ancient coinage nor a disquisition on *what* numismatic evidence adds to our knowledge of ancient history or classical archaeology; it is a discussion of method, of *how* (and how not) to employ numismatic evidence.

COIN FINDS

It is perhaps best to begin with an examination of the relevance of coin finds to problems of dating and attribution; I shall then move on to their relevance to problems of circulation and coin use. There are, however, three preliminary points which must be made.

First, coins are often misread. If one looks at a coin in

isolation, if it is worn, it is often quite hard to discern exactly what its types and legends are; coins are sometimes published with an inaccurate description and a publication of a single specimen may be misleading. One has to be careful therefore to check, by looking at several examples.

As soon as ancient coinage began to be investigated and collected in the Renaissance as part of the study of Classical antiquity, modern forgeries appeared. These can be of two kinds – they can either be completely invented coins (of which the finest example is a coin of Caesar with the legend VENI, VIDI, VICI) or they can be copies of existing coins. Although the latter do not in a sense falsify the picture totally, they can falsify it to a certain extent because they can give a wrong impression of how common a particular coin is, and by way of a fictitious provenance assigned by a vendor or dealer a wrong impression of where a coin comes from. The problem of deciding whether or not a coin is a modern forgery can often be extremely difficult: an example is the gold coin struck by the Italian rebels against Rome in the Social War of 90–89 BC. There is one extant example in Paris, sometimes accepted, sometimes doubted; in this case the argument can, I think, be settled because the piece bears an Oscan legend, and the coin is attested as early as 1840, at a stage when scholarly knowledge of Oscan could not have produced (except by accident) a correct Oscan legend. In general, if one is concerned with a coinage, it is worth starting with provenanced specimens, as they are almost certainly antique. Occasionally, finds are falsified, but not very often; by looking at a number of finds one can build up a reliable picture of the structure of a coinage.

The third problem is posed by ancient forgeries. The commonest form of ancient forgery is that of a coin with a bronze core and a silver exterior; within this class one sometimes gets coins with no genuine prototype at all, sometimes cases of so-called hybrids – a plated silver coin will often combine an obverse of one period and a reverse of another period; unless one is aware that this is an ancient forgery one may make quite invalid deductions about chronology.

9. Denarius of Domitian
(courtesy of the Department of Coins and Medals, British Museum)

10. Nummus of Diocletian
(courtesy of the Department of Coins and Medals, British Museum)

Only occasionally is a coin dated and mint-marked. Large parts of the Roman Imperial coinage are dated, often to within less than a year, by tribunician years and imperatorial salutations (Fig. 9); a coin of Domitian, for instance, can usually be dated to within a year or less, and for most purposes that is close enough. Again, the coins of the late Empire systematically bear the name of the mint at which they were produced; TES indicates the mint at Thessalonica, CON that at Constantinople and so on (Fig. 10). But most ancient coins carry no indication of date and many no indication of where they were struck; and before one can make use of an ancient coin as evidence one has to establish at least this minimum'– date and place of issue.

In assigning a coin to a date and a mint, there are eight considerations that may be relevant:[1] (1) considerations of style, type, legend and related factors; if one picks up an Athenian tetradrachm of the late fifth century BC, even if one

[1] Compare C.M.Kraay, *Archaic and Classical Greek Coins* (London, 1976), xxv.

has only a very minimal eye for style, one can place it in the fifth century and not in the sixth or earlier by reason of the classical profile of the head of Athena. (2) Types are sometimes borrowed from one issue for another and clearly, if one can be certain that one type is derived from another, the derivative type must be later than the type copied. (3) One can be more sophisticated and consider the letter forms used for the legend of a coin: thus, for instance, an archaic form of sigma is three barred, S; during the fifth century it becomes S, not only on Greek inscriptions, but also on coins. Similarly, the changing form of the ethnic used on a coinage may help in its classification. (4) Considerations of fabric: the physical make-up of a coin. Coins of one mint and date may vary enormously in mere shape from those of a different origin. More sophisticated techniques are also available, involving the analysis of metal content; for experience shows that within a particular series, such as the coinage of Carthage, coins of the same metal content belong together and that coins of different metal content are to be placed apart either in time or in space. (5) Overstrikes can be aids to dating; instead of melting down a coin, making a new blank and striking it, an ancient mint could overstrike an existing coin; one can often make out the old type below the new and thus establish a relative sequence. (6) One can sometimes place coins in a sequence on the basis of changes in weight standard. (7) There is also the historical context; but arguments from it are likely to be circular and are to be used with caution – when one has exhausted all other methods, with great care one can say that a coin probably 'belongs' in a particular historical context.

But the most important evidence for the dating and attribution of ancient coins is that provided by coin finds and archaeological evidence in general.[2] Obviously, there is an element of interpretation involved in the use of coin finds and hoards as evidence, but it entails a very large mechanical

---

[2] The fundamental modern discussion is that of P.Grierson, *NC* (1965), Proceedings I; *NC* (1966), Proceedings I.

element, which is quite independent of subjective criteria; I hope that this will become apparent when I talk about the different ways of using the evidence of coin hoards.

A coin hoard is a group of coins the circumstances of whose discovery – for example, in a purse or other container – make it clear that the hoard was deliberately buried in a group. The evidence of a single hoard must be used with care and is clearly less good than the evidence of a number of hoards; one hoard may be a freak, whereas the picture revealed by ten hoards, all of which produce exactly the same pattern, is more likely to be trustworthy. Coins in the ancient world both travelled far from their mint of origin and remained in use sometimes for several centuries. The contents of a hoard will thus often include coins of very diverse origins and cover a very long period. Mere association of coins in a hoard does not allow one to say that all the coins in this hoard belong even approximately to the same date; thus, almost any Roman Imperial hoard closing under Septimius Severus will contain coins from M. Antonius onwards. So what one wants to establish is the closing point of any hoard and the latest issues in it, and one needs then to arrange the remaining contents of the hoard in chronological order. As a general rule – which obviously cannot be applied rigidly, but which is of some validity and usefulness – in a hoard the least worn coins are the latest and the most worn coins are the earliest.[3] Roman Imperial hoards validate the hypothesis, because the coins contained in them can be dated at least to individual reigns. Thus if a hoard closes under Septimius Severus one finds that the coins of Severus are in good condition, almost uncirculated, the coins of Commodus have some wear on them, those of Marcus Aurelius more wear and so on right the way back. Greek coinage of course consists of a number of separate sequences of *polis* or royal issues.

Two hoards may be taken as an example of the sort of

---

[3] It also sometimes happens that the latest coins in a hoard include whole groups which must have been produced recently because they are struck from the same pairs of dies, see C.Boehringer, *SNR* (1975), 37 and 55 n.2.

evidence one can derive from coin finds for absolute dating. One of the major problems in the study of Hellenistic coinage is the date at which the so-called Athenian New Style coinage begins. From some time in the late sixth century, for at least three centuries Athens struck coins with basically the same types, Athena head/Owl, and then some time in the Hellenistic period it introduced coins which are quite different in fabric: whereas the early ones are dumpy and thick the late ones are very flat and outspread, and they also have a wreath on the reverse, around the owl (Figs. 11–12). First of all, the Anthedon hoard (*IGCH* 223): this includes coins of Chalcis and Eretria which we know on other grounds to belong to the first half of the second century BC; they are in very good condition and the hoard also has some of the earliest New Style coins of Athens, likewise in very good condition; so there is a strong supposition that the two groups of issues are contemporary. Second, the Sitochoro hoard from Thessaly (*IGCH* 237) closes with coins of the First Macedonian Region (of 167 BC at the earliest) and has no New Style coins of Athens, although the hoard comes from an area where they certainly circulated and contained eleven Old Style tetradrachms; the inference is that the New Style coinage post-dated 167 BC, but probably not by very much.

Analogous to a hoard which includes dated coins, and which allows inferences to be made about the dates of undated coins also present in the hoard, is a site or a part of a site with a known *terminus ante quem*. Thus it is clear from the archaeological evidence, including that to be derived from

11. Old Style Athenian tetradrachm
(courtesy of the Department of Coins and Medals, British Museum)

12. New Style Athenian tetradrachm
(courtesy of the Department of Coins and Medals, British Museum)

dated coins, that Gela was effectively abandoned by 282 BC; isolated later finds occur, but the coins of Syracuse with Zeus Hellanios/Eagle, which occur at Gela in large numbers, were almost certainly brought there before 282.[4] The classic example of this type of argument relates to Morgantina; a destruction-level which can be dated on archaeological grounds to the late third century may be linked to a mention in Livy of a revolt of Morgantina in 214 or 211, almost certainly the latter; since the destruction-level includes some of the earliest issues forming part of the denarius coinage and no later issues, the beginning of the denarius coinage may be dated to just before 214 or 211.[5]

Coin hoards also provide vital evidence when it comes to establishing a relative dating for a sequence of issues; the paradigm case is perhaps the coinage of the Roman Republic. The composition of hoards of dated Roman Imperial coins suggests that a hoard may normally be expected to contain a representative selection of issues struck before its deposition, a large hoard all or almost all the issues struck as far back as a century or so before its deposition (a few very rare issues may be missing). With the Imperial pattern in mind, one may proceed to the Republic. Only two major qualifications are necessary: hoards normally contain coins of only one mone-

[4] P.Orlandini, *AIIN* 9–11 (1962–4), 49.
[5] T.V.Buttrey, *Quad. Tic.* (1979), 149, 'Morgantina and the denarius.' Compare the all too rare evidence provided by coins from dated foundation deposits, such as that of Darius I from Persepolis (*IGCH* 1789).

Figure 13   Hoard Table: Coinage 49–45 BC

	Villette	Collechio	Padova	Ossolaro	San Nicholo	Sendinho	Vernon	Surbo	Dračevica	San Giuliano	Carbonara	San Cesario	Cadriano
49 BC													
MN.ACILIVS[1]	5	+	36	42	·	3	+	2	6	26	30	+	+
CAESAR with Elephant/Pontifical emblems[1]	38	+	65	21	·	6	+	2	2	24	6	+	+
L.LENTVLVS, C.MARC COS	·	·	·	3	+	·	·	1	·	·	·	·	·
CN. PISO PRO Q. MAGN PRO COS	·	+	·	·	+	·	·	·	·	·	·	·	·
VARRO PRO Q. MAGN PRO COS	·	·	2	·	+	·	·	·	·	·	·	·	·
48 BC													
L.HOSTILIVS SASERNA	3	+	14	20	+	1	·	2	3	9	9	·	·
C.VIBIVS C.F.C.N PANSA	6	+	27	40	+	1	+	1	1	1	2	·	·
ALBINVS BRVTI.F	4	+	20	20	+	1	+	1	2	1	·	·	·
C.PANSA, ALBINVS BRVTI.F	·	+	1	2	+	·	+	·	·	·	·	·	·
CAESAR with LII	1	+	1	2	+	·	·	1	2	·	·	·	·
47 BC													
L.PLAVTIVS PLANCVS	1	+	19	17	+	1	+	·	1	·	·	·	·
A.LICINIVS NERVA	·	·	5	5	+	·	·	·	1	·	·	·	·
C.ANTIVS C.F. RESTIO	·	+	2	2	+	·	·	·	·	·	·	·	·
A.ALLIENVS PRO COS, C.CAESAR IMP COS ITER	·	·	·	·	·	·	·	·	·	·	·	·	·
CAESAR with Venus/Aeneas carrying Anchises	13	·	44	3	+	·	·	5	1	·	·	·	·
Q.METEL PIVS SCIPIO IMP (alone)	6	+	3	·	+	1	+	·	·	·	·	·	·
Q.METELL PIVS SCIPIO IMP (with Legates)	·	+	5	·	+	1	+	·	·	·	·	·	·
M.CATO PRO PR	·	·	2	·	·	·	·	·	·	·	·	·	·

46 BC

Issue													
MN.CORDIVS RVFVS	.	.	.	.	6	2	+	2	+	8	120	+	23
T.CARISIVS	.	.	.	.	1	3	+	3	+	12	128	+	17
C.CONSIDIVS PAETVS	.	.	.	.	2	2	+	2	+	4	35	+	12
(CAESAR) with COS TERT DICT ITER	.	.	.	.	.	.	.	.	+	.	26	.	1
CAESAR with Venus and Cupid/Trophy	.	.	.	.	.	.	+	10	.	3	3	+	2
M.POBLICI LEG PRO PR, CN.MAGNVS IMP[1]	.	.	.	.	.	.	.	4	.	.	2	.	1
M.MINAT SABI PR Q, CN.MAGNVS IMP F[1]	.	.	.	.	.	.	.	.	.	1	.	.	.
45 BC													
L.PAPIVS CELSVS	.	.	.	.	.	.	.	.	+	4	4	+	3
PALIKANVS	.	.	.	.	.	.	.	.	.	.	.	+	.
L.VALERIVS ACISCVLVS	.	.	.	.	.	.	.	.	.	.	.	.	1
SEX. MAGNVS PIVS IMP	.	.	.	.	.	.	.	.	.	.	.	.	.
(Totals of Roman coins in each hoard)	3000	730	426	1758	109	140	1208	76	1000	1520	659	400	360

+ indicates issues known to have been present, number of coins not recorded.

[1] Examples of these two issues, already recorded from the Cadriano hoard, are therefore not recorded for the San Niccolo hoard, but were doubtless present in it.

Source: adapted from *RRC*, 90–1.

The table, and with it the chronology of the period, is constituted as follows:
The issue of Mn. Acilius, a moneyer, and the military issue of Caesar with Elephant/Pontifical emblems, both very common, are both present in the Cadriano and San Cesario hoards; they begin the period together and the issue of Caesar may be regarded as following his crossing of the Rubicon in 49. The three issues which follow may be dated to 49 from what we know of the careers of the men who produced and signed them. They are very rare and were not produced in Italy; hence it is not surprising that they do not occur until the large San Niccolo hoard. The Carbonara and San Giuliano hoards add two, then three issues of the following year; the joint issue of C. Pansa and Albinus is very rare and does not appear at once; the military issues of Caesar with LII are common and are therefore later than the moneyers' issues of 48. And so on. . .

tary area; and if a major change in the nature of the coinage being produced has taken place shortly before the closing date of a hoard, the hoard may reach back only to that point.

The basic method of using hoard evidence to establish a relative sequence of issues is straightforward. Of two hoards with some issues in common, that which was buried later will contain more recent issues which do not occur in the other hoard, as well as issues which are common to the other hoard, but which are more worn. A relative order of issues follows almost automatically (see Fig. 13, with commentary), provided due sensitivity is deployed in dealing with issues of great rarity.

A dramatic example of re-dating as a result of proper attention to hoard evidence is provided for the Roman Republic by the issue of M. Brutus with the simple legend BRVTVS and types advertising Libertas (*RRC* no. 433/1); it is dated in the older handbooks to the period of the Civil Wars in which he was involved, 43–42 BC. The issue in fact belongs in the late 50s BC and advertises Libertas in opposition to Pompeius, not to the heirs of Caesar.

Sites occupied in succession for short periods of time may provide evidence similar to that provided by sequences of coin hoards. The issues of the moneyers – junior magistrates in charge of the production of coinage – striking under Augustus pose particularly acute chronological problems: few are dated, the historical reference of the types and legends are often equivocal, arguments from the later careers of the moneyers are inconclusive, and hoards provide little help. In these circumstances it is valuable to have the demonstration of K. Kraft on the basis of the finds in the sequence of Roman camps on and near the Rhine that the issues of A. Licinius Nerva and his colleagues and of P. Lurius Agrippa and his colleagues are later than the first issue of the Altar series of bronze struck at Lugdunum in 10–6 BC.[6]

Given the usefulness of hoards, it is unfortunate that the circumstances of their discovery often militate against adequate recording. The interest of the finder of a hoard or of the

---

[6] *Mainzer Zeitschr.* (1951–2), 28.

owner of the land where the find occurred may clash with a claim of the state to the hoard; fear of apprehension may prevent complete recovery of the hoard from the ground and may lead to fragmentation of a hoard before any record is taken.[7] One is therefore often dealing with records of parts of hoards, which may be of two basic types; what is recorded may be a random selection from the whole, in which case we have the less useful, but unbiassed evidence of a small hoard instead of a large one; alternatively the record may enumerate pieces selected for the fineness of their condition, or the pieces left after such a selection has been made. Such hoards must be used with caution and their uncorroborated evidence accorded little weight.[8]

The vicissitudes suffered by a hoard between its discovery and its being recorded may also lead to the association with it of extraneous pieces; careful examination may make it possible to segregate these because of their different physical appearance (e.g., patination) or because they contradict the pattern to be expected of the hoard in the light of other hoards of the same period.

Not the least of the merits of hoard evidence is that the discovery of new hoards, particularly hoards found in the course of controlled excavation, confirm and add precision to the inferences to be drawn from hoards already known. Thus the Stobi hoard,[9] discovered in two contiguous pots in the course of meticulously controlled excavation, precisely confirms the evidence of the Riccia, Maserà, and San Giovanni Incarico hoards (*RRCH* 161–3), discovered casually and sometimes treated as providing untrustworthy evidence for the dating of the Republican coinage of the second century BC.

The most interesting side, however, of the study of coin hoards lies in what can be deduced from them, and from coin finds of other kinds, for the history of a particular site or for

[7] See M. Amandry and C. Carcassonne, *SM* (1979), 79, for the use of a chi^2 test to see whether two suspected lots of a single hoard have structures coherent with each other.

[8] See p. 199 for single hoards buried in two lots.

[9] *Stobi Studies* I (Belgrade, 1973), 1.

economic history in general. One spectre that needs to be exorcised at an early stage is the obsession of much earlier scholarship with the classification of coin hoards according to the purposes of their depositors,[10] a subject on which neither the ancient literary sources nor the circumstances of discovery of hoards shed much light. It is true that Theophanes records the loss of a military pay-chest in AD 801 and that the Lay hoard may well be one such, closing with coins of Severus Alexander; it was found in a military outpost and the coins were neatly arranged as a cylinder presumably once contained in a wooden box.[11] But hoards do not come with labels attached and guesses as to their original destinations are usually worthless; the internal evidence of the hoards themselves tells us very little, though occasionally the diversity of an assemblage may suggest a piratical owner.

What the internal evidence may sometimes reveal is something of the principles according to which a hoard was put together. It is clear that where coinage was depreciated in weight or purity, a man putting a hoard together sometimes chose *as far as possible* coins of the higher intrinsic value; the qualification is important, because it was presumably preferable to hoard a coin of the lower intrinsic value than not to hoard at all. Thus after the reduction of the weight of the tetradrachm by Ptolemy I, hoards for some time tended to exclude pieces of reduced weight; the Rennes hoard, buried under Aurelian,[12] largely excludes aurei of reduced weight, by then struck in substantial numbers. But selection of good coins is by no means a universal phenomenon and it would be rash to suppose that the ancient world as a whole always acted in accordance with Gresham's Law. Roman hoarders seem sometimes to have selected on the basis of a political preference for one emperor over another as well as on the basis of the good preservation or the metallic purity of the pieces hoarded.

[10] J.G.Milne, *Finds of Greek Coins in the British Isles* (Oxford, 1948), 14–17; *Greek and Roman Coins* (London, 1939), 91–9.
[11] *Rev.Arch.Est Centre-Est* (1950), 175.
[12] *RN* (1843), 11.

A special case is where selection is reflected in the use of more than one receptacle[13] for the hoard. Thus the Phacous hoard (*IGCH* 1678) was concealed in two jars, one containing Alexander tetradrachms down to 305 BC (*ipso facto* of full weight), the other containing Ptolemaic Alexander/Athena tetradrachms of full and reduced weight, but the latter so few in number that they must have been deliberately eschewed.

Classification of coins prior to hoarding, however, does not support the notion of a rigid distinction between 'circulation' hoards and 'savings' hoards. Seneca (*De vita beata* XXIV 2) talks of a 'thensaurus alte obrutus, quem non eruas, nisi fuerit necesse', 'a hoard hidden away, which you would not bring out unless it were necessary'; and one may hypothesise that some of the hoards of which we know are of this type, consisting only of an accumulation of coins from which none has ever been taken away. At the other extreme lies a hoard such as the Minturno hoard (*RRCH* 98), the contents of a shop-keeper's till, lost in the fire of 191 BC. Between these two extremes there is surely an infinite gradation, as J.-P. Callu rightly observes,[14] with the vast bulk of hoards being partly accumulations, partly reflecting to a certain extent the changing pattern of circulation.[15] It is obvious that many hoards include pieces not in normal circulation, though valid and capable of circulating; but that fact does not deprive the hoards concerned of all contact with the circulating medium. Pure accumulation hoards are surely very rare; even if one can be identified, there is no reason to suppose that it can reveal anything of the process of accumulation. Coins may be placed in an accumulation hoard some years after being struck and may also be stored by several owners without becoming worn and before reaching their final resting-place. Thus it is impossible to *assume* even in a hoard of perfectly preserved coins that they were accumulated in the hoard in question in the years of their production. It is equally rash to

---

[13] See in general J.-P. Callu, in *Fundmünzen der Antike*, ed. M.R. Alföldi, (Berlin, 1979), 5, 'Cachettes monétaires multiples (IIIe–IVe siècles)'.
[14] J.–P. Callu, *La politique monétaire des empereurs romains* (Paris, 1969), 4–5.
[15] Note G. B. Rogers, *Gallia* 1975, 257 (pushing his case too far).

assume that a hoard containing a sequence of good quality coins ending just before a devaluation is *necessarily* a 'savings' hoard.

We are on rather firmer ground when it comes to the reasons for the non-recovery of hoards in antiquity; ancient literary evidence, such as that relating to the arrival of Cassius at Rhodes in 43 BC, makes it clear that fear of armed violence was a major factor leading to the concealment of coin hoards; examples found in the destruction levels of settlements tell their own sad tale of the fate of the owners. Though few individual hoards can be related to particular acts of violence, the pattern of many hoards may be more significant; thus, for the last two centuries of the Roman Republic there is a remarkably close correlation between periodic concentrations of coin hoards in Italy and the incidence of war and revolution;[16] it is important to be clear that the violence which led to the death of the owner of a hoard and hence to its non-recovery did not necessarily occur where the hoard was buried; a soldier could be recruited, bury his money, and be killed at the other end of the Mediterranean.

Concentrations of hoards with the same or a similar closing date may also be revealing for the chronology of the coinage concerned. Thus there is a group of hoards of Athenian New Style coinage from Delos which close on the traditional chronology sometime in the 80s BC, on that of Margaret Thompson in the 120s BC; the former chronology, linking the non-recovery of the hoards with the sack of the island during the First Mithridatic War, is far more probable.

Much thought and energy have been devoted to attempting to detect behind the pattern of non-recovery of hoards a pattern of hoarding; it is obvious *a priori* that reasons other than fear may lead at some periods to a greater rate of withdrawal of coins from circulation, presumably in intention only temporary. The period and place for which the most persistent attempts have been made to recover a pattern

[16] See *PBSR* (1969), 76, 'Coin hoards and the pattern of violence in the late Republic'.

of hoarding is third-century Roman Britain; with its problems in mind, R.G. Collingwood remarked that 'when the value of money is falling sharply, users find that it will not buy as much as they are accustomed to think it should; they therefore allow it to hang on their hands, and thus hoards everywhere tend to accumulate'.[17] The argument of H. Mattingly is similar, that coins were hoarded because they had been demonetised.[18] But it does not seem to me plausible to maintain that hoards admittedly of devalued coinage, but often of many pounds of metal, were not recovered because it was not worth while.

Equally important is the evidence provided by hoards for the study of coin circulation in its widest sense, not just the coinage in circulation at the moment when a hoard was deposited, but the whole pool of coinage which was available for circulation and which to a greater or lesser extent did pass from one person to another. Of course an isolated hoard may be a freak, the possession of a stray traveller, and inferences about circulation must only be based on a whole series of hoards.[19] Coin finds of types other than hoards here become relevant, some of which have their own problems and significance: chance single finds, finds from excavated sites, finds from graves (whether grave-goods or obols for Charon) and votive deposits. In the study of such finds, as in their use for dating their archaeological contexts, it is of the utmost importance to remember that a single coin could circulate for centuries and be deposited or lost long after its date of issue. It

[17] *The Archaeology of Roman Britain* (London, 1930), 192; (second edition, London, 1969), 231; the experience of the two great inflations in twentieth-century Germany suggests precisely the opposite.

[18] *JRS* (1932), 88, 'Hoards of Roman coins found in Britain', at 91; endorsed by B.H.St J.O'Neil, in *Arch.Journ.* (1935), 73; revived by H.B.Mattingly, *N.Staffs. Journal of Field Studies* (1963), 26.

[19] Freaks may of course sometimes be revealing: a hoard of bronzes of Leontinoi from mainland Greece (IGCH 26) presumably reveals a citizen of Leontinoi on his way back to his mother-city of Chalcis after the destruction of his own city by Syracuse in 422 BC; and an odd influx of coins struck in the Peloponnese early in the third century AD into Syria reveals the movement of a group of auxiliaries raised in small rural centres by Severus to defend the Parthian frontier (*ANRW* II.2, 572).

is also important to remember that small coins not only became worn more quickly than large ones, but were also much more likely to be lost and not re-found; likewise low value coins were more likely not to be recovered than those of high value. In general, of the circulating medium, hoards are likely to contain high value pieces, site finds to consist of low value pieces. Finds on sites also normally include a number of deliberate losses, such as forgeries, which were not legal tender, and may well include scattered hoards not immediately recognisable as such.

With these cautions in mind, the numismatic evidence may be used not only to date individual strata, but also to date the occupation of a whole site, as demonstrated by J.W. Müller in a difficult, but important article.[20] The principle involved may be roughly stated thus: the occupation can be identified as beginning with the first year for which the available coinage in the area is fully reflected on the site. For coinage may be presumed to begin to disappear from circulation by loss or hoarding immediately after being issued.[21] If then a site comes into use on 1 January of a certain year, the coinage issued in that year will be the first one which is available in its entirety as a preliminary to representation on the site. If one plots, year by year, for the site and for the area as a whole, the volume of coinage as a percentage of the totals from the site and from the area, the date at which occupation of the site begins is indicated by the point where the two graphs coincide for the first time (see Fig. 14). The recovery of coins from a site must of course produce a representative sample before the process can be applied; in particular, calculation can be skewed by leaving some strata unexcavated.

Find evidence may also be used to produce solid and important information of a different kind; thus A. Pautasso has been able to identify the tribes and the societies producing and using the pre-Roman silver coinage of Cisalpine

[20] *SNR* (1968), 105.
[21] R.Reece, in *Coins and the Archaeologist*, J.Casey and R.Reece, eds. (Oxford, 1974), 78, obscures the issue by considering the coins of an entire reign.

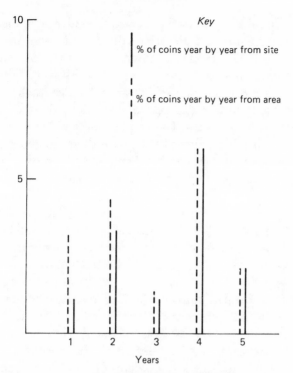

14. Graph illustrating site use

For Year 1, the earliest year for which coins are known from the site, those coins form 1% of the total, whereas in the finds from the area the coins for that year form 3% of the total, for example. The two percentages come closer to each other, and occupation of the site may be regarded as beginning in the year in which they become identical.

Gaul;[22] M.J. Price has been able to attribute bronzes with AΘH, previously regarded as belonging with other early bronzes of Athens, to a military mint of the Athenian general Timotheus during the siege of Olynthus; C.M. Kraay has identified Magna Graecia as an area within which the coins of any one *polis* circulated everywhere, contrary to the normal pattern of Classical Greek coinages, according to which the coins of one *polis* circulated only within its territory.[23] One

[22] A.Pautasso, *Le monete preromane dell'Italia settentrionale* (Milan, 1966).
[23] M.J.Price, *NC* (1967), 1; C.M.Kraay, *JHS* (1964), 76, 'Hoards, small change and the origin of coinage'.

Michael Crawford

must remember, however, that find evidence alone may provide an incomplete picture of the coins known to a particular area. P. Grierson has shown that Muslim coins known from documents but not from hoards were used in thirteenth-century England;[24] literary references make it clear that the gold coin of Philip II of Macedon, the *Philippeios, Philippus*, was known to late Republican and early Imperial Italy, though it was certainly not used there. In general, it is important to remember that literary texts, inscriptions and papyri, as well as coins, provide evidence for patterns of circulation.

The speed with which coins reached the periphery of the area within which they circulated, if they were minted in the centre, is also a substantial problem. Dated deposits such as those at Morgantina, Alesia, and Pompeii show that those places were reached relatively rapidly; the greater degree of wear on the Roman coins in the Cordova hoard, compared with that on the Iberian issues, suggests that Roman coinage in the second century BC was relatively slow in reaching Spain, a conclusion borne out by the gap between the dates of the latest coins and the known dates of the Roman camps at Numantia; in Britain the Weston hoard contained Republican denarii with native issues of the mid first century AD; in Germany, even the latest coins in the Niederlangen hoard were very worn; and the Roman camp at Oberaden, occupied from 12–8 BC, contained only one as of a moneyer of Augustus.[25]

In areas where coins arrived slowly even the latest coin in a hoard may thus be worn; but unfortunately there is no accurate way of assessing to how many years of circulation the degree of wear on a coin corresponds. More can perhaps be done with the weights of a group of coins. If one constructs a frequency table of a group of newly issued pieces (p. 223), it

---

[24] *Studies G.C.Miles* (Beirut, 1974), 387, 'Muslim coins in thirteenth century England'.

[25] Morgantina: M.H.Crawford, *RRC*, p.32; Alesia and Pompeii: *idem, JRS* 60 (1970), 43 and 42; Cordova: *idem, NC* (1969), 79; Weston: *RRCH* 476; Niederlangen: *RRCH* 452; Oberaden: *FMRD* VI, 5, 2080–2.

is likely to occupy a relatively restricted spread and to show a pronounced peak; the same group after a period in circulation is likely to occupy a much wider spread and to show a much flatter peak.

A discussion of circulation raises also the problem of hoards which are anomalous in respect of their internal composition; the problem is as important as that of the anomalous penetration of coins to areas where they do not normally circulate. The Agrinion hoard (*IGCH* 271) may be taken as an example: the bulk of the hoard consists of blocks of issues of Achaea, Athens and Rome; each block fits quite intelligibly into the sequences of other hoards of coins principally of each mint, but no conceivable dating system for each mint allows the same date to be adopted as the closing date for each of the three blocks. It remains mysterious why the cut-off point is not the same for all the coinages in the hoard.

An area of study where coin finds are a major historical source is that of the economic life of ancient cities, provided one can be reasonably sure that the excavations involved have yielded a representative series of the coins in use during the period in which the site was occupied, representative both in terms of the areas of the site covered and in terms of the whole period of its occupation. Thus a site where only the upper levels of the forum or only the wealthy quarters have been excavated is a dangerous subject for study. It is also salutary to be reminded by John Casey that the coins found at a site such as Corbridge represent only an infinitesimal fraction of what must have been paid out over the years to the troops there.[26]

Even in a partially excavated site such as Corinth, however, attention to the numismatic evidence can be very revealing of ancient economic history; after 200 BC, Corinth, like most ancient states preoccupied with fiscal concerns rather than with providing a coinage suitable for economic activity, did not strike in bronze; large numbers of bronze pieces therefore found their way to Corinth from Sicyon,

---

[26] In *Coins and the Archaeologist* (n. 21), 37.

contrary to the normal pattern.[27] Indeed, the normal tendency in the Greek world for small bronze coins not to travel far from their place of origin can sometimes lead to the identification of a city site whose name is not directly attested.

A serious problem arises from the fact that, as we have seen, a coin may have been lost long after its date of issue. The example of Pompeii, destroyed in AD 79, shows that Roman Imperial quadrantes were then available in large quantities; and a large number were also found at a crossing of the River Liris near Minturnae, presumably thrown in as offerings by travellers. By contrast, the forum area of Minturnae produced only one Imperial quadrans and the explanation is likely to be that the bulk of the Imperial coins there were lost at a stage when the quadrans no longer circulated. There is, however, no obvious single occasion for such a loss to parallel the fire of 191 BC and another of the mid first century BC, which doubtless caused the loss on both occasions of disproportionately large quantities of Republican bronzes.

In considering the monetary circulation on any site, it is naturally necessary to know something of the whole pattern of circulation of the coinage or coinages found there; this is particularly true for the Roman world where any one city is part of a Mediterranean-wide monetary system, and R. Reece has gone a long way towards building up an ideal type of the monetary circulation of the Roman Empire against which that of individual cities can be studied.[28] But above all one must remember that there are many things which the numismatic evidence can never reveal. It can almost never reveal the social class of the user of a particular coin or the owner of a particular hoard, and unaided it can tell us little of the economic function of coined money in a particular society. In this context the warning sounded by P. Grierson in a brilliant article of 1959 is of undiminished relevance;[29] the fact that we know of the existence of traders in itself tells us nothing about the overall pattern of the sale of goods, which

[27] See M.J.Price, *Hesperia* (1967), 367; see p. 203 above.
[28] *Britannia* (1973), 227; the graph in K.Hopkins, *JRS* (1980), 101, 'Taxes and trade in the Roman Empire', at 113, depends on such material.
[29] *Trans.Roy.Hist.Soc.* (1959), 123, 'Commerce in the Dark Ages: a critique of the evidence'.

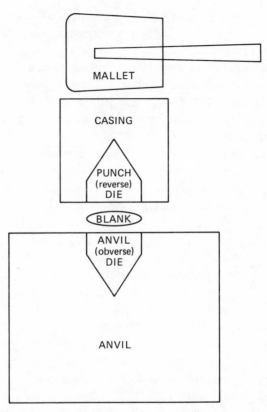

15. The process of minting

One die is set in an anvil (it may be known as the anvil or lower die); it strikes the obverse side of the coin. Another die is set in a casing and is hit with a mallet. Since it strikes the coin it is known as the punch die; it may also be called the upper die. It strikes the reverse, or upward facing side of the coin.

may still be largely in the hands of primary producers and to which gift exchange may be an important alternative; and as far as the distribution of goods, including coins, is concerned, plunder and gift and such things as indemnities may be much more important than trade as a vehicle.

DIE STUDIES

Coin finds also provide much of the material necessary if one is to attempt to study the dies used to produce an issue or

Michael Crawford

group of issues, material which must of course be supplemented by that which is now in public and private collections and that which is recorded in the catalogues of coins for sale published by dealers. (Some museums maintain classified files of such material as well as collections of plaster casts of coins shown at the museums.) Studies of dies have a variety of uses, serving to date or attribute an issue or to provide an estimate of its size.

The mechanism for the production of a coin in antiquity was very simple (see Fig. 15): one die was mounted in an anvil, a blank was placed on it, a second die was held over it and hit with a hammer (the blank, if heated, was manipulated with a pair of tongs).

Each die was individually made[30] and therefore had a different life expectancy, but there was a general tendency for anvil, or obverse (upward-facing), dies to last longer than punch, or reverse (downward-facing), dies, since these were unprotected and subjected to greater stress. The fact of varying die life means, for instance, that within an issue an obverse die may be used with one reverse die, which wears out, and with a second reverse die, which outlasts it and is used with a second obverse die; it is thus often possible to establish and number parallel sequences of obverse and reverse dies (see Fig. 16). It is often possible to see that a die has suffered wear or damage between its first and its last appearances and sometimes that a die has been repaired or recut in the course of its life. The provenance of two coins from the same die is established by careful comparison of the details of the type and the legend.[31]

The establishment of a sequence of die-links is a standard technique in the establishment of the chronology of any coinage where an identical obverse or reverse type is shared by more than one issue; thus the arrangements of the coinage

---

[30] See *NC* (1981), 176; for the infrequent artists' signatures on Greek coins see M.Guarducci, *Epigrafia Greca* III (Rome, 1974), 530; the artists who engraved coin dies were perhaps normally not specialists, but jewellers etc.

[31] T.Hackens and R.Beck, *Leitz-Mitteilungen für Wissenschaft und Technik* IV.7 (March 1969), 208; B.Schärli, *SM* (1979), 9, for various technical aids.

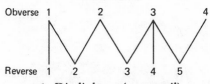

Obverse 1　　2　　3　　4

Reverse 1　2　　3　　4　　5

16. Die linkage (one anvil)

Since obverse and reverse dies were not normally paired, each could be individually discarded and replaced as it wore out or broke up. In most series the reverse dies are found to be more numerous than the obverses, and therefore had shorter lives; they suffered the direct impact of the hammer, whereas the obverse die was not only cushioned from its force by the intervening flan, but was also supported by the surrounding mass of the anvil. This inequality between the lives of obverse and reverse dies can produce a series of die-combinations, linked by common obverse or reverse dies, in which the number of reverse dies will be higher than that of the obverse dies.

of archaic and classical Abdera by J.M.F. May or of Hellenistic Athens by M. Thompson lean heavily on this kind of evidence; certain early issues of the denarius coinage may be placed together because of shared obverse dies, as well as some issues of the Triumviral period; die-links provide a basis for classifying the 'autonomous' coinages of AD 68–9 and also the *aes* coinage of Galba. For Asia Minor in the third century AD, the fact that several neighbouring towns often used the same obverse die may sometimes be used to settle problems of attribution and location: the site of an unidentified town should probably be sought near the sites of towns with which it shares a die or dies.[32]

Studies of dies may also reveal significant facts about the internal structures of issues which do not actually share dies. Thus an issue where only one anvil is in use at any one time will produce a pattern of die use like that of Fig. 16, an issue where several anvils are in use at any one time will produce a different pattern (see Fig. 17). If two issues with the two different patterns are broadly comparable in size, it may then be possible to argue that they are not likely to have been produced at the same time and in the same place.

Other inferences may be made from information about the

[32] L.Robert, *Villes d'Asie Mineure*[2] (Paris, 1962), 366; K.Kraft, *Das System der kaiserzeitlichen Münzprägung* (Berlin, 1972), 102 n. 21; A.Burnett, *JRS* (1978), 173.

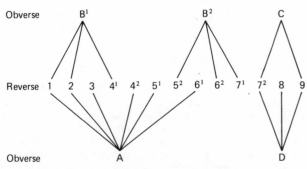

17. Die linkage (two anvils)

Large establishments had several anvils working together. For most of its history the Corinthian colony Leucas regularly operated two anvils at the same time, which shared a common stock of reverse dies, and since the number of surviving specimens is large, the pattern of its work can be reconstructed in some detail by the careful observation of the deterioration of both obverse and reverse dies. A typical sequence from the mid-fifth century is shown in the diagram above, where the small figures show the successive states of wear on each die.

internal structures of different issues: thus the different survival rates of coins per die for the earliest Athenian coinage, the so-called *Wappenmünzen*, and for the early owl coinage which followed, are one pointer to different functions for the two coinages, small-scale internal use and large-scale export. *Relatively* few owls survive because so many were exported to countries such as Egypt where they were treated as bullion and melted down.

Similar internal structures, on the other hand, make it quite clear that the two main issues of the Italian rebels against Rome in 90–89, with ITALIA and with the Oscan legend VIꓶƎTꟼꓛ, were not produced at separate mints, as often supposed, but at the same mint, and were a genuine bilingual coinage. The fact that in the third century AD fractional bronze coinage was sometimes produced with dies also used for gold coinage perhaps reveals something of the hand-to-mouth existence of the mints of that period.[33]

One special form of die-link requires a brief discussion, that apparently subsisting between pieces of pure silver and

[33] P.Strauss, *RN* (1954), 19; P.Bastien, *Le monnayage de l'atelier de Lyon* I (Wetteren, 1976), 27–8.

those plated with silver. These have been used to argue that an official mint could produce both genuine pieces and 'forgeries'. It is, however, clear that it was possible by a process of copying from a coin to make a die which could produce coins almost indistinguishable from the real thing, and I regard die-links between silver and plated pieces as probably in most cases only apparent.[34]

Finally, the ratio between obverse and reverse dies varies widely from one period or mint to another, providing valuable information on dating and attribution and, sometimes, raising questions about mint organisation.

The dies of an issue once identified, the knowledge may be used to help towards a study of the volume of ancient coinage. Such a study is by no means impossible. The Lohe hoard of Swedish coins from Stockholm, published by B. Thordeman in an epoch-making article of 1948,[35] showed an almost perfect correlation between the numbers of coins of each year in the hoard and the numbers of coins known from mint records to have been issued each year. Such a phenomenon makes it likely that at any rate for an ancient coinage which circulated over a very wide area without interruption for a very long time there is a correlation between volume of coinage issued and volume now surviving. Very small issues may obviously have an erratic survival rate.

It is then in principle easy to establish the relative commonness or rarity of a particular issue, something which has been done up to a point for a century or more, whether by Mommsen, who listed occurrences in hoards of Roman Republican issues down to 49, or by Cohen and Babelon, who offered estimated modern values, or by the editors of RIC II onwards, who offered estimated degrees of rarity. Given that only for a few issues is it knowable how large they

---

[34] RRC, p. 560. It remains possible that dies occasionally 'escaped' from the mint to a forger's workshop.

[35] NC (1948), 188; Num.Medd. 31 (1973), 104, for an early eighteenth-century wreck from Heligholm which repeats the lesson of the Lohe hoard; P. Sarvas, NNÅ (1967), 31–2 and 143 with Diagram 2, discusses a group of finds which also accurately reflects production. See in general the discussion in AIIN 29 (1982).

were originally, two avenues exist, either to establish for as large a sample of issues as possible the relationship between original size and surviving specimens, or to establish the number of dies used and the number of coins struck per die. The first avenue is in theory available for certain rare Greek and Roman issues, but certainly not for the bulk of the Roman coinage, since it is clear from the amount of material which passes through the market that there is an unknowable, but large, number of pieces of common issues in inaccessible private (and for that matter 'public') collections;[36] whence the notion of counting dies for a sample of issues and extrapolating to other issues, in order to establish the number of dies used overall.

The problem at once arises of whether a count of dies is anywhere near complete; it is easy to tell when the count *within the body of material which survives* is nearing completion, simply by observing when the acquisition of further material from another museum visited ceases to produce new dies; the effect may be graphically represented (see Fig. 18). But it might be that the material which survives only reveals a fraction of the dies once used. For the coinage of the Roman Republic, however, this is clearly not so.

A number of Republican moneyers were considerate enough to use for denarii and quinarii numbered or lettered sequences of dies; and it is possible to observe without undue difficulty that in some cases a number or a letter never has more than one die. Now although the sequences in question are rarely complete, it is clear, for instance, that a sequence which goes with occasional gaps from I to LXXX is unlikely ever to have extended very far beyond LXXX. It is therefore possible to compare, for the issues under discussion, the number of dies from which specimens survive to be observed with a theoretical maximum. It emerges in the case of issues whose dies are counted exhaustively that the first figure is normally close to the second figure. We may therefore assert

---

[36] In fact, no agreed estimate exists for the survival rate of ancient coinages and the rate is most unlikely to be the same for different periods and places.

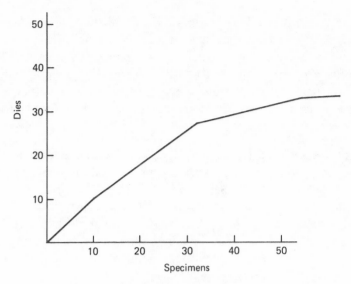

18. Emergence of dies

The first ten specimens known yield ten dies; as the number of specimens known increases, the number of new dies grows less rapidly and eventually ceases to grow at all. At this point it is futile to seek out new specimens.

with some confidence that if we count the number of dies used to strike the surviving specimens of an issue of denarii or quinarii during the Republic, the total will not be far from the theoretical maximum.

A practical problem remains: to count all the dies used to strike coins during the Republic would be the work of several lifetimes. One may therefore display the occurrence, in a representative sample of hoards, of all issues of denarii and quinarii struck under the Republic from c.157 onwards; it is then possible to estimate the numbers of dies used for issues where they have not been counted by comparing them with issues where the dies have been counted.[37]

---

[37] As an alternative approach, formulae exist for extrapolating from the number of dies known from a particular sample to the total number of dies originally used, see G.F.Carter, in *Scientific Studies in Numismatics*, ed. W.A.Oddy (London, 1980), 17 (the attempts to calculate the life of a die and the number of coins struck per die are based on wholly un-warranted assumptions); C.Carcassonne and T.Hackens (eds.), *Statistics and Numismatics* (Strasbourg, 1981).

Michael Crawford

If one knows or may estimate the numbers of obverse and reverse dies used for an issue or a coinage, one needs then to apply a figure of coins struck per die in order to discover the volume originally produced. It is normal to operate with coins per (longer-lasting) obverse die, and a number of serious estimates for precious metal coinage have been produced:

5,000–8,000	for cold striking in a modern experiment
10,000–16,000	for hot striking in a modern experiment (D.G.Sellwood, *NC* (1963), 229, imitating the production of a Greek coin)
23,333–47,250	P.Kinns, *NC* (1983), 1–22 at 18–19
c. 13,000	E.S.G.Robinson, *Museum Notes* (1960), 1 (with the calculations of M.H. Crawford, *RRC*, p. 698 n.6)
c. 30,000	M.H.Crawford, *RRC*, p. 694

More research and some lucky epigraphic discoveries which reveal the size of an issue are clearly needed; one should then be able to talk with some confidence about the financial history of the communities of the ancient world.

<h3 style="text-align:center">OVERSTRIKES AND COUNTERMARKS[38]</h3>

The norm, and presumably the ideal, when striking a coin in antiquity was to use a newly prepared blank or flan; but at certain periods actual coins were simply overstruck (sometimes after an adjustment to their weight) with new obverse and reverse types; an even more makeshift alternative to producing a completely new coin was simply to countermark one side of an existing coin with a design or legend covering part of the surface, as a prelude to paying it out.

An overstrike, then, is a coin treated as if it were a blank or flan; examples have been identified both in silver and in bronze, where the new types have failed to obliterate the old

---

[38] See in general G.Le Rider, in *Numismatique Antique*, J.-M.Dentzer et al., eds. (Nancy and Louvain, 1975), 46.

types completely. Often, the so-called undertype is insufficiently clear on obverse or reverse for the original issue to be identified. But where it can be identified, absolute priority of the original issue is established. Thus, it was once believed that the tortoise only appeared as the obverse type of the coinage of Aegina (instead of the turtle) in the fourth century BC; but a 'tortoise' then appeared, overstruck by Azbaal of Cition, no later than 425 BC;[39] the fifth-century dating was then confirmed by the occurrence of a 'tortoise' in a fifth-century BC hoard.[40] Similarly, the chronological evidence of overstrikes is of great importance in the dating of the early denarius coinage.

Where a coin is overstruck by an authority other than that which issued it originally, it must obviously have been available to the overstriking authority; but it would be rash to suppose that it necessarily arrived by way of normal circulation or that it was necessarily overstruck anywhere near its place of origin. Many of the foreign coins overstruck by Rome during the Second Punic War were acquired as booty; and the odd fact that all the cistophori of Hadrian are overstruck on cistophori of M. Antonius suggests that the coinage of Hadrian was produced by demonetising all surviving specimens of M. Antonius and calling them in for restriking.[41]

Coins can also often be regarded as having been overstruck precisely because they were unacceptable as they were to the overstriking authority, which wished to advertise its own sovereignty. For instance, numerous Sicilian cities chose to assert themselves after the mission of Timoleon by overstriking coins of Syracuse with their own types.[42]

A coin may be unacceptable to an overstriking authority

---

[39] S.P.Noe, *Museum Notes* (1954), 89 (a piece in the American Numismatic Society from the Side hoard); see also C.M.Kraay, *NC* (1969), 19–20.

[40] R.Ross Holloway, *Museum Notes* (1971), 20.

[41] W.E.Metcalf, *The Cistophori of Hadrian* (New York, 1980).

[42] R.J.A.Talbert, *Timoleon* (Cambridge, 1974), 180; the precise opposite is the case to the assertion of C.H.V.Sutherland, *NC* (1942), 6, 'coins are not normally overstruck by a second city unless they are themselves current in that second city'. See C.M.Kraay, *NC* (1960), 66–78, for a lucid discussion of overstriking in Magna Graecia and of Sutherland's

for other reasons than the character of the original authority. Thus, during the great inflation of the third century AD, denarii were eventually overstruck as antoniniani (double denarii), when the intrinsic value of the latter had declined to the level at which the denarius had once stood. And during the Second Punic War, as Rome reduced the weight standard of the as, the bronze unit, so she overstruck denominations of the preceding weight standard into their doubles of the new weight standard.

If a coin is melted down to be made into a new one to be paid out, it may be for a variety of reasons; the original coin may be a foreign one and not legal tender, it may be too worn to circulate, it may be of a weight standard or metal content no longer in use at the mint, it may actually have been demonetised, it may be unacceptable simply because the authority making a payment wishes for ideological reasons to pay out a new coin, with its own types. We have seen that overstriking may take place in many of these circumstances and, likewise, the only thing that can be said, *in general*, of countermarking in antiquity is that it is a makeshift alternative to striking a new coin, for all the purposes for which that may take place.[43]

Demonetisation is, of course, attested for certain occasions in antiquity, but there are no grounds for arguing that a countermarked coin would, without the countermark, *necessarily* have been demonetised. This is often true for the Greek world, but is less likely to be the case in the Roman world.[44] Quite apart from the astonishing level of government interference in monetary affairs which it would be necessary to postulate, there are numerous contexts in which

eccentric views; K.Regling, *ZfN* (1922), 166 n.5, for political overstriking in Parthia, by Timarchus of Miletus and by the Jews under Hadrian.

[43] Another kind of mark found on ancient coins is sometimes loosely called a countermark, namely a simple punch mark used by the people of the Levant and elsewhere to test the metallic consistency of Greek or Roman coins.

[44] H.Seyrig, *Syria* (1958), 187, 'Monnaies contremarquées en Syrie' (compare *RN* (1958), 173).

countermarked and uncountermarked coins circulated side by side. Countermarks *may*, of course validate coins which were not legal tender (because foreign or unacceptably worn) and revalue coins no longer of current weight or fineness; but these are by no means their only uses.

A whole group of countermarks may be associated with the fall of Nero: X̄ applied to his coins in Pannonia by the Legio X Gemina, ΓΑΛΒΑ in Moesia, SPQR in Gaul, ꟼ VES on the Rhine, ꟼ or an upright trident at Corinth; the phenomenon as a whole is remarkable evidence of men's dissociation of themselves from the fallen tyrant. But, needless to say, uncountermarked coins of Nero continued to circulate throughout the empire.[45]

Countermarking could be used, like overstriking, to raise the face value of a coin; the most conspicuous examples occur on city bronzes of the third century AD, as their intrinsic value in relation to the ever more debased denarius coinage rose.[46] There is also an odd case of countermarking apparently being used to affirm the face value of the coins of Corinth under the early empire, A being applied to asses, S to semisses and . · . to quadrantes, the marks presumably being applied to the coins as they passed through the city treasury because the denominations were otherwise insufficiently distinct. Apparently early in the reign of Tiberius, the application of the countermarks AVG (in Pannonia) and AVG (in the Rhineland) to some dupondii and sestertii was accompanied by their down-grading to asses and dupondii since they did not meet the new specifications which Tiberius intended to apply to the base metal coinage.[47]

An actual case of demonetisation seems to lie behind an example of countermarking at Byzantium in the Hellenistic period. At a certain point, the weight standard of the tetradrachm was reduced and earlier tetradrachms appear thereafter with a distinctive countermark; they had presumably been

---

[45] For the various countermarks see D.W.MacDowall, *NC* (1960), 103; (1962), 121.

[46] J.-P.Callu (n. 14), 68–9.

[47] D.W.MacDowall, *NC* (1962), 115; (1966), 125.

demonetised and called in, then restored to their owners after being countermarked and after the levy of a charge which reduced their value in Byzantium to that of the new pieces. Similar treatment was meted out to tetradrachms of full weight in the kingdom of Pergamum after the introduction of the reduced weight cistophori.

The examples of Byzantium and of the kingdom of Pergamum encourage the view that some countermarks applied by a Greek city to its own bronzes are also to be regarded as a device for raising money by demonetising an issue and re-issuing it after levying a charge.

The most conspicuous examples of countermarks simply serving to mark occasions of issue occur in the Rhineland during the Julio-Claudian period. The authorities there used a whole series of countermarks, in particular on asses of Augustus during the reign of Tiberius, as they passed through their hands, so that by the end of the reign of the latter the asses in circulation included pieces without counter-mark and pieces with one or more countermarks.[48] The often multiple countermarks applied to Persian silver produced in Asia Minor should also in my view be regarded as applied when the coins in question passed through the hands of one element or another of the Achaemenid administration.

It is clear that countermarks can not only, where a coin is countermarked elsewhere than where it was struck, reveal something of the movement of coinage (for whatever reason), but can also be remarkably informative on the monetary history of antiquity, particularly where a sequence of countermarks is applied to a single coin.

TECHNIQUES OF PRODUCTION

There is much more to the way a coin was made in antiquity than the pattern according to which the dies in use were deployed, and identified similarities in the various processes

---

[48] T.V.Buttrey, *Museum Notes* (1970), 57, 'Observations on the behaviour of Tiberian counterstamps'.

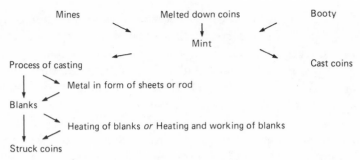

19. Sources of metal

The mint draws metal from three main sources. It may then cast coins directly, it may cast blanks directly, or it may cast sheets and rods from which blanks are cut. These blanks may be struck cold, or heated and struck, or else heated, hammered and struck.

involved can both serve to associate issues in date or attribute them to a single mint and provide much information on monetary and economic history. It is a field of study where an increasing range of scientific techniques is available.

The basic range of possibilities can be illustrated diagrammatically (see Fig. 19). Much may be discovered by a simple process of visual inspection, since individually cast blanks differ from those cut from a larger piece of metal, and blanks can be individually cast in a variety of ways at different times or places, for instance in a mould that produces a profile like this ⟨▭⟩ or in one that produces one like this ⟨▱⟩.

Important differences of approach at a later stage in the manufacture of an issue may also be detected simply by inspection, such as whether or not the obverse and reverse die are in a fixed relationship to each other. If the coins of which the issue is composed are held so that the type on one side is upright and are then rotated on their vertical axes, is the type on the other face exactly upright or exactly upside down or in no fixed position? (In catalogues of coins, the position of the reverse die in relation to the obverse die is indicated either by an arrow, for instance by ↓ or by assimilation to the hour-hand on a clock face expressed as a number, for instance by '6'.)

Regularity of die position helps to distinguish Punic coins struck at Carthage from those struck overseas; different forms of regularity of die position appear at different periods and at different mints under the Roman Empire from Tiberius onwards and help both with problems of attribution and with the elimination of forgeries.[49]

A third phenomenon which can be readily observed is the occurrence of various forms of mis-strike, of which the commonest is the so-called brockage, where a coin remains lodged in one die after being struck and the next blank is impressed by the other die (producing a type in relief) and the coin (producing the same type in intaglio). Such pieces are rare in the Greek coinage, but particularly common in the carelessly produced coinage of the Roman Republic and early Empire; in the late Empire, brockages were apparently re-struck before being issued.

More complex analytical procedures can also be important sources of evidence. One relatively simple procedure is to establish the specific gravity of a coin, by weighing it in air, then weighing it in water and then dividing the weight in air by the difference. The process serves at once to distinguish plated coins masquerading as coins of pure silver (whose specific gravity should be over 10); it has also revealed, along with actual analyses, that the quality of the electrum coinage produced under the terms of the monetary agreement between Phocaea and Mytilene (Tod 112 = *Epigraphica* II, 6) was remarkably consistent;[50] minor variations have also helped to individuate different chronological groups in series where it is hard to distinguish different dies and where there seem in any case to be few links between dies.

In the Roman coinage, analysis of metal content by a variety of techniques has made it possible to distinguish between Imperial dupondii and asses, often of similar weight

---

[49] P.Bastien and H.Huvelin, *BSFN* (1971), 30: 'Orientation des axes de coins dans le monnayage impérial romain'; C.Brenot, 135: 'Observations sur les orientations d'axes d'un groupe d'antoniniani de Victorin issus des mêmes coins de droit et de revers'.

[50] F.Bodenstedt, *Phokaisches Elektron-Geld* (Mainz, 1976); *Die Elektronmünzen von Phokaia und Mytilene* (Tübingen, 1981).

and size, the former, however, of zinc (*orichalcum*) and the latter of copper. Analysis of metal content also makes it clear that although Roman dupondii minted in Syria under Augustus are heavier than those minted at Rome, they are not of a higher intrinsic value since they are not of *orichalcum*.

Analysis of metal content is also beginning to help with some of the chronological problems of the base metal coinage of the early Empire. Thus G.F. Carter and T.V. Buttrey have shown that the quadrantes hitherto attributed to Augustus must be later than the rest of his base metal coinage and may not be Augustan at all.[51]

But perhaps the most spectacular information provided by analysis of metal content is precise information about the great debasements of antiquity. It is now clear that the Ptolemaic silver coinage was first significantly debased when Auletes was forced to raise the money to repay the loan which he had raised in order to bribe the *principes* of the late Republic to agree to his return to power in Egypt.[52] And the various stages of the debasement of the Roman coinage of the third century AD are also now gradually being revealed.[53]

An important field in which so far little has been done is in the detection of the sources of the metal used for ancient coinages. The pioneering work of C.M. Kraay and V. Emeleus on a number of Archaic Greek coinages has been followed up, by N. and S. Gale, and J. Diebolt and H. Nicolet-Pierre have demonstrated the difference in metal content between fourth-century Athenian tetradrachms and eastern imitations; and recent work by T.V. Buttrey has shown the nature of the advances that may be made by combining information derived from metal analysis with a proper understanding of the economic significance of the Athenian currency decree of 375/4 BC[54]. Given that the need for metal of all

---

[51] G.F.Carter and T.V.Buttrey, *Museum Notes* (1977), 49.

[52] D.R.Walker, *The Metrology of the Roman Silver Coinage* I (Oxford, 1976), 139.

[53] Principally by the work of L.H.Cope, see Bibliography in *Metallurgy in Numismatics* I (London: RNS, 1980).

[54] *SNR* (1977), 79; T.V.Buttrey, *Actes IX Congrès International de Numismatique, Berne* (Paris and Basle, 1982), 137–40; work cited in *La moneta in Grecia e a Roma*(Bari, 1982), 23; T. V. Buttrey, *QT* (1981), 71.

kinds is one of the constant factors in the economic history of Greece, the relative lack of analysis is more than unfortunate. G.F.Carter, however, has shown that in producing his new copper coinage Augustus went to the trouble of acquiring virgin metal.[55]

WEIGHT STANDARDS

The weight standard of an issue is the weight of the unit of which the various denominations produced are fractions or multiples.[56] Thus, silver coins which are struck on an Attic weight standard relate to a drachma whose modern equivalent is approximately 4.37 grammes; at Rome the libral weight standard was that of an issue of bronze asses and fractions where the as weighed a Roman pound. The weight standard of an issue may assist in attributing it by a process of association with other issues to a particular date or mint and the adoption, preservation or change of a weight standard may be historically significant, as may the extent to which a theoretical weight standard was observed.

The establishment of ancient weight standards is by no means easy, since although the theoretical standards of a number of issues are known from literary sources, the weights in terms of which these standards are expressed are themselves not absolutely certain. Thus we do not actually *know* the exact weight even of the Roman pound.[57] And even if we agree to work with an approximation, we still have to establish the actual weight standards for individual issues before we can identify these standards with those mentioned in the literary sources; for many issues a far more hazardous approach is necessary, to establish their actual weight standards and then to guess at their (unattested) theoretical standards. Any body of coins now surviving includes worn and corroded specimens and may exclude particularly heavy

[55] In R.H.Brill (ed.), *Science and Archeology* (Cambridge, 1971), 114.
[56] There is a good general discussion in P.Grierson, *NC* (1963), Proceedings I; *NC* (1964), Proceedings I.
[57] *RRC*, pp. 590–2.

pieces melted down in antiquity (but there is no way of knowing). It is therefore necessary to devise some way of expressing the weights of the individuals in a group of coins as a collective fact and then making some allowance for the difference between that figure and the figure demanded by an attested or hypothetical weight standard.[58]

One may take the coinage of the Roman Republic as an example. An issue of coinage was described by the Romans as struck so many to the pound and this terminology presumably reflected mint-practice; certainly no attempt was made to adjust the weight of individual pieces very carefully. Blanks were presumably made roughly the same size in the hope that they would turn out roughly the same weight and the size was reduced or increased towards the end of a batch depending on how the metal was lasting; thus the mean weight of a batch of coinage straight from the mint would be the same as its weight standard. But this is clearly not true of the coinage which survives today, for the reasons mentioned above. It has been argued that a frequency table may be a more reliable guide to the weight standard of an issue than an arithmetical averaging process.[59] But there is no reason why this should be so, and there are cases where a frequency table can be seen to be unreliable as an indication of weight standard. The best way, therefore, to discover the weight standard of an issue is to take the mean of the weights of unworn specimens; if this is impossible the only valid alternative is to take the mean of the weights of available specimens and attempt to estimate the mean loss of weight as a result of wear and corrosion.[60]

---

[58] Figures for weights of coins in circulation in antiquity are unhelpful and not necessarily accurate: in *P.Oxy.* 1653 (AD 306) twelve solidi are alleged to weigh on average 4⅚ grammata each, while the average weight of Diocletianic specimens ought to be 4⅘ grammata; in *P.Bremen* 83 (fourth century AD) 111 solidi are alleged to weigh on average 3⁹⁵⁄₁₁₁ grammata each, while the average weight of Constantinian specimens ought to be 4 grammata.

[59] G.F.Hill, *NC* (1924), 76.

[60] J.Lafaurie, *BSFN* (1970), 491, operates with a (not implausible) percentage to be added to the weight indicated by the peak of a frequency table.

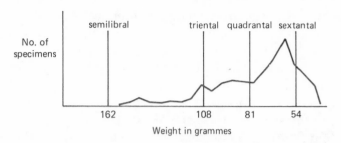

20. Frequency table of weights of Roman bronze coins

The weights of a sample of asses whose weight standard is lower than one based on a Roman pound are plotted at intervals of 1 gramme. The peaks in the resulting graph reveal a variety of different weight standards within the group.

Even if a frequency table is of no use in establishing the weight standard to which an issue was struck, it is remarkably efficient in the detection of two weight standards within an apparently homogeneous issue. If one simply plots the weights of all known specimens (compare p. 207 for the collection of material) at appropriate weight intervals (the lighter the weight standard, the smaller the intervals), one discovers, for instance, that a group of bronze coins of the Roman Republic with a weight standard between one based on an as of half a pound and one based on an as of two ounces was in fact struck in two stages with different weight standards (see Fig. 20).

The history of weight standards and their derivation is obscure and contentious.[61] Briefly, as far as Classical antiquity is concerned, the talent of about 26,220 grammes and its subdivision into 60 minae are of eastern origin; when they were borrowed in the Greek world, they had to be married to an already existing variety of drachmae or silver units. As a result, the number of drachmae to the mina varied from place to place, 100 at Athens, 70 on Aegina and so on. In addition,

---

[61] See the brilliant note of K.J.Beloch, *Griechische Geschichte* 1.2, 333, pointing out that the principles used by some scholars to derive one ancient weight system from another would serve also to derive the metric system from the ancient Egyptian.

the stater or standard piece contained a different number of drachmae from place to place.

Complications aside, it is a fact of the greatest importance that very early in their history the Greek *poleis* officially adopted a fixed drachma or silver unit; thus what is now known as the Attic drachma (from the most important mint to use it) was already the unit on Euboea when a colony was despatched to Pithecussae (Ischia) early in the eighth century BC.

A Greek community, however, did not necessarily keep the same weight standard for the whole of its history and one needs to be alert for changes of standard, often of political significance. Thus the issues of the erstwhile cities of the Athenian Empire, when they started up again late in the fifth century BC, systematically avoided the Attic weight standard. When Philip II of Macedon adopted this very standard for his gold and Alexander for his silver, it was an explicit assertion of their Greekness, part and parcel of the same policy which created Pella as a Greek city.

The origin of the Roman pound is unknown; it may be simply the weight of a handful of bronze. Apart from a few early silver and struck bronze issues, issues of Roman coinage were produced as its multiples or fractions down to AD 1453. Sadly, the interest in establishing weight standards is often in watching their decline in the face of financial pressure. Thus Rome drastically reduced the weight standard of its bronze coinage during the Second Punic War and the weight standard (as well as the purity) of its silver coinage during the third century AD; Constantine reduced the weight of the solidus as a result of financial difficulties in the course of his struggle for power. It is a bizarre irony that he should till recently have been regarded as its creator.

STYLE AND CHRONOLOGY

Style as a criterion for the dating and attribution of an issue is a veteran element in numismatic methodology; it is, however, imprecise and fallible, and its use is now largely secondary to that of the more precise criteria discussed above.

The derivation of the criterion, as far as Greek coinage is concerned, from the early methodology of classical art history and the value judgements which underlie it may be seen from the description of B. V. Head[62] of the periods into which Greek coinage falls:

Archaic
Transitional (=fifth century BC)
Period of Finest Art
Later Fine Art (=Early Hellenistic period)
Decline
Continued Decline

The only really scientific element in all this is the observation that between Archaic and Transitional the Greeks learnt to represent an eye seen in profile. However, given a few fixed points – dates in other art forms, occasional dated coins (such as those of monarchs), dates of the foundation or destruction of cities, some archaeological evidence – the bulk of Greek coinage had by the beginning of this century been assigned to roughly the right period.

The use of stylistic evidence to achieve precise dating was undermined by O. E. Ravel, who showed for the coinage of Corinth that reverses extremely diverse in style were often linked by a shared obverse die.[63] The opposite possibility may be illustrated by drawing attention to a coin of Carthage and a Republican denarius (Fig. 21–2), which must be at least a century and more apart in date, but which display profiles that are almost identical.

Style remains, of course, a criterion which has to be used at times, as in dating the unique denarius of Laterensis, for which hoard evidence is non-existent. Changes in letter forms also have their uses; though it must be recalled that not even in Greek epigraphy, where the material available is enormously greater in bulk, is appeal to letter forms uncon-

---

[62] *Historia Numorum*[2], lxi-lxiv.
[63] *NC* (1945), 117.

21. Denarius of Q. Cornuficius
(courtesy of the Department of Coins and Medals, **British Museum**)

22. Half-shekel of Carthage
(courtesy of the Department of Coins and Medals, British Museum)

tentious, and that in the Republican coinage the hooked Ⳑ took a generation to disappear.

Style can also be used with due caution to individuate mints, whether those of the enormous coinage of Alexander, where practice makes it possible to distinguish without undue difficulty closed stylistic groups, or those of the Roman emperors. Salutary warnings are to hand, however; die-links make it clear that the coins of Decius attributed to Milan by H. Mattingly were produced at Rome.[64]

Finally, it is worth drawing attention to a concrete result of minute stylistic analysis combined with a study of the dies of an issue. One die used early on in the production of the issue of P. Crassus M.f. displays an anomalous hair-style, otherwise found within the relevant period on the issue of Q.Cassius, which thus probably immediately or closely precedes it. Such minute stylistic analysis may also reveal the number of hands at work in the engraving of an individual issue.[65]

---

[64] K.J.Elks, *NC* (1972), 111.
[65] See *RRC*, p. 578 n. 6 and p. 95 for the two hands at work from the mid-eighties to the mid-seventies and for the engravers cutting dies for M.Antonius.

Michael Crawford

TYPES AND LEGENDS

Even if a coinage in which one is interested is as far as possible
dated and attributed, problems may still arise in the course of
an attempt to establish the significance of the legends and types
which occur thereon. It may seem unnecessary to reiterate that
one must be sure of what does appear; but there is as a warning
the experience of M. Grant, the basis for whose speculations
on Caesar as the founder of Corinth evaporated when C.H.V.
Sutherland pointed out that the supposed legend CREATOR
was in fact the result of mis-reading two monograms of
C(n).Publ(icius) and Ant(onius) Or(estes).[66]

Given certainty in the readings of the legends on a coinage,
much may be discovered of the administrative basis for the
coinage in question; but there are still considerable pitfalls.
Casual suggestions that the names appearing on Greek coins of
the Hellenistic period were those of men performing liturgies[67]
were developed by M. Thompson for the coinage of Athens
and A. Bellinger for that of Ilium.[68] Their theories were left in
ruins by L. Robert, in the course of a devastating critique of
their authors' ignorance of Hellenistic history and Greek *polis*
institutions.[69]

Similar inattention to the historical context has led to similar
disasters in the interpretation of types; the temptations are all
too obvious, since ancient coinage is a distinct class of ancient
material, to which distinctive methods of study are appropriate. But it can never be satisfactorily studied in isolation from
other material.

It is not my purpose here to refute the extravagant claims
made for the significance particularly of Roman Imperial coin
types as a means of propaganda; they seem to me to result

[66] *NC* (1947), 87.
[67] J.G.Milne, *Kolophon and its Coinage* (New York, 1941), 26; W.P.Wal-
lace, *Phoenix* (1950), 21; T.Gerassimov, *ANS Centennial Publication*
(New York, 1958), 276.
[68] M.Thompson, *The New Style Silver Coinage of Athens* (New York,
1961), 587; A.R.Bellinger, *Museum Notes* (1958), 23; *Troy. The Coins*
(Princeton, 1961), 26 n. 93.
[69] L.Robert, *Monnaies antiques en Troade* (Geneva and Paris, 1966), 83.

from concentration on the coin evidence to the exclusion of the rest of the evidence available.[70] A similarly unbalanced approach may be exemplified by the suggestion of A. Alföldi that a coin of Caesar with the legend DICT.QVART. shows the diadem rejected at the Lupercalia on 15 February 44;[71] quite apart from the other objections to this theory, it is incompatible with the record preserved by Cicero (*Phil.* II 87) that Caesar was already *Dictator perpetuus* at the Lupercalia.

For an earlier period, there is the equally fantastic suggestion of E.S.G. Robinson that the end of the Carthaginian series of silver coins struck in Spain during the Second Punic War was in fact produced for P. Scipio Africanus and bears his portrait.[72] There are decisive numismatic objections to this theory also; but it ignores the fact that whereas T. Quinctius Flamininus, for whom a portrait coin *was* struck, accepted extravagant honours in Greece, including cult, Africanus ostentatiously declined the title of king offered him by his Spanish troops.

Conversely, those unfamiliar with the coin material often wrongly attach individual significance to a type which is simply standard for the denomination in question. From the late third century BC to the end of the Republic, Janus was the standard obverse type of the as, Saturn of the semis, Hercules of the quadrans; the speculations of Richard on the relationship between Janus and peace, of Rowland on Saturn as an Italian symbol, of Bayet on Hercules and Sulla,[73] crumble in the face of this fact. An analogous error is that of R. Mac-Mullen, in attributing significance to the use of the legends LIBERTAS and BRVTVS under Trajan;[74] but these are

---

[70] See *Studies in Numismatic Method* (Cambridge, 1983), 47–64; also E. L. Bowie, *JRS* (1970), 204, for proper scepticism on the notion of 'anniversary' issues of coins.

[71] A.Alföldi, *Bull.Soc.Royale Lettres Lund* (1952–3), 1.

[72] E.S.G.Robinson, *Essays H.Mattingly* (Oxford, 1956), 34.

[73] J.C.Richard, *MEFR* (1963), 303; 'Pax, Concordia et la religion officielle de Janus'; R.J.Rowland, *Class.Phil.* (1967), 185: 'Saturn, Saturninus and the *socii*'; J.Bayet, *Bull.Acad.Belge* (1955), 453: 'Les sacerdoces romaines et la pré-divinisation impériale'.

[74] *Enemies of the Roman Order* (Cambridge, Mass., 1966), 33.

Michael Crawford

simply the legends of one issue out of a whole group of Republican issues 'restored' by Trajan for reasons quite unconnected with the legends of any one of them. It may seem invidious to cite the errors of others in order to make a methodological point, but it is surely better to be aware of the possible pitfalls; only thus is ancient coinage likely to be a reliable source for the history of the ancient world.[75]

APPENDIX

General handbooks

Both very out of date:
F. Schrötter, *Wörterbuch der Münzkunde* (Berlin and Leipzig, 1930)
S.W. Stevenson, C. Roach Smith, F.W. Madden, *A Dictionary of Roman Coins* (London, 1889)
Note also articles, of varying modernity, on numismatics in general and on specific topics in:
Dictionnaire des Antiquités Grecques et Romaines (1873–1919)
W.H. Roscher, *Lexikon der Mythologie* (1884–1937)
Pauly's Realencyclopädie (1894–1978)
Dizionario Epigrafico (1895–)
Reallexikon für Antike und Christentum (1950–)
Enciclopedia d'Arte Antica (1958–1970)
Der Kleine Pauly (1964–1975)
Oxford Classical Dictionary (1970)
Apart from the standard epigraphical and papyrological indexes, the numismatist should also be familiar with:
Vocabularium Iurisprudentiae Romanae (Berlin, 1903–39)
Heumanns Handlexikon zu den Quellen des Römischen Rechts (9th ed. by E.Seckel, Jena, 1907)
Vocabularium Codicis Iustiniani, R. Mayr and M. San Nicolo (eds.) (Prague, 1923–5)
A. Berger, *Encyclopedic Dictionary of Roman Law* (Philadelphia, 1953)

[75] See 'Roman imperial coin types', in *Studies P.Grierson* (Cambridge, 1983), 47. For important work combining numismatic and non-numismatic evidence see E. Lo Cascio, 'Oro e moneta in età traianea', *AIIN* 25 (1978), 75–102, with my reservations in *La moneta in Grecia e a Roma* (Bari, 1982), 147. K.Hopkins, 'Taxes and trade in the Roman Empire', *JRS* 70 (1980), 101.

Numismatics

General books

P. Grierson, *Numismatics* (London, 1975)

Handbooks on ancient coinage

The foundation of modern numismatics is J. Eckhel, *Doctrina Numorum Veterum* (Vienna, 1792–1826). The articles 'Münzwesen' by K. Regling in *RE* and 'Geld' by R. Bogaert in *RAC* are useful surveys. Note that catalogues of collections often function as handbooks, notably the catalogues of the British Museum collections, occasionally also the sale catalogues of great private collections.

Books on ancient coinage

F. Lenormant, *La Monnaie dans l'Antiquité* (Paris, 1878–9)
G.F. Hill, *Handbook of Greek and Roman Coins* (London, 1899)
E. Babelon, *Traité* I: *Théorie et Doctrines* (Paris, 1901)
P. Gardner, *History of Ancient Coinage* (Oxford, 1918)
M.H. Crawford, *La moneta in Grecia e a Roma* (Bari, 1982)

Handbooks on Greek coinage

E. Babelon, *Traité* II: *Description historique* (Paris, 1907–32)
G.F. Hill, *Historical Greek Coins* (London, 1906)
B.V. Head, *Historia Numorum* (Oxford, 1911)
British Museum, *Guide to the Principal Coins of the Greeks* (London, 1959)
C.M. Kraay and M. Hirmer, *Greek Coins* (London, 1966)

Books on Greek coinage

E. Babelon, *Les monnaies grecques* (Paris, 1921)
J.G. Milne, *Greek Coinage* (Oxford, 1931)
C.T. Seltman, *Greek Coins* (London, 1954)
G.K. Jenkins, *Ancient Greek Coins* (London, 1972)
C.M. Kraay, *Archaic and Classical Greek Coins* (London, 1976)

Handbooks on Roman coinage

G.F. Hill, *Historical Roman Coins* (London, 1909)
E. Babelon, *Description des monnaies de la République romaine* (Paris, 1895–6)

Michael Crawford

M. Bahrfeldt, *Nachträge und Berichtigungen* I–III (Vienna, 1897–1919)
E.A. Sydenham, *Coinage of the Roman Republic* (London, 1952)
M.H. Crawford, *Roman Republican Coin Hoards* (London, 1969)
M.H. Crawford, *Roman Republican Coinage* (Cambridge, 1974)
M. Bernhart, *Handbuch zur Münzkunde der römischen Kaiserzeit* (Halle, 1926)
H. Mattingly, E.A. Sydenham and others, *Roman Imperial Coinage* (London, 1923 onwards)

Books on Roman coinage

Th.Mommsen, *Geschichte des römischen Münzwesens* (Berlin, 1860)
M. Grant, *Roman Imperial Money* (London, 1954) (mainly in form of commentary on single issues)
H. Mattingly, *Roman Coins* (London, 1960)
C.H.V. Sutherland, *Roman Coins* (London, 1974)
J.P.C. Kent, *Roman Coins* (London, 1978)

Bibliography

The older material may be found in J. Friedländer, *Repertorium* (Berlin, 1885). Since then, nothing systematic has been produced. *Numismatisches Literatur-Blatt* runs from 1880 to 1939; *Numismatic Literature* runs from 1947. The war years are partly covered by articles, by S.L. Cesano in *Doxa* (1949), by R.A.G. Carson and G.K. Jenkins in *Historia* (1953–4), by C.C. Vermeule in *Middle East Supplement to Research Bibliography* (1957). Numismatics is also covered in *L'Année Philologique* (from 1914), *JdI* (from 1923), *Gnomon* (from 1925), *Fasti Archaeologici* (from 1946).

Earlier sporadic surveys may be found in W. Kubitschek, *Rundschau* (1890–4) and in *ZfN* (1901–6). Recent surveys are in the reports of the Congresses of Paris (1953) (note Spanish supplement in *Num. Hisp.* (1953) 171), Rome (1961), Copenhagen (1967), New York (1973) and Bern (1979).

Earlier regional surveys are those of S.L. Cesano, *Boll.Ist.Naz. Stor.d'Arte* I (1922), 2–3, 67, 'Bibliografia numismatica per gli anni 1914–21'; M. Karamessini-Oikonomides, *RN* (1967), 269, 'Bibliographie des travaux numismatiques publiés en Grèce de 1961 à 1967'; E. Bosch, *Türkiyenin antik devirdeki meskûkâtina dair.bibliografya* (Ankara, 1949); O. Iliescu, *Bul.Soc.Num.Rom.* 42–66 (1948–72), 29, on numismatics in Romania from 1950 to 1972; B. Saria, *Num.Zeitschr.* (1927), 10, 'Numismatischer Bericht aus Jugoslawien'; M.F. Fejer and L. Huszar, *Bibliographia Numismaticae Hungariae* (Budapest, 1977).

Specialist bibliographies are those of M. Bernhart, *Handbuch zur Münzkunde der römischen Kaiserzeit* I: *Bibliographischer Wegweiser*, and C.C. Vermeule, *Bibliography of Applied Numismatics* (London, 1956). *Jahrbuch für Numismatik und Geldgeschichte* and now *Chiron* produce *Literaturüberblicke* at intervals on Greek numismatics. There is a good modern bibliography by P. Grierson: *Bibliographie numismatique* (Brussels, 1979). For a provisional list of collections of ancient coins, see T. Hackens and P. Marchetti (Louvain, 1971).

Books on numismatic methodology

W. Schwabacher, *Neue Methoden in der griechischen Münzforschung* (Lund, 1964) (on 'series' as opposed to issues, on hoards and on die-links – but very insubstantial).

L. Breglia, *Numismatica Antica* (Milan, 1964)

L.R. Laing. *Coins and Archaeology* (London, 1969) (see review in *N.C* (1971), 356)

E. Bernareggi, *Istituzioni di numismatica* (Milan, 1973)

J. Casey and R. Reece (eds.), *Coins and the Archaeologist* (Oxford, 1974)

J.-M. Dentzer, T. Hackens, Ph. Gautier (eds.), *Numismatique antique: Problèmes et méthodes* (Nancy and Louvain, 1974)

R. Göbl, *Antike Numismatik* (Munich, 1978)

M.-R. Alföldi, *Antike Numismatik* (Mainz, 1978)

Index of names

Index of names

Plautus, 66–8
Plutarch, 41–5
Polybius, 4, 6–8, 11, 16
Pyrgi, Punic and Etruscan texts from, 96–7

Robert, L., 80; and J., 83

Sallust, 8–9, 17
Samothrace, sanctuary of the Great Gods, 178
Shapor I, 'Res Gestae' of, 89
Solon, 37–8
Sostratus of Aegina, inscription of, at Graviscae, 95–6
Statius, 39
Strabo, 27–8, 37
Syria, 161

Tacitus, 9
Tell-el-Amarna, 151
Theophrastus, 65–6
Theopompus, 10–11, 12
Thera (Santorini), 151
Thucydides, 5–6, 69; on Sicilian colonies, 152; on urbanisation, 160
Tripolitania, 161

Veii, 180
Velleius, 20
Vergina, tomb of (?) Philip II at, 181

Xanthos, Lycia, trilingual inscription from, 87

Index of subjects

Index of subjects